THE RENAISSANCE IN EUROPE: A CULTURAL ENQUIRY

The Impact of Humanism

THE RENAISSANCE IN EUROPE: A CULTURAL ENQUIRY

The Impact of Humanism

EDITED BY LUCILLE KEKEWICH

Yale University Press, New Haven & London in association with
The Open University

First published 2000 by Yale University Press in association with
The Open University

Copyright © 2000 The Open University

A catalogue card reference for this title is available from the Library of Congress.

ISBN 0-300-08216-9 (C)
ISBN 0-300-08221-5 (P)

Edited, designed and typeset by the Open University.

Printed and bound in the United Kingdom by Alden Press Ltd, Osley Mead,
Oxford, OX2 OEF.

This text forms part of an Open University course AA305, *The Renaissance in Europe:
A Cultural Enquiry*. The complete list of texts which make up this course can be
found on the back cover. Details of this and other Open University courses can be
obtained from the Course Reservations Centre, PO Box 724, The Open University,
Milton Keynes MK7 6ZS, United Kingdom, tel. (00 44) 1908 653231.

For availability of this or other course components, contact Open University
Worldwide Ltd, The Berrill Building, Walton Hall, Milton Keynes MK1 6AA,
United Kingdom, tel. (00 44) 1908 858585, fax (00 44) 1908 858787, e-mail
ouwenq@open.ac.uk

Alternatively, much useful course information can be obtained from the Open
University's website http://www.open.ac.uk

22339B/aa305b1i1.1

1.1

Contents

Preface

This is the first of three books in the series *The Renaissance in Europe: A Cultural Enquiry* which form the main texts of an Open University third-level course of the same name. This interdisciplinary course has been designed for students who are new to cultural history and the Renaissance as well as for those who have already undertaken some study in these areas. The purpose of this series is to introduce the idea of the Renaissance both as it developed during the fifteenth and sixteenth centuries and as it has since been interpreted. Through a wide-ranging series of case studies, we hope to provide a broad overview of current scholarship in the field of Renaissance studies. The subject is not tackled chronologically, although the earlier phases of the Renaissance tend to be considered in the first two books and the later in the third. Each book engages with different themes and aspects of the Renaissance and is self-sufficient and accessible to the general reader. This first book, *The Impact of Humanism,* begins with an overview of Jacob Burckhardt's seminal work *The Civilization of the Renaissance in Italy,* and continues to focus on the impact of humanism on scholarship, music, philosophy and politics in Italy and subsequently throughout Europe.

As part of the course, this book includes important teaching exercises which in most cases are followed by some discussion of the points raised. At the beginning of each chapter the expected outcomes for the reader are listed in the form of objectives. A bibliography has been prepared for each chapter and where applicable is followed by a source list for texts from the set Reader and Anthology (see below) and for musical extracts. At the end of the book is a glossary. Entries in the glossary are emboldened in the text, usually the first time they appear. A general map of Italy in the fifteenth century has been included on page xii to be used for reference throughout the book. The convention for dating adopted throughout the series is to use CE (Common Era) and BCE (Before Common Era) in preference to the more traditional AD and BC.

For each book in the series there are set texts that the reader will need access to in order to engage fully with the material. Throughout the series references to the two volumes of source material are to the 'Reader' and the 'Anthology' followed by an extract number; no page references to the Reader and Anthology are given. References to other set texts are in the standard author/date system. For this book the set texts are:

P. Elmer, N. Webb and R. Wood (eds) (1999) *The Renaissance in Europe: An Anthology*, New Haven and London, Yale.

K. Whitlock (ed.) (1999) *The Renaissance in Europe: A Reader*, New Haven and London, Yale.

Jacob Burckhardt (1990) *The Civilization of the Renaissance in Italy*, trans. S.G.C. Middlemore, introduction by Peter Burke, Harmondsworth, Penguin.

Alison Cole (1995) *Art of the Italian Renaissance Courts: Virtue and Magnificence*, London, Weidenfeld & Nicolson.

Niccolò Machiavelli (1999) *The Prince*, trans. G. Bull, introduction by Anthony Grafton, Harmondsworth, Penguin.

Michel de Montaigne (1991) *The Complete Essays*, ed./trans. and introduction by M.A. Screech, Harmondsworth, Penguin.

The three books in the series are:

The Impact of Humanism, edited by Lucille Kekewich

Courts, Patrons and Poets, edited by David Mateer

The Age of Reform, edited by Peter Elmer

The course editors were Christine Considine and Rachel Crease, picture research was carried out by Tony Coulson and the course secretary was Sam Horne. Roberta Wood was the course manager, Ruth Drage was the course designer, Ray Munns was the course artist and Robert Gibson was the compositor.

Introduction

BY PETER ELMER

The chapters in this book focus on what was arguably the most distinctive feature of Renaissance culture, humanism. Like the term 'Renaissance', humanism, as a historical phenomenon, has been the subject of wide-ranging debate. Attempts to define it, as well as locate its origins in and impact on western Europe, have preoccupied cohorts of scholars for generations and continue to provide intellectual stimulation for a new generation of researchers and writers. One of the prime functions of this book is to provide an overview of much of that scholarly debate, particularly as it relates to broad concerns that underpin the series as a whole. Of these, two in particular demand special attention.

In the first place, a consistent theme of this series is discussion of the extent to which we should see the Renaissance either as a period or a process. If we opt for the former, then we should expect to find evidence of discontinuity with the medieval past, none more so than in the learned cultural developments associated with the 'rise of humanism'. If, however, we envisage the Renaissance as principally a process of cultural innovation, it is unlikely to fit into the neat chronological categories which characterize much historical scholarship. Both the origins and impact of humanism on western thought and culture thus provide important opportunities to test this most fundamental of problems in Renaissance studies. Second, the whole question of the impact and spread of humanism in Europe raises a key area of recent research into the Renaissance, namely the issue of 'reception'. Recent scholarship has confirmed the view that the reception of the Renaissance as a whole in Europe was uneven, both in time and place. In seeking solutions as to why this should be so, attempts to assess the way in which humanist beliefs and values were received, rejected or modified in the process of transmission can provide vital clues as to the nature of the Renaissance and its place in European culture and history.

In attempting to address these and related questions, all of the chapters in this book adhere to the view that such issues are best pursued through an approach that eschews narrow disciplinary boundaries and attempts instead to recreate the culture of Renaissance Europe as a whole. Humanism, by its very nature, defies the simple categorization of disciplines which informs modern western approaches to learning. The development of interdisciplinary studies has to some extent provided a solution to this particular problem, and it is the approach which is adopted throughout this series. By its very nature interdisciplinarity suggests that we should treat cultures and societies as a whole, an approach that is now firmly embedded in modern scholarship in the form of cultural studies and cultural history. Taking our cue from Peter Burke – who accepts the view of culture as 'a system of shared meanings, attitudes and values, and the symbolic forms (performances, artefacts) in which they are expressed or embodied' [1] – we too acknowledge not only the rich variety of forms which culture might take in this period, but also the fact that Renaissance culture was only one of many vying for the attention of Europeans at the time.

This holistic approach to Renaissance culture was one which the founder of Renaissance studies, Jacob Burckhardt, intuitively understood and practised, even if the term 'cultural history' was alien to nineteenth-century scholars. In Chapter 1 of this book, Burckhardt's contribution to the debate over the origins, meaning and significance of the Renaissance is explored and placed within the context of more recent studies which have rejected, corrected or modified various aspects of his ground-breaking work. In Chapter 2, we address, albeit briefly, two issues central to Burckhardt's thesis, the 'revival of antiquity' and the 'discovery of the individual', and examine the range of evidence available to scholars in attempting to reassess the validity of Burckhardt's seminal approach to the Renaissance. Chapter 3 introduces the central theme of the volume, the place of humanism in Renaissance thought and culture. The reader is introduced to humanism through an assessment of its impact on two areas of learning, the retrieval of the past and textual criticism. Issues of style and content are addressed and an attempt is made to provide a working definition of humanism, and an assessment of its impact on Italy and other parts of Europe. This is followed in Chapters 4, 5 and 6 by case studies in the relationship of humanism to three areas of Renaissance culture: music, philosophy and politics. The book concludes with an in-depth evaluation of one of the most important texts of Renaissance political thought, Machiavelli's *The Prince*. Here, the aim is to contextualize Machiavelli's work, not just within the boundaries of political philosophy, but also by reference to contemporary political events in Italy in which Machiavelli was a minor actor.

One of the greatest difficulties encountered in teaching or writing about the Renaissance is the extent to which such activity is dependant upon a knowledge of the classical world of the ancient Greeks and

---

[1] P. Burke (1978) *Popular Culture in Early Modern Europe*, London, Temple Smith, Prologue.

Romans which provided so much of the inspiration for Renaissance writers, poets, artists and thinkers. As will become apparent in this and later volumes in the series, the debt of Renaissance Europeans to their ancient forbears was vast. Clearly, it is not possible here to do justice to the full extent of this influence, but in three critical areas – religion, politics and education – the impact was particularly noteworthy.

Greek stories and myths, adapted by the Romans, formed a veritable treasure-house for Renaissance scholars and artists which helped to inspire a range of cultural pursuits. Pagan gods and heroes were often invoked in philosophical debate where they were presented, in allegorical form, as the personification of moral qualities. Likewise, Renaissance historical scholarship frequently sought to appropriate classical heroes such as Hercules and the Trojan Brutus in order to claim a classical ancestry for the new nation-states of Europe.

In the field of politics, the rediscovery of classical orators and historians provided Renaissance commentators with a wide variety of concepts and debates which helped to shape the style and content of contemporary political discourse. Machiavelli referred constantly to Greek and Roman authorities in his discussion of the perfect form of government and the qualities most befitting a ruler (Chapter 6). Aristotle and Cicero were frequently quoted by humanists eager to demonstrate the ethical nature of government and Plato's ideal of the philosopher as ruler found expression in Thomas More's *Utopia* (Chapter 5). The various types of government developed in ancient Greece and Rome also provided Renaissance politicians and writers with classical prototypes which might be used to legitimate a whole range of political forms from republicanism to imperialism. The Renaissance understanding of concepts such as responsible citizenship, civilized society, freedom, duty and the rule of law were all derived from antiquity.

Obviously, education played a vital role in the dissemination of such knowledge of the ancient world and was itself modelled on classical precedents. The curriculum in the universities of medieval and Renaissance Europe, echoing the classical system, was based on the seven Liberal Arts (grammar, logic, rhetoric, arithmetic, geometry, music and astronomy). The term 'humanism' was itself derived from the study of the *studia humanitatis* or what we might refer to today as the 'arts', incorporating language, literature, history and moral philosophy. Skill in Latin, and to a lesser extent Greek, was considered the hallmark of an educated man in the Renaissance and provided access to a rich world of classical beliefs and values which helped to shape the culture of Europe in the fifteenth and sixteenth centuries. Just how successful humanism was in this process forms the backbone of this volume of studies.

Map of Italy in the fifteenth century. Adapted from C. Black et. al. (1994) *Atlas of the Renaissance*, Cassell, London. Reproduced by permission of Andromeda Oxford Ltd, Abingdon, UK ©

CHAPTER ONE

Inventing the Renaissance: Burckhardt as historian

BY PETER ELMER

Objectives

The objectives of this chapter are that you should:
- meet the basic concepts inherent in cultural studies of the Renaissance;
- gain some understanding of the **historiographical** and methodological assumptions that underlay Burckhardt's seminal work;
- assess the reaction of subsequent generations of historians of the Renaissance to Burckhardt's model;
- undertake the textual analysis of selected extracts from Burckhardt's *Civilization of the Renaissance in Italy*.

Introduction

The appearance in 1860 of Jacob Burckhardt's *The Civilization of the Renaissance in Italy* marks a defining moment in historical scholarship. Not only is Burckhardt's study still considered by many modern scholars to be *the* starting point for those studying the Renaissance, but it continues to attract the praise of those who are eager to promote the virtues of that broad school of historical thought signified by the term '**cultural history**'. Love or hate the work – and it is only fair to point out that historians are often bitterly divided in their appreciation of Burckhardt's *magnum opus* – it is impossible to ignore. So why is this the case? A major cause of dispute among those who have debated Burckhardt's continuing worth and relevance has been discussion of his own motives and assumptions in writing the book. In addition, specific aspects of Burckhardt's argument have attracted widespread critical attention. We will need to consider these in more detail if we are to arrive at a fair and just assessment of his place in modern scholarship. Before turning to these issues, however, we might wish first to clarify the central thesis of Burckhardt's seminal work.

Figure 1.1 Photograph of Jacob Burckhardt (1818–97), about 1892. Porträtsammlung, Oeffentliche Bibliothek, Universität Basel

In six highly original parts, Burckhardt set out what he saw as the defining features of the period in Italian history (roughly from 1350 to 1500) known to his contemporaries as the Renaissance.[1] Of these six parts, the first three in particular have attracted the attention of subsequent generations of scholars eager to test Burckhardt's equation of the Italian Renaissance with the origins of the state, modern individualism and secular society. In Part 1, 'The state as a work of art', he postulated the idea that the onset of the Italian Renaissance signified the end of the medieval political world. According to Burckhardt, the death of **feudalism** in Italy ushered in the age of the independent state (usually in the form of the **city-state**) whose defining characteristic was its rejection of feudal relations based on custom, privilege and tradition. He asserted that the 'modern' Italian city-state was founded upon 'reflection and calculation' (1990, p.20). Unlike their predecessors, the rulers of these new, independent city-states felt no compulsion to refer to medieval law, custom or religion in order to defend or justify their actions. And this might, and frequently did, result in outrageous, unrestrained and sometimes spectacular acts of political single-mindedness.

---

[1] Burckhardt did not invent the term 'Renaissance', which was first coined in sixteenth-century Italy. Nor was he the first scholar to demonstrate the importance of this epoch in European history. In many respects, his own work was a development of the interests of Enlightenment scholars such as Voltaire, and nineteenth-century historians such as Jules Michelet, who was the first to apply the phrases 'discovery of the world' and 'discovery of man' to the Renaissance.

For Burckhardt, then, the rejection of feudalism in Italy marked a major turning point in European history. And he detected similar forces in his enquiry into the origins of Renaissance individualism in Part 2 of his book, 'The development of the individual'. Clearly related to the presuppositions that informed his view on 'The state as a work of art', his espousal of the idea that the Italian Renaissance saw the birth of modern man, an individual rather than a product of the medieval, corporate identity, has proved to be one of his most profound, if contentious, insights. Here was the seed of one of Burckhardt's most celebrated creations, the idea of *l'uomo universale*, the multi-talented individual, who still stands today in the popular consciousness as perhaps *the* defining feature of the Italian Renaissance.

In Part 3, Burckhardt introduced that element of Renaissance culture which has formed the focus of so much recent scholarship on the subject: 'The revival of antiquity'. Unlike more recent generations of Renaissance scholars, however, he was at pains to point out that respect for, and appreciation of, the **classical** past was not the chief ingredient of the new cultural movement. Instead, pride of place in his hierarchy of values was reserved for 'the genius of the Italian people', which he saw as primarily responsible for 'the conquest of the Western world' (p.120). Throughout the work, the emphasis is firmly placed on the spirit and genius of the Italians as the seminal source of Renaissance culture. In Burckhardt's highly original conception of the Renaissance, **humanism**, with its respect for the classical past, was merely a convenient vehicle for the subtle genius of Italian scholars, poets and artists. This is further manifest, for example, in Part 4, 'The discovery of the world and of man', where he discusses the emancipation of the Italian mind with respect to the world of nature, and man's relationship to the natural world. It is also apparent in Part 5, 'Society and festivals', where Burckhardt discusses the impact of such ideas on society as a whole. Italian society, for example, is perceived as characteristically 'modern' in that it places talent and education above birth as the major determinant of social, cultural and political status. He also hints at the gradual disintegration of class boundaries in Italy, and even goes so far as to suggest that 'women stood on a footing of perfect equality with men' (pp.230–1, 250–1). Finally, in Part 6, 'Morality and religion', he attempts to address the paradoxical end-product of his analysis of Italian Renaissance society. In rejecting medieval custom and tradition, including the moral constraints of the church, the Italian spirit had fostered a secular approach to the things of this world which in its turn had created a moral vacuum. The outcome was the creation of a modern, secular society in which individuals were free to act and speculate in whichever way they saw fit. And though sometimes this produced remarkable works of art and culture, it also generated, as Burckhardt freely confessed, spectacular deeds of human wickedness.

Burckhardt as historian

In order to appreciate Burckhardt the historian, we need to know something of his personal background and the influences that helped to shape his distinctive approach to the writing of history. He was born in 1818 in the Swiss city of Basle, and much has been made of his attachment to his native city to which he returned in 1858, and where he remained until his death in 1897. Essentially a conservative man by nature and in his politics, Burckhardt loathed most aspects of nineteenth-century 'progress' in Europe, including industrialization and nationalism, which he saw as destructive of the cultural values that he prized so highly in his historical work. Hence his devotion to

Figure 1.2 Franz Theodor Kugler, *Jacob Burckhardt*, 1843, pencil drawing, 22.2 x 17.6 cm. Oeffentliche Kunstsammlung Basel Kupferstichkabinett Inv. No. XX 1948.45

Figure 1.3 R. Lehmann, *Leopold von Ranke*, pencil drawing, *The Graphic*, June 1886. Photo: Hulton/ Getty Images

Figure 1.4 *Georg Wilhelm Friedrich Hegel*. Photo: Bildarchiv Preussischer Kulturbesitz Berlin

the small but cosmopolitan 'city-state' of Basle, which he praised as a bastion of the true values of European civilization. It is probably safe to assume, then, that the events of his own age influenced the way Burckhardt wrote as a historian. What we can be less certain of is precisely how he arrived at his distinctive and original approach to the history of Renaissance Italy, one that has led successive generations of historians to applaud him as the founder of 'cultural history'.

One aspect of Burckhardt's career which has called for particular attention has been his early immersion as a student in the academic historical and philosophical debates raging in Germany in the 1830s. Berlin was the intellectual centre of Europe at this time, and, as a student at the University of Berlin, Burckhardt was taught by one of the most original and gifted historians of his generation, Leopold von Ranke (1795–1886). Here he would also have heard lectures by followers of the recently deceased philosopher Georg Hegel (1770–1831), whose ideas were to have such a profound influence on a fellow student of Burckhardt's, Karl Marx. Yet despite this Burckhardt seems to have been largely unaffected by the contemporary fascination for the work of both men. In particular he rejected the positivism of Ranke's historical method, which envisaged history as a form of science and laid claim to the idea that if one followed the rules of historical method (primarily the archival retrieval of undisputed 'facts') one would arrive at an objective and irrefutable view of the past. And though there is some evidence to suggest the influence of Hegel on his writing, on the whole it is clear that Burckhardt rejected the Hegelian idea that history followed a pre-ordained pattern, in the same way that he was loathe to accept any over-arching theory or system of beliefs which might explain historical causation.[2] Instead Burckhardt proposed the idea that history was neither a form of science nor of philosophy, but rather an art, a view best expressed in his celebrated dictum that 'history to me is always poetry for the greater part' (Brown, 1988, p.20).

One consequence of such an approach to the writing of history was the 'subjectivity' of Burckhardt's method, an issue which has resounded in the debates of historians ever since. Burckhardt himself was convinced that it was impossible to reach definitive conclusions about every aspect of the past. The best that could be achieved was a vivid and imaginative evocation of the spirit of the age, something that he felt was most successfully demonstrated by specific examples of the dominant *Zeitgeist* (literally, 'spirit of the age'). Writing cultural history was for him a creative enterprise: 'where others wanted to tell a story, Burckhardt's aim was to paint the portrait of an age' (Burke, 1990, p.5). This accounts in large part for his tendency to eschew academic historical conventions in his writing (e.g. the use of detailed evidence backed up by documented footnotes) and to focus instead on a narrative approach heavily dependent on anecdotal evidence and his own moral and aesthetic judgements. Occasionally, as a prisoner of his age and its conventions, he indulges in some embarrassing asides, as for example his allusions to the racial inferiority of Asian peoples (pp.20–21). But we must also concede that Burckhardt's view of history, and how it should be written, was never prescriptive or dogmatic. He himself confessed on numerous occasions in *The Civilization of the Renaissance in Italy* that each individual must be free to impose their own critical, subjective judgements on the evidence of the past. In this respect, his legacy has endured while Rankean positivism has receded as an influence on the discipline of academic history writing.

[2] The extent of Hegel's influence on Burckhardt is disputed. E.H. Gombrich (1979, pp.24–59), for example, is keen to suggest that Burckhardt was influenced by his deterministic view of history, in particular Hegel's notion of the *Volksgeist* or 'national spirit' as a predisposing factor in human history. Others have refuted such influence on the grounds that Burckhardt never subscribed to the idea of the inevitability of human progress in history.

Figure 1.5 Franz Gerhard von Kugelgen, *Johann Wolfgang von Goethe*. Photo: Bildarchiv Foto Marburg

Figure 1.6 Rausch, *Johann Gottfried von Herder*, engraving. Mansell Collection/Time Inc.

Arguably, the greatest influence on Burckhardt's approach to history was scholarly **German Romanticism** which flourished at this time and was represented by the work of the poet Johann Wolfgang von Goethe (1749–1832) and the historian, Johann Gottfried von Herder (1744–1803). Herder believed that history was a dynamic process of evolution in which each period was characterized by the particular 'spirit' of its various peoples or nations. The key to understanding history thus lay in the attempt to define those qualities which constituted a given group of people, one that Herder felt was most conveniently located in the literature of nations. Just as Herder sought the character or 'spirit' (*geist*) of the German nation in the moral, folkloric traditions of its people, so Burckhardt attempted to locate the 'spirit' of the Italian people in the abstract, mental qualities that he believed exemplified the period of the Renaissance. In so doing, he rejected the idea of history as the compilation and analysis of objective facts, and proposed in its place a new conception of the study of the past, one that emphasized the creative ability of the historian to capture the spirit of an age by reference to 'the constant, the recurrent, and the typical' (Burke, 1990, p.7).

History's verdict on Burckhardt

Rather than charting the history of academic reaction to Burckhardt's seminal work on the Renaissance since its publication, we might more usefully reflect on those aspects of his book that have endured or suffered with the passage of time. Unfortunately for Burckhardt's reputation, his critics tend to outnumber his defenders. Nonetheless, there is much in *The Civilization of the Renaissance in Italy* that continues to excite and stimulate the modern reader, none more so than his use of a wide range of sources and subject-matter to illustrate the general themes of the book. He was writing cultural history in a way that is still relevant to the concerns of present-day historians, as for example where he cites the Renaissance penchant for jokes, etiquette, festivals, astrology and magic. Moreover, his influence on subsequent generations of scholars is apparent, for example, in the work of the Warburg Institute, which was transferred from Hamburg to London in the inter-war period as a research centre specializing in the kind of interdisciplinary cultural history that Burckhardt had begun to popularize two generations earlier. But though most experts in the field of Renaissance studies today would feel comfortable with the subject-matter of Burckhardt's book, few would wish to emulate his methodological approach to the interpretation of historical evidence. And fewer still, I suspect, would accept some of the more sweeping assumptions that underlie the central thesis of his *magnum opus.*

With respect to this thesis, Renaissance historians of the twentieth century have raised a series of objections that threaten to dismantle some of Burckhardt's most cherished conceits. Serious caveats have been pronounced, for example, with regard to his excessive admiration for the originality and modernity of Renaissance Italians. The claim that they represented 'the first born among the sons of modern Europe' (p.98) is one that few historians, medieval or early modern, would today accept with equanimity. Not only is Burckhardt's emphasis on Italy as the home of all things modern seen as an extreme generalization, but many have questioned his attempt to locate the genesis of the modern world exclusively in the post-medieval period. Medievalists especially have been quick to charge him with a gross violation of the facts, resenting in particular his characterization of the **Middle Ages** as a period of intellectual sloth, superstition and torpor. Burckhardt was clearly of the opinion that the mid fourteenth century in Italy represented the beginnings of a major break with the past. Today few scholars would accept this neat periodization. Many, indeed, would reject altogether the idea that there was a discreet period in European history denoted by the term

'Renaissance'. Others have pointed out that prior to Burckhardt's Renaissance, Europe had witnessed numerous earlier periods of intellectual and artistic revival, some of which contained the seeds of Burckhardtian modernism and thus merit the term 'Renaissance'. Rather than acknowledging a single burst of creative cultural endeavour between the fourteenth and sixteenth centuries, most scholars consequently prefer to speak of a series of Renaissances beginning with that of Charlemagne (Charles the Great) in the eighth and ninth centuries and including further periods of *renovatio* (cultural renewal) in the twelfth and thirteenth centuries, culminating in the medieval rediscovery of the Greek philosopher and polymath, Aristotle.

Yet others have taken issue with what has proven to be one of Burckhardt's most contentious, though still thought-provoking, hypotheses: his views on the origins of individualism in Renaissance Italy. Here he has come under fire from two directions. First, from those medievalists eager to demonstrate the germs of a burgeoning European self-consciousness at least two centuries prior to Burckhardt's Renaissance (see Morris, 1972; Bynum, 1984; Benton, 1985). And second, from those Renaissance scholars who have criticized Burckhardt for the excessive weight that he placed on the death of corporate forms of identity in Renaissance Italy (see Kent, 1977; Verdon, 1990). According to this school of thought, those institutions that he assumed to have died an early death in Italy – the guilds, the clan and the church – continued to play an important social role throughout the fourteenth and fifteenth centuries. In the process, their continuing vitality stands as a warning to those who, like Burckhardt, have assumed the birth of the individual and the emergence of 'modern' self-consciousness in the period. Interestingly, despite this criticism, Burckhardt continues to attract support for his defence of the Renaissance as the birthplace of modern individualism. But even his defenders frequently feel obliged to moderate many of his more sweeping generalizations. While acknowledging the continuing relevance and vitality of much of his work, his critics and supporters alike point, in the last resort, to the failure of Burckhardt's arguments to carry full conviction. Thus Kerrigan and Braden – two of his greatest admirers – admonish him for failing to apply his analysis of individualism (with which they are in general agreement) to the whole of Renaissance Europe, and castigate him for 'the blindnesses and prejudices of [his] post-Romantic German scholarship' (Kerrigan and Braden, 1989, p.xi; see also pp.41–2, 46).

You may feel that the criticisms levelled against Burckhardt are unfair, given that most scholars now accept that he, like later generations of historians, was only working within the established conventions and limitations of his own age. Each era has its particular priorities and hobby horses which inevitably infect scholarship, despite the oft-repeated claims by academics that they shun partiality and bias. Burckhardt's equation of the power of the Renaissance church and religion with the forces of backwardness and superstition was likely to have been informed by his own lack of religious faith, which chimed in well with the general attack on religion in the second half of the nineteenth century.[3] Few historians today would doubt the crucial role played by the church and individual churchmen in propagating various aspects of Renaissance culture. In a similar vein, we might point to other omissions on Burckhardt's part without seeking to place too much blame on the shoulders of a single scholar. Perhaps, from the point of view of the modern student, the most obvious omission in *The Civilization of the Renaissance in Italy* is the lack of reference to any economic dimension to Burckhardt's thesis.[4] But equally apparent is Burckhardt's ignorance and insufficient treatment of a range of subjects which historians nowadays are eager to promote as vital to an understanding of the Renaissance. Consequently, students of music, philosophy and science in this period will find little in his work to satisfy their particular scholarly interests. Again, however, it is only fair to say on behalf of Burckhardt that in the case of philosophy and science, for example, he was simply reflecting a contemporary view – and one that continued well into the twentieth century – that nothing of significance took place in these two related fields of enquiry before the scientific revolution of the seventeenth century. Only recently have scholars in the history of philosophy and science begun to re-establish the significance of the Renaissance for these two disciplines, the work of Ernst Cassirer in the mid 1920s demonstrating how a Burckhardtian framework might be successfully applied to a reappraisal of the merits of Renaissance philosophy (Kristeller, 1964, pp.27–52; Cassirer, 1963).

Another key aspect of Burckhardt's conception of the Renaissance which has come under increasing scrutiny is its failure to address the issue of the Renaissance outside Italy. As early as 1919, the Dutch

[3] Particularly important in this respect were the criticisms of German biblical scholars such as Ferdinand Baur (1792–1860) whose philological researches undermined literal interpretations of the scriptures. Religious scepticism was further advanced by the publication of Darwin's *Origin of Species* in 1859.

[4] Crucial here is the contribution of those scholars of the so-called *Annales* school who have sought to locate the engine of change in pre-industrial Europe in the long-term movements of social and economic development which defy conventional periodization. See, for example, the work of the French historian Fernand Braudel, especially his three-volume history translated as *Civilization and Capitalism, 15th–18th Century* (1981–4).

historian Johan Huizinga demonstrated a northern European dimension to a revival of arts and letters in this period which was out of tune with Burckhardt's optimistic account of the Italian Renaissance (Huizinga, 1919). In Huizinga's work, the focus of developments in Europe at this time was seen as France and Flanders, which are shown to rival the Italian city-states in terms of artistic and cultural production. Subsequent research into the dispersal and reception of the Renaissance in fifteenth- and sixteenth-century Europe has stressed the non-Italian origins of much of the creativity of European scholars and artists in this period, as well as the fact that Italian models of craftsmanship and expertise were often modified and creatively repackaged to suit the needs and desires of non-Italian patrons. Consequently, though few would dismiss the crucial part played by Italy and its people in encouraging and shaping the revival of arts and letters in the Renaissance, most would equally wish to demonstrate the existence of a more complex network of cultural relations in Europe at this time, one that does not automatically privilege the role of Italian artists, craftsmen and scholars above their continental neighbours (see Burke, 1998).

Today it is probably fair to say that we have a far more nuanced picture of the Renaissance and its place in European history. Gone is the general Burckhardtian preoccupation with Italy as the home of a mythical modernism. In its place, historians now tend to depict the Renaissance as a curious hybrid of the old and the new, and of tradition and innovation. It is no longer fashionable to dismiss the Middle Ages, as Burckhardt once did, as the breeding ground of superstition, custom and tradition. Instead it is usual to acknowledge the continuity of the Renaissance with the medieval past, while at the same time recognizing the role of the Renaissance in fostering new and challenging approaches to the status quo. A good illustration of this process at work is afforded by developments in the religious history of Europe in the late fifteenth and early sixteenth centuries. There is little doubt that the challenge to papal supremacy which culminated in the **Protestant Reformation** would have been unthinkable without the contribution of Renaissance humanism, which helped to provide an intellectual justification for reform in an age of widespread religious conservatism. Yet, as Burckhardt himself acknowledged, humanism was essentially a conservative movement of ideas – one that looked back to the classical past for inspiration at the same time as it provided vital intellectual support for the forces of change.

Clearly then, much has changed since Burckhardt sat down to compose his account – in his own words, *ein Versuch*, or an exploratory essay – of the Renaissance. Today historians of the various disciplines are far more appreciative of the complex interaction of ideas in Renaissance Europe. And though many have acknowledged his privileged place as the first to attempt an overarching interpretation of what is meant by the term 'Renaissance', the majority have also developed Burckhardt's original conception of 'cultural history' far beyond the limits he envisaged in the nineteenth century. If this modest and unassuming Swiss professor continues to leave his mark on Renaissance studies today, it is probably most apparent in the fact that large numbers of contemporary scholars are still drawn to the idea of writing and researching within a disciplinary convention designated by the title 'cultural history'. The interdisciplinarity that Burckhardt took for granted in his own research has proved extremely appealing to subsequent generations. And though today many schools of 'cultural history' compete with each other for attention, all share a common commitment to the ideal of interdisciplinarity. Such was, and remains, the approach adopted by the followers of the German Renaissance specialist Aby Warburg. And it continues to flourish in academic circles today, most notably among a group of scholars from various disciplines who have come under the influence of **post-structuralist** and **post-modern** philosophy, as well as recent trends in cultural anthropology.

One of the ways, however, in which these modern scholars deviate from the approach to the Renaissance adopted by Burckhardt is in their perception of the role of language and culture in society. At the heart of their approach lies the idea that language and culture actively creates or constitutes the social reality that we inhabit, rather than passively reflecting it as writers such as Burckhardt, Marx and others assumed. The language we use, and the symbols and social practices we adopt, not only structure our world and give it meaning, but also provide the means through which power is exercised in society. Cultural objects function in the same way as texts and can be read in a variety of ways, thus constituting various systems of 'representation'. These are rarely politically neutral, and more often than not are potent 'signifiers' of real political import (Brown, 1995, p.8).

One result of this approach has been a growing sensitivity on the part of contemporary historians to the 'otherness' of Renaissance society and culture, that is, its essential difference from the world that we inhabit today. Rather than searching for the origins of modern society, historians of the Renaissance like Richard Trexler, Bill Kent and Peter Burke are far more attuned to detecting ways in which the world of Renaissance Europeans was different from our own. Just as the anthropologist of an alien culture attempts to avoid imposing their own, western-orientated, preconceptions on their observations and understanding of that culture, so the historian is admonished to do the same when approaching the study of our own pre-industrial ancestors. In the words of one of the foremost practitioners of this particular approach:

> If we, inhabitants of the world around the year 2000, are to understand the culture in which this movement [the Renaissance] developed, we would be well advised not to identify ourselves with it too easily. The very idea of a movement to revive the culture of the distant past has become alien to us, since it contradicts ideas of progress or modernity still widely taken for granted despite many recent critiques. At the very least – since there are degrees of otherness – we should view the culture of the renaissance as a half-alien culture, one which is not only distant but receding, becoming more alien every year.

> (Burke, 1998, p.4)

On a practical level, such an approach provides a wonderful challenge to the historian to explore the full range of meanings that cultural artefacts read as 'texts' or modes of 'representation' possessed for Renaissance Europeans. One good example of the way in which this approach has influenced modern Renaissance scholarship is the school of '**New Historicism**'.[5] Largely confined to specialists in the field of Renaissance literature, New Historicists such as Stephen Greenblatt (1980) have sought to turn the Burckhardtian notion of the discovery of the Renaissance self on its head by describing it as largely a fiction: 'a cultural artifact [and] a historical and ideological illusion generated by the economic, social, religious, and political upheavals of the Renaissance' (Martin, 1997, p.1315).

Nor is the search for understanding limited to the products of elite culture, a trend in earlier writing on the Renaissance which also owes much to the influence of Burckhardt. Paintings, buildings and scholarly manuscripts jostle alongside popular ballads and various elements of everyday life for the attention of the new breed of cultural historian. All evidence – whatever its origin – possesses potential value for Renaissance historians, who are increasingly drawn to the idea that their prime aim should be to reconstruct, as far as possible, the complete *mentalité* of the age. Though scholars continue to debate and argue among themselves as to what precisely this age and its actors were about, there can be little doubt that today we possess a far richer and more complex picture of the Renaissance, although one that continues to pay lip service to the founding father and pioneer of Renaissance studies, Jacob Burckhardt.

---

[5] For a brief account of New Historicism see the article by Richard Danson Brown in the Reader (no. 1).

Reading Burckhardt

The following exercises are intended to ease you gently into your study of the Renaissance. Having read my comments on Burckhardt, his work and Burke's introduction to it, and the reaction of subsequent generations of Renaissance scholars, you ought to be well placed to make constructive criticisms of your own of selected extracts from *The Civilization of the Renaissance in Italy*. Try not to worry too much about Burckhardt's style, which you may find disconcertingly alien. Concentrate instead on trying to unpick his fundamental arguments, and juxtapose these with your own critical comments. Six extracts have been selected for discussion and analysis, each from a different part of Burckhardt's work. They are:

1 Part 1, 'The state as a work of art': pp.19–20, from 'This work bears the title' to 'offered by the despotic states'.

2 Part 2, 'The development of the individual': pp.98–101, from 'In the character of these states' to 'a vast circle of spiritual interests'.

3 Part 3, 'The revival of antiquity': pp.120–23, from 'Now that this point' to 'most advanced nation in the world'.

4 Part 4, 'The discovery of the world and of man': p.185, from 'Freed from the countless bonds' to 'bore among the Teutons'; pp.187–9, from 'For the position of the Italians' to 'devote themselves to tranquil research'; pp.198–9, from 'To the discovery of the outward' to 'strangely out of date in the Italy of the sixteenth century'.

5 Part 5, 'Society and festivals': pp.230–31, from 'Every period of civilization' to 'the belief in nobility vanished forever'; pp.250–51, from 'To understand the higher forms' to 'moderate male impulse and caprice'.

6 Part 6, 'Morality and religion': pp.271–3, from 'The relation of the various peoples' to 'Yet the two sentiments are essentially different'; pp.289–91, from 'The morality of a people' to 'a fact characteristic of Italy'; pp.312–14, from 'But in order to reach' to 'matter of such vast importance'.

Exercise

Read the six extracts from Burckhardt and, in each case, attempt to answer the questions that follow:

(a) What are the essential points that Burckhardt wishes to make?

(b) Subjecting these points to critical evaluation, what further questions might you wish to ask of Burckhardt in order to clarify his views?

(c) How do you think modern historians might react to Burckhardt's judgements and historical presuppositions?

Discussion

1 Part 1, 'The state as a work of art'

(a) Two points are worth noting. First, one cannot fail to be impressed by Burckhardt's exemplary opening, which sets out the limitations of his own approach and invites the reader to make their own judgements as to the merits of his argument. Second, we are introduced to some of his most cherished and fundamental ideas which will inform the rest of the book, such as the central role of Italy in the Renaissance, the demise of feudalism in the Italian states and the notion of the 'state as a work of art'.

(b) While acknowledging Burckhardt's apparent humility and honesty in his approach to his subject – an open acknowledgement on his part of the 'subjectivity' of history – we are left wondering what are the alternative views of the Renaissance in 1860. In other words, how does Burckhardt's conception of the Renaissance differ from that of his academic contemporaries? With respect to his introduction of the idea of the 'state as a work of art', perhaps, from the modern vantage point, the single most apparent omission is his failure to define critical terms such as 'feudalism' and the 'modern state'. It is taken for granted that the reader will understand what is meant by these terms, which are presented as unproblematic.

(c) Without appearing to be overly critical of a work written around 140 years ago, there is little doubt that most historians today would adopt a very different style and approach if they were to set about producing a history of the Renaissance. One would certainly expect some form of historiographical essay to introduce the book (similar, perhaps, to that which I have attempted above), as well as discussion and definition of problematic terms. One might also reasonably expect a more detailed summary, not only of the author's intentions in writing the book, but also of their intended approach. The bold assertion of the idea that during the Renaissance 'a new fact appears in history – the state as the outcome of reflection and calculation, the state as a work of art' (p.20) demands further clarification and has certainly attracted the criticism of subsequent generations of historians who have disputed many of Burckhardt's underlying assumptions. In particular, medievalists have taken him to task for what they have seen as his crude stereotyping of the Middle Ages (an age of superstition and cultural retrogression), while Renaissance specialists have increasingly questioned his implicit faith in the radical newness of the post-medieval era.

2   Part 2, 'The development of the individual'

(a)   Here we are introduced to what has proved to be one of Burckhardt's most disputed and controversial claims: that the political conditions in Italy described in Part 1 provided the perfect conditions for the emergence of modern individualism. The Renaissance Italian was, in Burckhardt's celebrated phrase, 'the first-born among the sons of modern Europe' (p.98). Again the burgeoning modernity of the Renaissance is contrasted starkly with the intellectual and cultural backwardness of the Middle Ages. The Renaissance Italian is typically characterized as cosmopolitan and free-spirited, unhindered, that is, by the fetters of 'race, people, party, family, or corporation' (p.99). And when Italian individuality is combined with cultural precocity, the archetypal figure of Renaissance man – *l'uomo universale* – emerges into the full light of day (p.101).

(b)   Perhaps the most pressing point of debate here is to pin down exactly what Burckhardt means by the 'individual' and 'individualism'. Nowhere is this made clear, though we can find some important clues in this extract. It is probably fair to say that Burckhardt, reflecting contemporary notions of the self, took for granted the objective existence of individualism, which consequently did not require further elucidation or proof. Note, for example, his comment that 'documentary evidence' for the existence of what he terms 'the private man ... cannot of course be required' (p.99). But this still does not answer the question of what he meant when he spoke of the individuality of the Italians of this period. A further important clue can be found where he speaks somewhat tentatively of the feasibility of tracing 'the increase in the number of complete men during the fifteenth century' (p.101). In the comment that follows, he clearly demonstrates that his own conception of individuality did not of necessity include a sense of self-awareness or self-consciousness. Instead, for Burckhardt, human individuality is equated with the achievement of completeness or fame. As a result, it is the ability of Renaissance artists, writers and others to achieve through their life and works a posthumous celebrity which lies at the heart of his ill-defined concept of individualism.

(c)   Not surprisingly, historians, sociologists and others have taken him to task for his rather vague and unsatisfactory definition of what constitutes the modern self. Most assume (as Burckhardt did not) that a degree of self-consciousness and self-reflection was, and remains, a vital ingredient of human individuality. Few, however, are in agreement as to how this might best be demonstrated from the documentary evidence of the past. Others, such as the school of New Historicists, have rejected the entire notion of the modern self as little more than a fiction whose creation ('self-fashioning') was dependent on specific social, religious, political and cultural factors. Finally, many historians today, regardless of what precise definitions they might adopt in discussing the origins of individualism, have pointed to the idea that the fact of individuality is not necessarily incompatible with the existence of other corporate modes of existence such as race, people, party, family or corporation. None of the above, however, has precluded historians from continuing to debate and search for the origins of individualism. Many in the process have acknowledged Burckhardt's pioneering role in first raising these issues, and his ideas on the subject continue to prompt much speculation (see Martin, 1997).

3   Part 3, 'The revival of antiquity'

(a) Burckhardt's central point here is that the revival of antiquity and rediscovery of the classical world was not essential to the Renaissance. His starting point remained the 'genius' of the Italian people and the peculiar social and political circumstances prevailing in Italy from the fourteenth century onwards. The prime role of the recovery of the classical world of the ancient Romans and Greeks was to provide a vehicle for Italian genius. In Burckhardt's words, it 'coloured' the Italian Renaissance and helped to make it manifest to subsequent generations (p.120). Other points worth noting here are his comments on the manner of the dissemination of Renaissance ideals and culture from Italy to the rest of Europe (p.120); the restatement of his revulsion at the horrors of all things medieval (p.120); and his suggestion that the Renaissance marked a critical juncture in the growing split between 'popular' and 'elite' cultures in Europe (p.121). Equally noteworthy is his grudging acknowledgement of the existence of earlier Renaissances, including that of Charlemagne. Their influence on subsequent events, however, is neatly side-stepped (p.121).

(b) We are left pondering some familiar themes and dilemmas here. Again, Burckhardt's depiction of the Middle Ages and the implied suggestion that the Italian Renaissance marks a major break with the past begs a number of questions – not least the role of the earlier Renaissances to which he alludes. Most questions, however, will probably focus on his fascinating suggestion that the Renaissance, as he understands it, was conceivable without a revival of antiquity.

(c) These are all points that have been taken up by historians in the twentieth century. We are now far more appreciative of, and sympathetic to, the notion of the Renaissance as representing a gradual rather than a sharp break with the medieval past. The various

Renaissances of the seventh to eighth, twelfth and thirteenth centuries all have their advocates, many of whom would wish to place far greater emphasis on these earlier manifestations of classical revival than on that which occurred in Italy from the fourteenth century onwards. Equally susceptible to criticism is Burckhardt's automatic assumption that the revival of the antique was a case of one-way traffic between Italy and the rest of Europe. The dissemination of the Renaissance throughout Europe from the fourteenth century onwards is now seen as far more complex than he envisaged. Nonetheless, one of the merits of his approach here is his interesting insight that the process of classical rediscovery was not simply one of imitation, but also emulation, as for example where he writes that the Renaissance should be seen not merely as a 'fragmentary imitation or compilation, but [rather as] a new birth' (p.122). This idea has proved particularly influential in recent attempts to understand the Renaissance as a 'process'. Burke, for example, has extended the idea of emulation to what he terms 'transformation', whereby something new is created from the initial reverence for some aspect of the classical past (1998, pp.5–10).

4 Part 4, 'The discovery of the world and of man'

(a) Two interrelated concepts are introduced here: the Renaissance discovery of the natural world and the discovery of man. Again, Italy is proposed as the birthplace of the new spirit of scientific enquiry which underpins both. Burckhardt even goes so far as to extend Italian inquisitiveness in the realm of science to the 'whole people' of the peninsula (p.188). Nothing is allowed to get in the way of this thesis. Thus in Italy the church is described as either more lenient in condemning scientific innovation, or alternatively, Burckhardt hypothesizes, its power is so circumscribed as to make it an ineffectual opponent of the new science. Either way the spiritual and intellectual freedom of the Italian people is evident in their tendency to speculate anew on the nature of the creation and man's unique relation to it. The Italian Renaissance marks a turning point in man's understanding of the natural world.

(b) Burckhardt's admission that when he writes on the subject of science, he does so as a non-specialist, with little knowledge of what he speaks, should alert us to several difficulties here. His view of the history of science as merely the chronicling of who was first to invent or discover this or that particular scientific fact or solve some problem is typical for a man of his age. Equally predictable is his dismissal of what he terms 'pseudo-science' (in this case, astrology, p.188) and his embarrassment at attempting to vindicate the workings of the free Italian spirit within the constraints of Renaissance humoural psychology (the widespread view that all men were predisposed by astrological necessity to one of the four humours; p.199). The fact that Burckhardt here is frequently reduced to speaking in terms of 'conjecture', or without full knowledge of the subject, increases one's doubts as to the soundness of his grandiose claims.

(c) Indeed, from the 1970s on, historians of Renaissance science and medicine have shown themselves increasingly hostile to many of the assumptions which underlie Burckhardt's analysis of this subject. Many now would dispute the notion that the main role of the historian of science is to map the glorious achievements of men of genius, while ignoring or deprecating all those aspects of past science that have failed the test of time. Individual scientists, particularly those who are held to have made vital breakthroughs in their understanding of man and the natural world, are no longer typically seen as one-dimensional geniuses, whose scientific work was somehow divorced from the social and political worlds they inhabited. On the contrary, the practitioners of past science are increasingly viewed as men of their time, whose work and research was frequently shaped and guided by the pressing religious, political and cultural forces at work in Renaissance society. Consequently, Burckhardt's suggestion, for example, that humanism undermined the urge to investigate science is one that few would now take seriously (p.189).

5   Part 5, 'Society and festivals'

(a) Building on an earlier conceit, Burckhardt makes what seems from the vantage point of the first decade of the twenty-first century an astonishing claim on behalf of the Italian Renaissance. Referring yet again to the radical disjuncture between the Renaissance and the Middle Ages, he suggests that the former was the site of a social revolution. Not only does he propose that social status in Italy at this time was increasingly predicated on education and ability rather than birth and pedigree, but he also affirms that 'the main current of the time went steadily toward the fusion of classes in the modern sense of the phrase' (p.230). He later expands this theme of the classless society to include women within its compass (pp.250–1).

(b) Again we are faced here with a number of assumptions which, I feel, demand close scrutiny. What, for example, does Burckhardt mean when he talks of class 'in the modern sense of the phrase'? And what hard evidence does he provide in this chapter for the existence of that western chimera, the classless society? Moreover, his view of Renaissance women is laced with all manner of personal and moral judgements which would not fail to raise the hackles of even the most moderate feminist today! Is Burckhardt's understanding and analysis of Renaissance society convincing? And to what extent is it shaped by the hopes, prejudices and fears of his own age?

(c) Modern historical scholarship, as one might imagine, has not reacted positively to Burckhardt's image of Renaissance Italy as a proto-modern, some might say utopian, society. Today, not only are historians increasingly loathe to use categories like 'class' to describe a pre-industrial society such as Renaissance Italy, but they would also shy away from the idea that this period marked the end of social distinctions based on wealth, inheritance and birth. All of these continued to exert considerable influence on all parts of Europe including Italy throughout the era of the Renaissance, notwithstanding the fact that Italy undoubtedly possessed a more sophisticated and highly developed economy and society than its neighbours. Though Burckhardt is not without his supporters in perceiving Italian society as progressive and less bound by social and economic traditions than other parts of Europe, the consensus of opinion suggests that his depiction of Italy is not borne out by the surviving evidence. As to his view of women, and their supposed equality with men, this, not surprisingly, has found few advocates. While one might admire Burckhardt's desire to see women integrated within his vision of the Renaissance, doubts remain as to the nature and extent of female participation in the movement (see Jardine, 1985). As for his 'feminist' principles, these are, by and large, the object of derision, originating as they do in the nineteenth-century view of woman as essentially destined to imitate the superior qualities of men.

6   Part 6, 'Morality and religion'

(a) We catch a glimpse here of Burckhardt's profound concern to understand what for him stood as a paradox: the fact that one of the end products of the Renaissance was a collapse of morality. One way out of the dilemma was to deny the right of the historian to make moral judgements on the past (pp.270–1), advice that Burckhardt himself found almost impossible to follow. On the other hand, he was able to point the finger of blame at two major contributory factors. First, he confessed that the Renaissance desire to emulate the pagan heroes of antiquity may have eroded moral propriety (p.272). Second, and far more important, there was the example of the church, which Burckhardt consistently depicted as corrupt and held responsible for driving the people 'into the arms of unbelief and despair' (p.290). The church, in his eyes, was spiritually and morally bankrupt. Small wonder, therefore, that Italians of this period were tempted to seek redemption in such 'superstitious' practices as astrology and magic (p.313).

(b) Is it possible, we might ask, to write the history of morality? And what of Burckhardt's treatment of the Italian Catholic church? Are we convinced by his explanation of the failure of the Protestant Reformation to take root in Italy?

(c) With all the usual provisos, most historians would today feel comfortable with the idea of reconstructing the moral universe of past societies. Influenced by social anthropology, it is possible, we learn, to rediscover how our European forbears thought of moral issues and how this influenced their actions. Morality, we are reassured, is culturally constructed just like other forms of knowledge. Burckhardt, who rightly suggested that we, as historians, might be best advised to refrain from passing moral judgements on past peoples, signally failed, however, to heed his own advice in his treatment of the Italian church. Though most historians of the pre-Reformation church in Italy would not doubt the existence of various forms of corruption at various levels of church governance, the picture that emerges today is one far more balanced than that provided by the sceptical Burckhardt. Indeed, we now know that many of the church's personnel, including its fiercest critics and would-be reformers, were themselves profoundly influenced by humanist values. Consequently, it is not deemed valid, as Burckhardt presupposed, to present the church (in all its myriad forms and manifestations) as antithetical to the Renaissance. Religion and a deep yearning for spiritual piety were as likely to be found in supporters of Renaissance values as they were in members of the clergy. In some cases, the two coincided. ❖

Bibliography

BENTON, J.F. (1985) 'Consciousness of self and perceptions of individuality' in R.L. Benson and G. Constable (eds) *Renaissance and Renewal in the Twelfth Century*, Oxford, Oxford University Press.

BRAUDEL, F. (1981–4) *Civilization and Capitalism, 15th–18th Century*, 3 vols, London, Collins.

BROWN, A. (1988) 'Jacob Burckhardt's Renaissance', *History Today*, vol. 38, pp.20–6.

BROWN, A. (1995) 'Introduction' in A. Brown (ed.) *Language and Images of Renaissance Italy*, Oxford, Clarendon Press.

BURCKHARDT, J. (1990) *The Civilization of the Renaissance in Italy*, trans. S.G.C. Middlemore, Harmondsworth, Penguin; first published 1858.

BURKE, P.(1990) 'Introduction' in J. Burckhardt, *The Civilization of the Renaissance in Italy*, Harmondsworth, Penguin.

BURKE, P.(1998) *The European Renaissance: Centres and Peripheries*, Oxford, Blackwell.

BYNUM, C.W. (1984) 'Did the twelfth century discover the individual?' in *Jesus as Mother: Studies in the Spirituality of the High Middle Ages*, Berkeley, University of California Press.

CASSIRER, E. (1963) *The Individual and the Cosmos in Renaissance Philosophy*, Oxford, Blackwell.

GOMBRICH, E.H. (1979) *Ideals and Idols: Essays on Values in History and Art*, Oxford, Phaidon.

GREENBLATT, S.J. (1980) *Renaissance Self-fashioning: From More to Shakespeare*, Chicago, University of Chicago Press.

HUIZINGA, J. (1999) *The Waning of the Middle Ages*, Mineola, NY, Dover Publications; first published 1919.

JARDINE, L. (1985) ' "O decus Italia virgo": the myth of the learned lady in the Renaissance', *Historical Journal*, vol. 28, pp.799–819.

KENT, F.W. (1977) *Household and Lineage in Renaissance Florence: The Family Life of the Capponi, Ginori and Rucellai*, Princeton, NJ, Princeton University Press.

KERRIGAN, W., and BRADEN, G. (1989) *The Idea of the Renaissance*, Baltimore and London, Johns Hopkins University Press.

KRISTELLER, P.O. (1964) 'Changing views of the intellectual history of the Renaissance since Jacob Burckhardt' in T. Helton (ed.) *The Renaissance: A Reconsideration of the Theories and Interpretations of the Age*, Madison, Wis., University of Wisconsin Press.

MARTIN, J. (1997) 'Inventing sincerity, refashioning prudence: the discovery of the individual in Renaissance Europe', *American Historical Review*, vol. 102, pp.1309–42.

MORRIS, C. (1972) *The Discovery of the Individual, 1050–1200*, London, SPCK for the Church Historical Society.

VERDON, T. (1990) 'Christianity, the Renaissance and the study of history: environments of experience and imagination' in T. Verdon and J. Henderson (eds) *Christianity and the Renaissance: Image and Religious Imagination in the Quattrocento*, Syracuse, Syracuse University Press.

Reader source

Richard Danson Brown, 'From Burckhardt to Greenblatt: New Historicisms and Old': original work commissioned for the Reader. (no. 1)

CHAPTER TWO

Evidence for Renaissance culture

BY LUCILLE KEKEWICH, NICK WEBB AND
ANTONY LENTIN

Objectives

The objectives of this chapter are that you should:

- gain some knowledge of the great range of new artefacts and ideas which were produced in Europe during the fifteenth and sixteenth centuries;
- assess some evidence for the phenomenon of the revival of antiquity as a central feature of Renaissance culture;
- appreciate the diversity of traditional and new styles, practices and attitudes which coexisted during the Renaissance;
- consider how the portraits of Michel de Montaigne and his *Essays* relate to the claim that the discovery of the individual was characteristic of Renaissance culture.

Introduction

This chapter addresses two of the main claims that Jacob Burckhardt made for the Renaissance. The first was that it was radically shaped by the revival of antiquity. We review this by examining some of the evidence for that revival as well as other developments in the culture of the Renaissance. The second was that the Renaissance was the time of the discovery of the individual, in contrast to the western Middle Ages when individual aspirations were seemingly inhibited by a domineering church. Michel de Montaigne produced his autobiographical *Essays* in the second half of the sixteenth century. By considering his aims and attitudes as a writer in relation to examples of Renaissance portraiture, we can try to assess the significance of his attempts to depict his personality and discover his own identity.

Fonts, forks and fireworks

If you were asked to think of some representative examples of culture from the Renaissance, you would probably name a famous painting, sculpture or building – perhaps a statue by Michelangelo or a painting by Raphael; you might mention a writer, Shakespeare or Cervantes; or a musician such as Josquin or Byrd. Yet we might equally point to developments in everyday culture whose influences are still felt today such as: the lettering on this page, the table fork and fireworks.

Script and style

The text of this book is printed in a version of Roman lettering, which is distinguished by its serifs (drawn lines finishing off the ends of letters) and wedges, balanced proportions, uprightness, regular spacing, uniformity and lack of joined letters. It is quite similar to the lettering adopted by the Florentine humanist Giovanni Francesco Poggio Bracciolini (1380–1459) in his copy of a poem by the Roman author Catullus (Plate 1). For us, the main peculiarity of Poggio's handwriting is the tall 's' which could be confused with an 'f'.

Humanism had a significant impact on the development of Renaissance culture and will be discussed in depth in Chapter 3. Here we are interested in one characteristic attributed to humanists – their veneration for classical antiquity and attempts to retrieve the past. Poggio and other Florentine humanists, including Coluccio Salutati (1331–1406) and Niccolò Niccoli (1363–1437), produced versions of *lettera antica* – ancient script as opposed to the 'modern' style of the Middle Ages. They were influenced by the poet and humanist Francesco Petrarch (1304–74), who during the fourteenth century had recommended a style similar to Roman lower-case script in preference to the often illegible, over-abbreviated Gothic handwriting used by medieval scholars. Such black lettering could also be difficult to read because there was insufficient distinction in the shape of individual letters, as shown by the joke example illustrated in Figure 2.1.

Figure 2.1 Example of formal Gothic hand. From M. Drogin (1989) *Medieval Calligraphy, Its History and Technique*, New York, Dover Publications Inc., p.67. Reproduced by permission of the publishers

By the time the first printing press in Italy was installed at the Benedictine monastery of Subiaco near Rome in 1465, the new humanist script was well established. It was adopted by printers from 1467 onwards and became the normal lettering for book publishing in print and manuscript throughout Europe, except for German-speaking areas, during the course of the sixteenth century. The Venetian printer Aldus Manutius (*c.*1450–1515) used a version of this script for a small-scale series of classical texts which were published from 1501. This series was intended for the growing humanist audience.

Isabella d' Este, among others, owned a copy of the *Opera* (collected works) of the Roman poet Virgil, which is now in the British Library (Plate 2). Aldus, the printer-publisher, intended his new Latin type to complement the continuous script he had already devised for Greek texts. In his dedications Aldus mentioned the manuscripts belonging to the father of the famous humanist Pietro Bembo (1470–1547), which he had seen and used as textual sources. He also praised the 'Daedalus-like' hands of the sculptor who carved the typeface (Daedalus was an ingenious craftsman in classical mythology). The letters of the Latin text are characterized by their regular slope, together with the restrained use of combinations and joining of letters. The script style derives from the fast handwriting associated with humanist secretaries, often working in the papal *curia* (court). The angled version of humanist script is now called italic, which indicates the English recognition of where it came from. The opening pages of the Virgil text that you see in Plate 2 were illuminated by hand in the same way as if it was a manuscript book. Pre-Gothic medieval manuscripts were used as models for Renaissance script and illumination partly through a mistaken belief that they reflected the appearance of classical books. Nevertheless, the reformation of handwriting was bound up with the humanist recovery of, and desire to imitate, antique culture. This is also evident in the attitude of scribes and artists towards upper-case letter forms, for they regularly used the square capitals found on Roman inscriptions. The reform of letters was complemented by a perceived return to a classical standard in language. Epitaphs in stone were now mainly written in prose, often incorporating Latin quotations, in carefully laid-out compositions, instead of crammed letters and dull hexameter verse, which had been the norm during the Middle Ages.

We shall look at the career of one assiduous inscription-hunter, Ciriaco of Ancona, in the next chapter. However, some of his connections are worth noting here as evidence for the diffusion of Renaissance culture. A friend of Niccoli and Poggio, he also visited Padua in the 1440s, where an antiquarian interest in epigraphy (the study of inscriptions) was fostered by the local university lecturers and clergy. A number of these were friends or patrons of the budding young artist Andrea Mantegna (1431–1503), who throughout his life remained fascinated by different forms of writing, ranging from cipher codes to Hebrew. Both Ciriaco and Mantegna were close friends of the eccentric antiquarian, Felice Feliciano (1433–80) of Verona, who wrote the first treatise on the Roman alphabet, using epigraphic examples. Feliciano copied the drawings Ciriaco had made of antique monuments which were then used as models in Mantegna's work. Mantegna's collection of antiquities was remarkable, the more so, according to Feliciano, because he was such a bad Latinist.

In his painting Mantegna's approach to antiquity ranges from careful archaeological reconstruction to fantastical improvization. From 1464 he was working for the Gonzaga family, a dynasty of **condottieri** (mercenary captains) whose court was based in Mantua. (The art and politics of Renaissance courts are investigated in more detail in Book 2 of this series. Here we are looking at an aspect of the subject which relates to the use of the forms of classical antiquity.) Mantegna's style is a typical example of what was known in Italy as **all' antica**, meaning that it looked back to antiquity for its formal models, rather than to the 'modern' **Gothic style** of late medieval art. He used this antique style in much of his work, regardless of whether he was depicting the lives of saints, subjects from Roman history, moralizing allegories or even contemporary portraits. The cultural authority associated with antique references appealed equally to republican states, such as Venice, and to princely regimes. It was, however, in the latter context that Mantegna was best able to develop his distinctive genius, as court artist, friend of humanists, antique collector and cultural adviser to the Gonzaga. The comparison with ancient art provided a standard for measuring both the magnificence of patrons and the genius of their artists (see Cole, 1995, pp.36–43).

Exercise

Some understanding of Mantegna's imaginative reformulation of an 'antique' style can be seen in his painting commissions for the Gonzaga. Read pages 148–59 in Cole and look at the related plates. The three Gonzaga commissions discussed by Cole, the *Camera Picta*, the *Triumphs of Caesar*, and the *Madonna della Vittoria*, were all influenced to some extent by classical antiquity. As you read note down the features that demonstrate this influence. They should be apparent in the choice of subject-matter, the motifs of subsidiary decoration and the style throughout.

Discussion

All three painting commissions combine idealized representations based on antique sculptural models with a degree of naturalistic realism. In the case of the *Camera Picta* (fresco, 1465–74) the degree of realism was sufficient to make the portraits appear immediately recognizable and the fictive architecture was extended as part of the actual room. However, Mantegna represented the antique elements with similar conviction. These included well-known Roman monuments in the city in the background of the 'Meeting Scene' (Cole, pl. 113); scenes from the lives of classical heroes in the spandrels painted as relief sculpture; and the heads of Roman emperors as if in medallions on the ceiling (Cole, pl. 111). The framework provided by the fictive architecture is similarly articulated through decorative classical motifs. For Ludovico Gonzaga this painted audience chamber was a dynastic statement, whereas for Mantegna it was a virtuoso performance which won him a reputation as the best artist in Italy within ten years of its completion.

A representative example of the way texts played a role in Mantegna's pictures can be seen in the *Triumphs of Caesar,* a set of nine canvas paintings (1489–1506). They were based on a mixture of ancient visual and literary sources and contemporary descriptions of Roman triumphs. The inscription may be an allusion to Julius Caesar's conquest of Gaul. The reference to 'envy scorned and overcome' would relate to the opposition to Caesar in the Roman senate, a suitably imperial sentiment for the Gonzaga. Of the three commissions, the *Triumphs* is probably the most strictly accurate recreation of antiquity.

The third commission described by Cole, the *Madonna della Vittoria* (1496), is a votive altarpiece dedicated to the Virgin Mary. It is full of Christian imagery but much of the detail is classical in style, for example, the armour of the marquis Francesco and the saints, the base of the Virgin's throne and the swags of fruit around and above it. ❖

Several of Mantegna's paintings became widely known through prints. They were a relatively cheap method of collecting works of art which effectively promoted an artist's reputation over a wide geographical area. At the same time the prints distributed *all' antica* models in reproduction to patrons who had never seen Roman art. These indirect means of transmission were especially important in communicating Italian ideas to northern Europe. For instance, Mantegna's early admirers included the German artist, Albrecht Dürer.

Mantegna's concern for the spirit of antiquity, as opposed to the letter of antiquarian imitation, can be illustrated by an anecdote recorded by Feliciano. In September 1464 Mantegna and Feliciano went, with other friends, on a two-day expedition. Feliciano wrote:

Worth Remembering:

... Starting out together, with Andrea Mantegna the Paduan,
incomparable friend, Samuel de Tradate, and myself Feliciano of
Verona, for the sake of relaxing our thoughts, we came from a field
as lovely as the Tusculan, [reference to Cicero's villa in Tusculum] by
way of the lake of Garda, to greenswards like heavenly gardens in the
most delicious dwelling places of the Muses. We found them not only
pleasant and fragrant with red and purple flowers, but also with the
leafy branches of orange and lemon trees everywhere, when we gazed
at the islands through fields that were overflowing with springs, and
adorned with tall old leaf-bearing laurels and fruit trees. There we
saw a number of remains of antiquity, and first, on the island of the
monks, one with highly ornamental letters on a marble pillar.

Celebration

On the [next] day ... under the rule of the merry man Samuel de
Tradate, the consuls being the distinguished Andrea Mantegna of
Padua and John the Antenorean [Paduan], with myself in charge with
the bright troop following, through dark laurels taking our ease.
Having crowned Samuel with myrtle, periwinkle, ivy, and a variety of
leaves, with his own participation, and entering the ancient precincts
of St. Dominic, we found a most worthy memorial of Antoninus Pius
Germanicus surnamed Sarmaticus ... Having seen ... these things, we
circled lake Garda, the field of Neptune, in a skiff properly packed
with carpets and all kinds of comforts, which we strewed with laurels
and other noble leaves, while our ruler Samuel played the zither, and
celebrated all the while.

At length, having gloriously crossed over the lake, we sought safe
harbor and disembarked. Then entering the temple of the Blessed
Virgin on the Garda, and rendering the highest praises to the most
high thunderer and his glorious mother, most devoutly, for having
illuminated our hearts to assemble together and opened our minds to
seek and investigate such outstanding places, and caused us to see
such worthy and varied diversions of objects, some of them
antiquities, and allowed us such a happy and prosperous day, and
given us fortunate sailing and good harbor, and our wished-for
conclusion. Especially for seeing such great wonders of antiquities;
anyone of great soul should on just that account take the road to
see them.

(Gilbert, 1980, pp.179–81)

Here we have a group of men, at least two of whom are in their forties,
playing at being ancients, while looking for inscriptions and

archaeological remains on the shore of Lake Garda. Feliciano's statement that there were 'all kinds of comforts' and they 'celebrated all the while' suggests that wine was drunk. While they did go to church during the field trip, pilgrimages were often regarded as an opportunity for a holiday. The proximity of Roman remains to the Christian religious sites is noticeable and reflects the common medieval practice of reusing classical inscriptions and masonry. Feliciano is evidently writing in a deliberately classical tone when he refers to Lake Garda as 'the field of Neptune' and Christ as 'the most high thunderer'.

Manners and courtesy

A private picnic, such as that described by Feliciano, was not bound by the same degree of formal decorum as indoor dining. The interior decorations, the plate, drapes and furnishings, together with table manners all contributed to a highly-ritualized performance art which formed a distinct component of Renaissance culture. An example of this is the use of the table fork. The Italian nobility were accustomed to using forks to eat sweets, salads or fruit; although the practice was considered decadent by some northern visitors. A Medici inventory of 1492 refers to eighteen spoons and eighteen forks of silver, and paintings of the period provide further evidence of their use. You can see some young ladies skewering nuts with a two-pronged fork during dessert in a Botticelli painting for a Medici marriage in 1483 (Plate 3), and Salome's unexpected platter appears to have put King Herod off the next course, which required a knife and fork in the picture by Botticini (Figure 2.2).

Figure 2.2 Francesco Botticini, *Herod's Feast*, *c.*1485, tempera on panel. Galleria della Collegiata, Empoli. Photo: Alinari

During the thirteenth and fourteenth centuries a few aristocratic inventories from northern European countries mention forks alongside spoons as luxury objects. Generally, though, people ate with a knife, bread mops and their fingers, and, except for the most privileged guests at a formal meal, the diners would share eating bowls. The water to wash their hands would be scented with rosemary, marjoram or rose petals. In Italy, however, the practice of eating with forks was not confined to the nobility. In 1376 ordinary Italians were using them to wrap spaghetti, and the sumptuary laws (regulations concerning conspicuous display) promulgated in Florence in 1472 forbade peasants to own silver forks weighing more than eight ounces. Michel de Montaigne reports seeing the table of a Roman cardinal laid with bread, knife, fork and spoon in 1581, and he thought the etiquette of the meal was comparable to that observed by the nobility of his own country.

Taking their cue from the classical moralists who saw courtesy as the reflection of inward virtue, Italian Renaissance authors sought to codify social manners: using a fork was considered part of decorous eating. The following passage is taken from a treatise on manners (*On Conviviality, c.*1493) by Giovanni Pontano (*c.*1426–1503), the humanist prime minister to the Aragonese kings of Naples. It is one of a series of treatises about virtues of public life, originally recommended by the Greek philosopher Aristotle. At a theoretical level Aristotle proposed the ethical doctrine of the Golden Mean (the good between two bad extremes of behaviour, for example, excessive indulgence and abstemiousness) and Pontano explores how this works in practice:

> When ... banquets are held solely for the sake of splendour, then not only is there no need to leave out or dispense with anything, but the reins should even be loosened; and instead of proceeding at a stately pace, as the saying goes, things should move at a gallop. This is the time for all the domestic trappings to be on display, with the sideboards and back-boards decked out with gold and silver, the dining-halls decorated, the floors covered over and everything arranged so that, as Horace says, 'the house itself laughs' [*Carmina* IV.11.6]. Added to this is the splendid and lavish livery of the servants, who should be trained to do everything on the nod; for is there anything more awkward than being served at table in a boisterous manner?

> With regard to the banquet and all its fixtures, I can offer, in this section, the following general advice. All the components should appear to be in competition with each other, so that the domestic trappings do not outshine the abundance of the food, nor does the abundance outstrip the sumptuousness and elegance. Local and

national dishes will not suffice, unless accompanied by many foodstuffs which appear to have been imported, with great difficulty, from abroad, so that a kind of deliberate variety, sought out with elaborate care, is apparent ... The courses themselves should be plentiful and varied; for variety adds much to the sumptuousness and provides great pleasure during the meal; and splendour and abundance are not readily evident without a number of courses.

Nevertheless, everything should be done according to the appropriate measure. Striving for effect, especially when it is excessive, is in no way admissible. Is there anyone who praises such behaviour in banquets, given that good and well-reputed men do not even permit it in the worship of the gods? Is there anything more deserving of condemnation than immoderate religious zeal? It seems a proper and splendid practice to precede the arrival of the food with trumpets and flutes, which entertain the guests and servants with music, as well as signalling the appearance of the dishes, so that order is combined with pleasure; for if order is lacking, everything is necessarily disorganized and confused. It contributes also to the order if the servants and waiters observe the discipline appropriate to banquets: not only should there be no sullen or disturbing words but no such gestures either. For this reason, it seems to me a good idea that musicians should be in attendance at banquets, for they will give pleasure with their songs and, moreover, will entice the servants to listen to them, thus producing silence, and from silence will come a serene atmosphere. The management and running of the whole affair seems to reside, above all, in the careful planning and attention to detail of the steward and master of ceremonies.

(Tateo, 1970, pp.138–55; translated by J. Kraye, 1998)

The scene described by Pontano is illustrated in many *cassone* (marriage chests) panel depictions of feasting (Plate 4). In this chapter he is concerned with the meat course; afterwards there would be a dessert course of sweet foods, wine, more music and gift-giving. The banquet is a typical instance of the conspicuous consumption associated with courts like that of Naples and with those who wished to be courteous: that is say, to behave in the correct courtly manner. The inclusion of forks in the dining service would have formed part of the overall effect of magnificence and decorum. Pontano's recommendations for good taste can also be applied to other contexts where splendour could be shown, such as architecture, antique collections or jewellery.

Banquets could last for the best part of a day, sometimes longer. Surviving accounts of the menus describe the visual arrangement of the food as 'representations', often depicting a recognizable subject

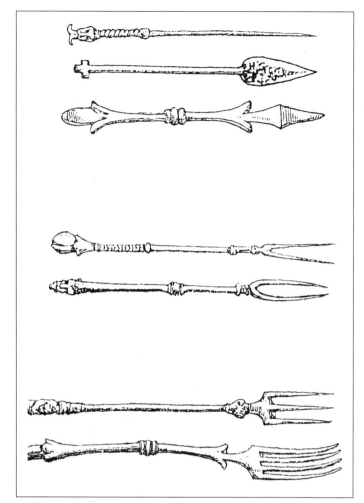

Figure 2.3 Forks and related cutlery from the fourteenth to the seventeenth centuries. From P. Marchese (1989) *L'invenzione della forchetta*, Catarzano, Rubbettino Editore, plate 1, p.15

(see a Sforza banquet menu in the Anthology, no. 29). Food sculpture was made possible by imports of sugar in the fourteenth century. Usually the banquet comprised a series of fish, fowl and meat courses, interspersed with salads and different wines, followed by sugar or marzipan desserts and fruit. The forks were used for the meat and fruit.

The distinct advantages of eating with forks were that they were cleaner, more elegant and encouraged the diners to use separate plates, thereby creating a sense of formal individuality. The hierarchical arrangement of the tables and the displays of wealth by the host and guests would have accentuated the distinctions in status.

The fork had its origin in antiquity, but it was less overtly a revival of classical culture and more a sign of the pre-eminence of Italian fashion during this period. It had been taken up in France during the reign of Henri III (1574–89), following his holiday in Italy between 1574–5 and under the pervasive influence of his mother, Catherine de' Medici. The Englishman, Thomas Coryat, writing in 1610, considered eating with a fork to be an Italian characteristic (Marchese, 1989, pp.37, 161). To this extent the fork and its associated social etiquette ranked alongside those widely-dispersed other stereotypes of Italian culture: the Petrarchan sonnet, Machiavellian politicking, double-entry book-keeping and the art of poisoning.

Festive fireworks

Whether the introduction of fireworks into Europe should be credited to the Italian oriental traveller Marco Polo (1254–1324) is unclear, but it certainly had no connection with classical antiquity. Fireworks originated in China, where missiles which exploded in mid air were being used by 1232. Gunpowder, of which the saltpetre of fireworks is the main ingredient, was known in the west by the fourteenth century, and it became a decisive feature of warfare in the next century. The fall of Constantinople in 1453 is largely credited to Turkish fire-power. Fireworks were first used at the civic festivals associated with patron saints, such as St John the Baptist in Florence, and by the late fifteenth century they had become a fashionable component of many Renaissance festivals. The military associations meant that the designers and presenters of firework displays were usually experts in the practical science of ballistics and gunnery. The fireworks were either designed as small 'table' pieces to be let off at private gatherings or as public displays within an architectural or sculptural setting, the most common form of firework being the *girandola* or 'whirler', which came in small and large versions.

Fireworks continued to be part of the St John the Baptist's day festivities under Duke Cosimo de' Medici from 1537. He required a more structured display than that which had been organized by the Florentine republican government, with the fireworks arranged in the classical shape of an octagonal Temple of Peace or representing a narrative subject associated with fire, such as Dante's *Inferno* or the Hades of Orpheus. The longest surviving *girandola* is still held at the Castel Sant' Angelo – the papal fortress that controls access to the Vatican from the city of Rome – on the feast day of saints Peter and Paul, and at the coronation of a new pope. The first reference to the event dates from 1463. By the time the manual on pyrotechnics of Vanoccio Biringuccio (1480–1537) was published in 1540, Nuremberg and Bologna were the recognized centres for firework manufacture. Nuremberg specialized in the small-size rockets, wheels and fountains that we know today, whereas the Bolognese Ruggieri family had a European reputation for the production of set-piece displays. Similarly by the end of the century fireworks had become a feature in the more private setting of court masques as well as retaining their older use as mass entertainments at public festivals. The engraving in Figure 2.4 shows the papal display of 1579. The accompanying caption tells how all the windows, church towers, and palaces of the cardinals, lords and gentlemen were lit and boxes with fire burnt in the streets and squares, so that it seemed that the whole of Rome was alight. The height and the position of the fortress overlooking the river Tiber would have enhanced the visual effect. Here is the description of the display given by Biringuccio in his *Pirotechnia*:

> If you have never seen a girandole, as perhaps you never have, you may understand what it was when you hear it named. Indeed, although it was a beautiful thing and cost much money, it was a useless thing to make. Nevertheless those times were truly golden, that is, they had much gold to spend for things without consideration of the expense, and fireworks had no other purpose than amusement

and endured no longer than the kiss of a lover for his lady, if as long. Now, so that you may know exactly what they are, I shall tell you how they are made and how they are operated. First they selected a fable or historical scene. Then, in order to represent it, they made four, six or eight figures which with their posture or appearance should represent that fable or story. To make these figures they first built a framework of wood with arms and legs and then proceeded to enlarge it to shape by tying hay on all its parts. Then they put on the head, feet, and hands that they had made by moulding in plaster of Paris. Then they clothed them with heavy linen cloth and painted them elsewhere with fresh-coloured tints ...

When this had been painted and made beautiful, they had two or three thousand rockets of various kinds and sizes, some to make explosions, and some arranged to move upwards toward the sky, others level, and others to strike the ground. Among these, in the mouths of animals or figures or whatever seemed best, were put some squibs which project tongues of fire two or three *braccia* [between one and two metres] long. Elsewhere fire tubes were put which would expel balls made in the way that I have described to you before. In other places they put small girandoles each one of which consists of two little squibs tied individually one on each end of a stick of wood ... with a hole in the middle, so that it can turn when fastened loosely with a nail to the end of a pole. The holes should be made near the diameter, as are those in guns ...

Now these things were put in place according to the opinion of the master, and the more of these there were and the more varied, the more beautiful this thing was judged. Therefore they made some of these rockets which, no sooner were they extinguished than they seemed to give birth to four or six others in the air. Likewise the masters made various powders that took fire, and ten or fifteen lights at one time made out of a composition of turpentine, pine resin, ship's pitch, and gunpowder, with dry laurel sawdust. And, to conclude, they applied the fire to this contrivance with a fuse made of cotton boiled in vinegar mixed with sulphur, gunpowder, and saltpetre. A master fuse was joined to all the fuses that were to do the igniting.

As I told you, it was customary to make this thing in many places, and the ones I know most of were in Florence and Siena. Truly it was an ingenious and beautiful thing to see it produce so many effects in fire, just as living things do by themselves. Now for all the said festivals, only this one has remained in Rome in Castel Sant' Angelo when popes are elected or crowned or at other great celebrations. But instead of constructing this edifice they make use of the whole castle, which is

Figure 2.4 Ambrogio Brambilla, *Firework Display at the Castel Sant' Angelo, Rome*, 1579, engraving. Biblioteca Apostolica Vaticana, Ris.S.6, fig. 112

indeed a very pleasing shape. They ornament it by placing in each embrasure and on top of each merlon [parapet] two small lanterns made of a sheet of white paper over a mound of clay in which a tallow candle is put. When they are lit at night it is a very beautiful thing to see that shining and transparent whiteness in many rows as far as the eye can reach. As soon as the lanterns are lighted, two salutes are fired from a large number of short guns, all of which hurl into the air balls of fire made like those that are put in the tube I have already described to you. These make a clear fire in the air that appears like stars, finally bursting. At the third round they shoot many rockets [which] hold three to four ounces of powder each. These are constructed so that after they have moved upwards with a long tail and seem to be finished they burst and each one sends forth anew six or eight rockets. Fire tubes are also made and small girandoles, flames, and lights, and even the coat of arms of the Pope is composed in fire. Up on the highest peak of the castle where the angel is attached to the flagpole the shape of a great star containing many rays is erected.

Thus, in short, when all the fire is lit and the guns go off, and the rockets, fire tubes, squibs, and balls go hither and thither nothing can be seen but smoke and fire, and verily it seems then to be the fire imagined in hell. As far as I know, I have never seen such a thing in any other festival ...

(Gaudi and Smith, 1978, pp.441–3)

Exercise

How might fireworks have enhanced papal authority?

Discussion

As we can see from the engraving and Biringuccio's description, the Castel Sant' Angelo *girandola* was a grand affair. While it is associated with 'civic religion' in celebrating the Roman patron saints, the ruler–subject relationship between the papacy and the city of Rome was also reinforced by this public festival at the fortification controlling the access to the Vatican from the secular city. The patterning of the fireworks includes the outline of the papal coat-of-arms. Like banquets, fireworks are a form of conspicuous consumption: they go up in smoke. While fireworks were often thought of as part of the deregulation of society associated with communal festivals, they also represented a form of patronal splendour. The visual appeal of fireworks were an extension of the dazzling brightness and sumptuousness of the court, the *son et lumière* of the ephemeral event literally highlighting the permanent authority of the papal fortress. ❖

A process, a period or both?

The inventors of humanist script were members of the intellectual elite of republican Florence: Niccolò Niccoli was a scholar, Poggio Bracciolini and Coluccio Salutati both became chancellors of Florence. Yet by the end of the fifteenth century this script would have been familiar to any literate Italian. It was considered to be classical in origin, even if it depended on the humanists' collections of early medieval manuscripts. The table fork became widely established through the culture of the hereditary nobility who adopted Italian manners. Fireworks were initially communal and popular, but were increasingly used in extravagant pageants and celebrations organized by the aristocratic and princely courts. These distinctions about the origin and transformation of a cultural artefact help us to understand how its meaning can change within different contexts. Niccoli and Poggio were humanists for whom the revival of antiquity was a conscious aim. The same was true of the artist Mantegna and his circle of friends. Stylistically, the ornamental scrolls and cartouches of some surviving forks have parallels with *all' antica* design, but the use of the fork itself was not developed in imitation of antiquity. Fireworks, although they acquired their popularity during the fifteenth and sixteenth centuries, have little direct connection with the Renaissance, if it is conceived as a process associated with the revival or emulation of antiquity.

Issues of definition are a constant preoccupation of this series. Should we envisage the Renaissance primarily as a process – the adoption of a distinct set of cultural practices and values by the people of post-medieval Europe? Or is it fairer simply to use the term Renaissance for the period which followed the Middle Ages? Both approaches have attracted their critics. Burckhardt would appear to have envisaged the Renaissance as both period and process. Others have questioned its existence in either form.

A further issue which we shall need to explore is the vexed problem of the spread and reception of Renaissance culture outside of Italy. Evidence of Renaissance values and beliefs can be found throughout Europe. However, their dispersal across the continent was anything but uniform. Most nations and peoples not only selected those aspects of Renaissance culture which best suited their specific ends and aspirations, but cross-fertilization with indigenous cultures produced curious hybrid and localized versions of the Renaissance. Moreover, there is often little evidence that this process proceeded systematically. Instead, reception was more often than not characterized by an *ad hoc* approach, the recipients opting to accept those Renaissance forms and styles which were most relevant to their particular community (Fish, 1980, pp.14–16). More often than not, this meant that Renaissance values were admired and imitated for reasons which had little to do with aesthetic judgements. Ethical and political considerations also figured prominently, the symbolism of classical art providing a wealth of potential references which rulers might exploit to legitimize their authority. The end result was a complex 'language' of classical allusions and images which, by the sixteenth century, had successfully insinuated itself into the cultural life of Europe's elite.

Portraits, self-portraits, Montaigne's *Essays* and 'the Reader'

Burckhardt claimed the discovery of the individual as a hallmark of the Renaissance (1990, pp.98–119). We can consider this claim through the work of one Renaissance Frenchman, Michel de Montaigne (1533–92). In his *Essays* Montaigne made a unique attempt to understand human nature through the study and discovery of one individual – himself. In his preface entitled 'To the Reader', Montaigne declares: 'I myself am the subject of my book' (Screech, 1991, p.lix; all subsequent references to the *Essays* are to this edition unless indicated otherwise). What Montaigne was doing was highly original, so original that he gave it a novel title which, though familiar to us, puzzled and intrigued his contemporaries. The French word *Essais* meant, among other things, attempts, tests, trials, experiments. Attempts at what? Experiments in what? His professed aim was a kind of self-portrait – 'drawn from life' – but drawn in words; and on almost every page of the *Essays* he offers some touch of himself, some random but deliberate piece of self-revelation. In some chapters he gives more detailed and extended self-portraits.[1] In 'To the Reader' Montaigne explicitly uses the metaphor of painting: 'it is my own self that I am painting' (even simpler in the French: *c'est moy que je peins)* – and he claims to offer a 'natural', realistic self-portrait. It must be realistic and truthful (or 'honest') if it is to have any value and to be recognizable by his 'friends and kinsmen' and 'keep their knowledge of me more full, more alive' (p.lix).

Having one's portrait painted was common in the Renaissance among the wealthy, powerful or important. One purpose, as Montaigne says of his *Essays*, was to be remembered by friends and family, 'so that, having lost me (as they must do soon) they can find here again some traits of my character and of my humours' (p.lix). Montaigne had

---

[1] See the *Essays* Book 1, Chapter 26; Book 2, Chapters 8, 10, 17; and especially Book 3, Chapter 2.

Figure 2.5 Anon., *Montaigne as mayor*, 1581–5, oil on panel. Musée Condé, Chantilly. Photo: E.T. Archive

several portraits painted of himself. One was an anonymous portrait as mayor of Bordeaux, an office he held from 1581–5 (Figure 2.5).

Why did Montaigne not select a portrait of himself to accompany his *Essays*?

Ever since the invention of printing, portraits of the author had become conventional in books published in the Renaissance. Given this, and Montaigne's interest in and claims about the *Essays* as self-portraiture, it may seem odd that none of the editions published in his lifetime included his portrait. This was not through any apathy towards the presentation of his work: he took a close interest in the design and format of the *Essays* as they went to press, including the frontispiece, making frequent amendments and suggestions. The first portrait of Montaigne to appear with the *Essays* – by the fashionable Flemish engraver Thomas de Leu (1560–1612) – appeared only after his death, in the edition of 1608 (Figure 2.6). Why, if his intention in the *Essays* was self-portraiture, did Montaigne himself not take the obvious step of showing 'the Reader' what he looked like, by including a portrait in the frontispiece? Several reasons are possible.

When we think of Shakespeare's appearance, we almost always think of the famous engraving by Martin Droeshout in the frontispiece to the first folio edition of his works of 1623 (Figure 2.7). This portrait must have been reasonably life-like, since the editors of this edition were the playwright's old friends and fellow-actors; and in his prefatory lines 'To the Reader', which these first editors placed opposite the engraving, Ben Jonson (1572–1637) claimed that it was indeed remarkably lifelike:

> This Figure, that thou here seest put,
> It was for gentle Shakespeare cut;
> Wherein the Graver had a strife
> with Nature, to out-do the life:
> O, could he but have drawn his wit
> As well in brass, as he hath hit
> His face; the Print would then surpass
> All, that was ever writ in brass.
> But, since he cannot, Reader, look
> Not on his Picture, but his Book.

Montaigne's posthumous editors did exactly the same as Shakespeare's. Beneath the engraving by de Leu, which is clearly taken from the anonymous mayoral portrait of Montaigne (Figure 2.5), they placed four lines of verse attributed to the poet and critic François de Malherbe (1555–1628). In English they read as follows:

> Here is a complete portrait of the great Montaigne,
> The painter depicted his body, and he [Montaigne] his intelligence (or 'wit'):
> The former equals Nature by his art,
> But the latter surpasses Nature in everything he writes.

The prefatory verses by Jonson and Malherbe are very similar in their message. Both agree that the portraits are highly realistic, 'natural', a true likeness of the author. But they stress that portraits, however lifelike, can only convey the author's outward appearance; they cannot depict his mind ('wit' or intelligence). The picture can tell us what Shakespeare or Montaigne looked like; but only their writings can tell us what they were like, what kind of men they were. The portrait is no substitute for the book. Evidently this was also Montaigne's view.

Let us put this claim to the test (something Montaigne was always doing, and a key meaning of *'essais'*). Does the portrait of Montaigne as mayor in Figure 2.5 tell us much more than that he *was* mayor? It shows us his outward appearance, that (like Shakespeare) he was bald, had a moustache, and so on. But what about the inner man? Perhaps it is just a rather uninspiring, feebly

Figure 2.6 Thomas de Leu, *Montaigne*, engraving. Bibliothèque Nationale de France, Cabinet des Estampes

Figure 2.7 Martin Droeshout, *William Shakespeare*, engraving, published on the title page of the first folio of 1623. The British Library

executed work, a bad portrait. A better portraitist, a Rembrandt, say, might have given us more profound insights into his character. But both Jonson and Malherbe insist that the likenesses are *good*. Therefore, even the best portrait must be inherently inadequate to the task of representing the real man. Evidently Montaigne agreed. Why was this?

Portraiture and role-playing

The portrait of Montaigne as mayor shows him in his official capacity. The office was no sinecure. Montaigne took over an important and politically delicate position at the request of King Henri III at a time of acute religious strife, civil unrest and periodical bloodshed. But while he could have gone down to posterity as mayor of Bordeaux, Montaigne did not wish to be associated solely or even largely with this image. It did not represent the real 'me' that he sought to depict in his *Essays:* 'Here I want to be seen in my simple, natural everyday fashion.' He was conscious of important differences between his official and unofficial self and of the 'role' that we all play in society, 'the role of a character which we have adopted'. In his own case, he insists, 'The Mayor and Montaigne have always been twain, very clearly distinguished' (p.1144). He would have disapproved of the inclusion of the engraving with his *Essays,* because it was 'Montaigne' and not just 'the mayor' that was 'the subject of my book' (p.lix).

Portraiture, beauty and truth

The portrait of Montaigne by Étienne de Martellange (Figure 2.8) suggests something more intimate, informal and individual than the mayoral portrait. It shows Montaigne in 1588, when he published the fullest edition of the *Essays* to appear in his lifetime. But does it tell us much about his personality?

Again, Montaigne queries the reliability even of the most accurate portrait as a guide to the character of the sitter. In Book 3, Chapter 12, 'On physiognomy', he asks: should we judge by appearances, given how deceptive appearances can be? He contrasts the beauty of Socrates' character (Socrates is one of Montaigne's heroes) with the notorious ugliness of his features (Figure 2.9).

Figure 2.8 Étienne de Martellange, *Montaigne at the age of 54,* 1588, oil on canvas. Private collection. Photo: Archives Photographiques Larousse

Figure 2.9 Marble head of Socrates (copy), late fourth century. Antikensammlung, Staatliche Museen zu Berlin Preussischer Kulturbesitz

He notes the same paradox in his beloved friend Étienne de La Boétie and wonders about it. He agrees that 'there is nothing more probable than the conformity and correspondence of the body and the mind' (p.1198), and considers 'beauty to be only two fingers away from goodness' (p.1200). But he admits that in practice 'looks are a weak guarantee', while adding 'yet they have some influence' (p.1200). So a portrait, however genuine and life-like, does not necessarily tell the truth about the sitter's character.

Artifice and truth: the mayor of Bordeaux again

The mayoral portrait was a formal, official portrait of the 'public' Montaigne, a nobleman. His title, 'Le Seigneur de Montaigne' (lord of Montaigne) is painted across the top of the canvas in large capital letters, and his coat-of-arms features prominently just below on the left. We know that Montaigne was extremely proud of his title, but kept quiet about the fact that it was a very recent acquisition, dating back only to his grandfather, who was in the food and wine trade. Montaigne dropped his bourgeois surname, Eyquem. The portrait shows Montaigne in an elaborate ruff, richly decorated doublet with gold-braided buttons, and a scarlet gown over his left shoulder. Around his neck is the order of St Michael with which the king had honoured him. It is a portrait clearly designed to impress, to show the sitter off and, as Montaigne says in 'To the Reader' 'to serve ... my reputation' (p.lix). But what about its quality as a portrait? As Peter Burke argues, portraits like this, commonplace in the Renaissance, 'are more often institutional than individualistic. The portrait usually represents social roles rather than individuals.' The subjects of the portrait are 'weighed down by their cultural baggage, by such accessories as robes, crowns, sceptres', or, as here, by ruff, gown, medal and coat-of-arms (1995, p.395).

Even if well executed, this type of portrait can give a misleading impression. Sometimes deliberately so. Anthonis Mor (*c.*1519–*c.*1577) was a Dutchman employed by Philip II at the Spanish court. In 1554 he was sent to England to paint a portrait of Philip's future wife, Mary Tudor, for which he was knighted. In his self-portrait of 1569 (Plate 5), Mor gives no indication that he was only a court-painter, however eminent. Rather he presents himself as a gentleman, 'Sir Anthony More': rich, successful, anglicized and ennobled; fashionably apparelled, a sword at his waist, a chain of honour around his neck, a hunting-dog at his side; courtly, aristocratic and heroic.

In 'To the Reader' Montaigne makes it clear that this kind of self-portrait is not what he has in mind in his *Essays*. He rejects the formal pose as staged, stiff, artificial and unnatural. Mor in his self-portrait is demonstrating – putting on a show. Note his dramatic gesture of right hand on hip, the thumb imperiously extended, accentuating both the sumptuous velvet of the sleeve and Mor's haughty stare.

Montaigne, as he emphasizes in 'To the Reader', is not interested in showing off. He wants to portray himself as he is, not to serve his reputation: 'If my design had been to seek the favour of the world I would have decked myself out better and presented myself in a studied gait',[2] i.e. like Mor. 'Here [i.e. in his *Essays*] I want to be seen in my simple, natural, everyday fashion, without striving or artifice' (p.lix).

In a very different self-portrait painted some years later (Plate 6), Mor did portray himself in a more workaday pose as an artist. But the very contrast between Mor as nobleman and Mor as painter could have prompted a thinker such as Montaigne to raise further questions as to which, if either, was the real man: Anthonis Mor or Sir Anthony More?

Montaigne's 'official' portrait in de Leu's engraving (Figure 2.6) immortalizes him as the author of the *Essays*. But again remember that its inclusion was a decision of later editors. It was never authorized by Montaigne and was not how he wished to be remembered. He was mayor, of course, but he was more than mayor: a highly proficient Latin scholar, a judge for a dozen years and a man of letters. But, just as he did not feel that his 'role' as mayor represented his entire self, so he did not want to be thought of as a 'mere' writer, not even (so he says) as the author of the *Essays*! These were aspects of his life, but he felt his real self to be something apart

---

[2] In his first edition Montaigne added 'with borrowed beauties, or would have tensed and braced myself in my best posture'.

from all of them. In Book 3, Chapter 2, 'On repenting', he emphasizes the uniqueness of his self-portraiture as the first man ever to attempt not only to portray his many-sided self, but also to distil its essence, its 'universal being, not as a grammarian, poet or jurisconsult [legal expert] but as Michel de Montaigne' (p.908).

Montaigne, moods and melancholy

Montaigne considered himself to be partly a 'melancholic', a recognizable psychological type, based on the Renaissance theory that a man's 'character' was determined by the balance of his physical constituents, the 'humours' mentioned in 'To the Reader'. The symptoms of melancholy were thought to include moodiness, forgetfulness, neglect of one's appearance and general eccentricity. Melancholy was also sometimes a fashionable affectation, since it was also associated with genius! In Book 1, Chapter 8, 'On idleness', Montaigne indicates that he began to write the *Essays* in a particular mood of melancholy madness and as a way of snapping out of it (pp.30–31).

Exercise

Take another look at the portrait of Montaigne by de Martellange (Figure 2.8) and compare it with Isaac Oliver's portrait of a melancholy man (Plate 7). Does the comparison suggest that de Martellange's portrait represents Montaigne as a 'melancholy' man in the Renaissance sense of a psychological type? Or does it at least represent Montaigne in melancholy mood?

Discussion

It is difficult (and perhaps unwise) to attempt to draw profound conclusions. Perhaps the most one can say is that both sitters look abstracted, withdrawn and pensive. Even if either portrait is a realistic depiction of a melancholic, we may by now conclude that Montaigne did not want to be labelled as a single type of man, since he was, like all of us, a person of many moods. The *Essays* would convey him in a variety of 'humours'. ❖

Perhaps Montaigne wished to be thought to be in a melancholy mood rather than to be tied permanently to a melancholy humour. As he says:

> I feel quite a different person before and after a meal; when good health and a fine sunny day smile at me, I am quite debonair; give me an ingrowing toe-nail [or simply 'a corn' – A.L. / ed.] and I am touchy, bad-tempered and unapproachable.

(p.637)

Finality and openness

Every portrait has an element of finality. There was no finality about Montaigne's attitude to his *Essays,* which he was continually revising and 'touching up', going through the printed text with his pen, adding, crossing out, substituting, annexing huge chunks of afterthoughts for the printer to include in the next edition. For Montaigne there was never a final edition, for what he recorded was not static, but dynamic: his own development. 'I am not portraying being but becoming', he wrote, 'not the passage from one age to another [...] but from day to day, from minute to minute. I must adapt this account of myself to the passing hour. I shall perhaps change soon ...' (pp.907–8). The portrait of himself was not complete until his life was over. He never had the last word on himself until he ceased to write. Or rather, until his latest additions were published (which they were posthumously). To find out the latest about Montaigne, 'the Reader' must acquire the latest edition. As Montaigne wrote in his 1588 edition (which contained numerous additions to the existing two books plus a completely new volume, Book 3): 'Reader: just let this tentative essay, *this third prolongation of my self-portrait,* run its course' (p.1091; emphasis added). In effect, he is saying: if you want to see what I am like today, read on.

So while the de Martellange portrait may show what Montaigne looked like in old age, again it did not tell the whole story, because the story was not yet over and perhaps would never be told in full. But Montaigne felt that his method of telling it had turned out to be more authentic, more truly revealing of his character: 'By portraying myself for others I have portrayed my own self within me in clearer colours than I possessed at first' (p.755). Montaigne was conscious of changing with age, though not necessarily maturing. In one of his additions, published posthumously, he states:

> My first edition dates from fifteen hundred and eighty: I have long since grown old but not one inch wiser. 'I' now and 'I' then are certainly twain, but which 'I' was better? I know nothing about that.

(p.1091)

His 1588 self-portrait is thus as truthful as that of 1580, or at least as truthful as he could make it; but it was *different.* Montaigne points out the contrast by musing whether the convention that age brings wisdom is true in his case.

For Montaigne, then, conventional painterly portraiture had serious drawbacks. It was not true that the portrait (like the camera in our day) never lies. Even when it is an honest portrait (like his book, 'a book whose faith can be trusted'), it may tell *some* of the truth about its subject, 'some traits of my character', but it can never tell the whole truth and nothing but the truth, because the truth about human-beings is complex, variable and elusive (p.lix). So convinced of this did Montaigne become that he constantly questions how we apprehend, or can apprehend truth at all, about ourself or anyone else. Profoundly concerned with this problem, he devised for himself the suggestive maxim: *'Que sçais-je?'* – What do I know?

Montaigne, the naked truth and 'the Reader'

What Montaigne set out to do – 'to draw a portrait of myself from life' – he considered not only far more true to life than any portrait in oils, but also a wholly novel and unique undertaking – 'the only book of its kind in the world' (p.433). In 'To the Reader' he claims to offer the truth about his innermost self, warts and all – 'Here, drawn from life, you will read of my defects and my native form'; so candid a self-portrait that if convention allowed, he says, 'I can assure you that I would most willingly have portrayed myself whole, and wholly naked' (p.lix).

He refers to 'those peoples who are said still to live under the sweet liberty of Nature's primal laws', i.e. the recently discovered 'Indians' of South America – the 'New World' – who reportedly ran about naked, to the horror of most of their European observers. Montaigne, who was amazingly open-minded and receptive to all kinds of human experience, was enormously interested in the Indians as a novel example of the variety of humankind. He wrote about them sympathetically in 'To the Reader' and discusses them at length elsewhere. In Book 1, Chapter 31, 'On the cannibals', after expressing considerable admiration for them, he ends the chapter on a note of irony: 'Ah! But they wear no breeches. ...' (p.241).

Now Montaigne says that he *would have* portrayed himself naked had 'social convention' allowed. It didn't, of course, and he didn't. The only nudity allowed by social convention in the Renaissance was in the visual arts. And in any case, how could nudity be represented adequately in words, or at all except through the visual arts: sculpture, drawing and painting? Renaissance art is of course full of nudes, chiefly mythological or biblical. The only Renaissance artist known to have actually done what Montaigne claimed that he himself would have done had circumstances permitted, to portray himself wholly naked, was Albrecht Dürer (Figure 2.10). Dürer, notes Burke, was 'a man whose many self-portraits suggest his obsessive concern with his appearance' (1995, p.398).

But would even a pictorial representation of this kind have told us any more about the inner Montaigne than the conventional portraits

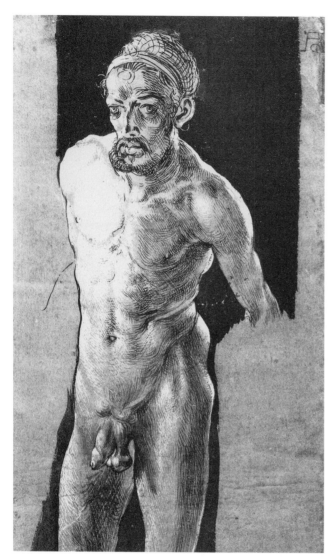

Figure 2.10 Albrecht Dürer, *Self-portrait*, c.1500–7, black and white pen and pencil on green prepared paper, 29.1 x 15.3 cm. Schlossmuseum, Weimar. Photo: Kunstsammlungen zu Weimar Fotothek/Roland Dreper, Weimar

which he repudiated as inadequate? Malherbe described the de Leu engraving (Figure 2.6) as 'a *complete* portrait of the great Montaigne'. But, as we have seen, Montaigne does not seem to regard any kind of conventional representation as 'complete'. The best we can achieve are steps towards, *attempts* at, completeness – *essais*, in fact.

What, then, does Montaigne mean about portraying himself naked? What about the *tone* of 'To the Reader'? What about Montaigne's initial claim that in publishing the *Essays* 'I have set myself no other end but a private family one'? If he meant that, why publish? What about his first sentence: 'You have here, Reader, a book whose faith can be trusted'? Where does this leave Montaigne? And the Reader?

At the same time Montaigne also claimed a universal validity for his self-portrait (or self-portraits) since 'every man carries in himself the complete pattern of human nature' (p.908; I have here preferred the translation by Cohen, 1958, p.236). As a human being, Montaigne shared elements common to every other human-being (including primitive peoples and cannibals). So, if his self-portrait in the *Essays* is true, 'the Reader' too will find something in common with Montaigne. In this sense the *Essays* tell 'the Reader' something about himself or herself and are to this extent a reflection or portrait of 'the Reader'.

Montaigne's presentation of his own individuality, then, was richer and more complex than the discovery of the individual that Burckhardt saw in the careers of the great figures of the Italian Renaissance. The next chapter examines the phenomenon of humanism, an approach to thought and literature which was to enable Montaigne to write his *Essays* in such a free spirit.

Bibliography

BURCKHARDT, J. (1990) *The Civilization of The Renaissance in Italy*, trans. S.G.C. Middlemore, Harmondsworth, Penguin; first published 1858.

BURKE, P. (1995) 'The Renaissance, individualism and the portrait', *History of European Ideas*, vol. 21, no. 3, Oxford, Pergamon, pp.393–400.

COHEN, J.M. (ed./trans.) (1958) *Montaigne: Essays*, Harmondsworth, Penguin.

COLE, A. (1995) *Art of the Italian Renaissance Courts: Virtue and Magnificence*, London, Weidenfeld & Nicolson.

FISH, S. (1980) *Is there a Text in this Class? The Authority of Interpretative Communities*, Cambridge, Mass., Harvard University Press.

GAUDI, M.T. and SMITH, C.S. (trans.) (1978) *Pirotechnia*, Cambridge, Mass., MIT Press

GILBERT, C.E. (ed.) (1980) *Italian Art 1400–1500, Sources and Documents*, Englewood Cliffs, N.J., Prentice-Hall.

MARCHESE, P. (1989) *L'invenzione della forchetta: spilloni, schidioncini, lingule, imbroccatoi, pironi, forcule, forcine e forchette dai Greci ai nostri forchettoni*, Soveria Mannelli, Rubbettino.

SCREECH, M. (ed./trans.) (1991) *Michel de Montaigne: The Complete Essays*, Harmondsworth, Penguin.

TATEO, F. (ed.) (1970) *Giovanni Gioviano Pontano: I Trattati delle Virtù Sociali*, Rome, Edizioni dell' Ateneo.

Anthology source

A Sforza banquet menu: *Ludovico il Moro: La sua città e la sua corte (1480–1499)*, Archivio di Stato di Milano, Como, New Press, 1983, pp.171–3, translated (with footnotes) for this edition by Dorigen Caldwell. (Anthology, no. 29)

CHAPTER THREE

Humanism

BY LUCILLE KEKEWICH

Objectives

The objectives of this chapter are that you should:

- be able to define the meaning of 'humanism' both for Burckhardt and for subsequent generations of scholars up to the present day;
- be able to evaluate the impact of humanist methodologies on learning during the fifteenth and sixteenth centuries;
- be able to explain how and why humanist methods were disseminated from Italy throughout the rest of Europe;
- have read representative examples of humanist texts and be able to recognize the features of their style and content which made them important and distinctive;
- understand some of the areas of controversy concerning the phenomenon of humanism and relate them to the search for a satisfactory account of the Renaissance.

Introduction

> those who acted as mediators between their own age and a venerated antiquity, and made the latter a chief element in the culture of the former.
>
> (Burckhardt, 1990, p.135)

Burckhardt's epigram is a good starting point for an introduction to the movement which embodied a new approach to the cultural heritage of Christendom. A proper definition of 'humanism', however, is almost as difficult as the more general questions about the nature of the Renaissance that were raised in Chapters 1 and 2. In order to give a fuller account of humanism than the one offered in the Burckhardt quotation above, I will initially provide a working definition and then develop it throughout this chapter.

From the time of Petrarch onwards, a number of Italian scholars, poets, ecclesiastics, lawyers and officials can be claimed as humanists if we accept the following definition of their calling: an engagement with the *studia humanitatis* (the humanities), that is, grammar, **rhetoric**, poetry, history and **moral philosophy**. These were approached in a spirit of enquiry often entailing little respect for the

Figure 3.1 Andrea del Castagno, *Francesco Petrarch*, 1440s, fresco, from the convent of Sant' Apollonia, Florence. Photo: Alinari

intellectual authority traditionally exercised by the Catholic church. Humanism also involved the culture and institutions of classical antiquity and a desire to restore them in the contemporary world: the wish to communicate new and revived knowledge by reformed educational practices, improved texts and learned discourse in academies, universities and informal gatherings.

Why is the phenomenon of humanism so important in a study of the Renaissance? It was suggested in Chapter 1 that Burckhardt minimized the significance of humanism in literary and artistic developments, preferring instead to emphasize the interaction of the 'genius of the Italian spirit' with the legacy of the past. However, as soon as scholars, including Burckhardt, started to analyse how these developments came about they invariably identified humanism as a key factor. Nearly all the Renaissance figures whom you will be studying either were humanists or were strongly influenced by their methods and attitudes: many were directly concerned with the preservation of texts and/or the transmission of the learning and artistic forms of the classical past. In this chapter the origins of humanism will be considered through a discussion of the retrieval of classical antiquity, and some key aspects of humanist learning – such as textual criticism and the writing of history – will be addressed. The question will be asked as to whether the study of women humanists is an example of 'tokenism' or whether their achievements merit serious consideration. The reaction of scholars, since the time of Burckhardt, to the phenomenon of humanism is discussed throughout the chapter and this will contribute to our attempt to provide a satisfactory account of the Renaissance.

Few would disagree with the statements made in my working definition of humanism (pp.51–2). But the significance of statements like these and the way they have been interpreted have been debated since the middle of the nineteenth century. Apart from the question of when the practices we describe as 'humanist' were adopted, the motivation and nature of the work of scholars during the Renaissance are matters of controversy. This partly arises from the fact that this period has been intensively studied since the mid nineteenth century and each generation has brought its own priorities and values into play. During the second half of the twentieth century, for example, there was a lively historical debate about the extent to which the ideas and structures of classical antiquity influenced the thought of Italian Renaissance political commentators. This centred on the work of Hans Baron and his concept of 'civic humanism', which will be discussed later in this chapter. For the moment we will concentrate on how accounts of humanism have changed since the time of Burckhardt.

Exercise

Read Burckhardt pages 135–9 and then refer to paragraphs one and two on page 136 and answer the following questions:

1   How are humanists characterized by Burckhardt?

2   To what extent does Burckhardt's description of humanism coincide with the working definition given above? And how, if at all, does it differ?

Discussion

1 'They formed a wholly new element in society', had an 'unstable existence', held 'free views of life', showed 'pagan tendencies', promoted a new civilization which was a 'competitor with the whole culture of the Middle Ages' and successfully modelled their work and thought on classical antiquity.

2 Most humanists, as you will already have gathered from your readings of Burckhardt, occupied conventional situations in late medieval society as priests, lawyers, cultivated gentlemen, officials, *condottieri* and princes. The 'free views of life' that Burckhardt attributes to humanists could be seen as a spirit of enquiry and criticism, and a number of humanists were accused by contemporaries, with varying degrees of justification, of holding irreligious or heretical opinions, which may have originated in the same spirit of enquiry.

The claim that humanists sought to promote a new civilization in competition with that of the Middle Ages is a large one; it is not a claim made in the working definition and is, in fact, at odds with the many continuities between the former and the latter which will be identified in this series of books. While the emulation of classical antiquity is the basis of all major accounts of humanism, Burckhardt claims that humanists made a distinct break with traditional culture and beliefs and that they were an estranged minority in society at large. He seems to question the possibility of continuity with the past and suggests that humanists had little stake in the society in which they lived. None of these factors are implicit in the working definition of humanism. ❖

John Addington Symonds, an English scholar, published a series of books on the Italian Renaissance during the mid 1870s and was aware of Burckhardt and other Europeans working in the field. His view of the Renaissance was enormously influential in the English-speaking world for the next 70 years. You may find his style somewhat florid in comparison with the translation of Burckhardt by Middlemore, yet an interesting point to note is that the latter was completed in 1878, only a year after Symonds wrote his *Renaissance in Italy.*

Exercise

Read this extract from Symonds on humanism and identify in what respects its conclusions are similar to or different from Burckhardt's:

> what gave its deep importance to the classical revival, was the emancipation of the reason, consequent upon the discovery that the best gifts of the spirit had been enjoyed by the nations of antiquity. An ideal of existence distinct from that imposed upon the Middle Ages by the Church, was revealed in all its secular attractiveness. Fresh value was given to the desires and aims, enjoyments and activities of man, considered as a noble member of the universal life, and not as a diseased excrescence on the world he helped to spoil ... The intellect, after lying spell-bound during a long night, when thoughts were as dreams and movement as somnambulism, resumed its activity, interrogated nature, and enjoyed the pleasures of unimpeded energy. Without ceasing to be Christians (for the moral principles of Christianity are the inalienable possession of the human race), the men of the Revival dared once again to exercise their thought as boldly as the Greeks and Romans had done before them ...
>
> That more and nobler use was not made of the new light which dawned upon the world in the Revival; that the humanists abandoned the high standpoint of Petrarch for a lower and more literary level; that society assimilated the Hedonism more readily than the Stoicism of the ancients; that scholars occupied themselves with the form rather than the matter of the classics; that all these shortcomings in their several degrees prevented the Italians from leading the

intellectual movement of the sixteenth century in religion and philosophy, as they had previously led the mind of Europe in discovery and literature – is deeply to be lamented by those who are jealous for their honour.

(1937, pp.33–4)

<table>
<tr><td>Discussion</td><td>The ideas about the revival of antiquity and the discovery of the individual are certainly there; Burckhardt, like Symonds, was prone to take a distinctly anti-Catholic line in parts of his book, as you have probably discovered in your reading. Where Symonds diverged is in the sharpness of his criticism of Italians, not just in the sixteenth century, but by implication a hundred years earlier when Burckhardt describes them as suffused with a fine and noble spirit. This was not only because of his strong religious beliefs but because he thought less of rhetoric (form) and far more of philosophy, a discipline to which Burckhardt, the aesthete, paid very little attention (even though he had been a friend and colleague of the German philosopher Nietzsche at the University of Basle). ❖</td></tr>
</table>

Views on humanism are hard to disentangle from general interpretations of the origins and nature of the Renaissance. During the last part of the nineteenth and first half of the twentieth centuries most writers still subscribed to Burckhardt's thesis. The only major exception was the growing acceptance that the Renaissance was not the first period in which the cultural development of Europe received a stimulus from the revived knowledge and use of classical texts and images. The concept of the **Carolingian** and twelfth-century 'Renaissances' enabled humanism to be explained in terms of a far greater continuity of cultural experience than had been possible for Burckhardt and his contemporaries. This approach has also been supported by a greater understanding of late medieval scholarship and education, often described by the umbrella term **'scholasticism'** (which derives from the 'schools', including the universities, all dominated by the Catholic church). It is now recognized that scholastics such as Peter Abelard (1079–1142) and Roger Bacon (*c.*1214–92) relied extensively on classical learning, and that they were capable of daring and innovative thought. Even those humanists who condemned the methods of these scholars were, to some extent, reliant on their legacy.

It was not until the 1930s and 1940s that new light was thrown on the origins of humanism. Hans Baron saw the late fourteenth and early fifteenth centuries in northern Italy as a time when a vital element in the new approach to scholarship was developed. He described this as 'civic humanism', finding in the works of public servants, lawyers and

Figure 3.2
Coluccio Salutati, portrait in an initial letter, second half of fourteenth century. Biblioteca Medicea Laurenziana MS. Laur. Plut. 53.18. c.1

historians like Coluccio Salutati (1331–1406) and Leonardo Bruni (1370–1444) evidence of a new consciousness of the uniqueness of republican institutions in states like Florence. Baron also identified a humanist belief that it was their destiny to restore to Italy the greatness it had enjoyed in Roman times. Eugenio Garin, an Italian contemporary of Baron, adopted a similar approach to the phenomenon of humanism, stressing the importance to its development of an awareness of the historical background to classical texts. He has also been one of the most prolific publishers of good editions of Renaissance texts, and their increasing availability has improved the opportunities for scholarly understanding of the period.

Exercise

Read the extract that follows from Garin. Does he add anything to Burckhardt's account of humanism?

> The essence of humanism is most clearly defined by its attitude to the civilization of the past ... The 'barbarians' were not barbarous because they had remained ignorant of the classics, but because they had failed to understand them as a historical phenomenon. The humanists, on the other hand, discovered the classics because they managed to detach themselves from them and comprehend their Latin without confusing it with their own Latin. It is for this reason that it is true to

Figure 3.3 Bernardino Rossellino, tomb of Leonardo Bruni, Chancellor of Florence, 1440s, Church of Santa Croce, Florence. The inscription translated reads: 'After Leonardo departed from life, history is in mourning and eloquence is dumb, and it is said that the Muses, Greek and Latin alike, cannot restrain their tears' (Borsook, 1973, p.99). Photo: Alinari

say that antiquity was discovered by the humanists, even though both Aristotle and Virgil were equally well known to the middle ages. It was humanism which placed Virgil back into his historical context; and which tried to explain Aristotle in terms of the problems and the sciences of the Athens of the fourth century before Christ. For this reason one should never seek to distinguish between the humanistic discovery of antiquity and the humanistic discovery of man – for they amount to exactly the same thing. For the discovery of antiquity implied that one had learnt to make a comparison between antiquity and oneself, to take a detached view of antiquity and to determine one's relation to it. And all this implied, further, the concept of time and memory and a sense of human creation, of human work in this world and of human responsibility. It was indeed no accident that the majority of the great humanists were statesmen and men of action, accustomed to participate freely in the public life of their age.

This point of view assumed concrete shape in the critical discussion which was started about the documents of the past. Such a discussion, whether or not it was to have any specific results, made it possible to establish a proper sense of distance between the humanists and the past. And in between, the humanists discovered those seven centuries of darkness – for no less were counted by

Leonardo Bruni. During those centuries the spirit of criticism had been in abeyance, and all knowledge of history as a story of human activity had been absent. The 'philology' of the humanists gave concrete shape to that crisis which was occasioned by the new awareness of the past as past, by the new vision of reality as something earthly and by the new attempt to explain history as the story of men.

(1965, pp.14–15)

Discussion

Garin distinguishes between the knowledge of antiquity which was retained in the Middle Ages and the capacity of the humanists to take a detached, analytical view of it. This marks a development from Burckhardt's 'revival of antiquity' and an appreciation of how the study of history developed. He goes on to suggest that the value they placed on human work and responsibility encouraged many humanists to participate in an active public life. Burckhardt described despotic and republican regimes at length and he adopted a narrative approach as well as giving some recognition to the importance of **philology** – Valla figures along with Poggio Bracciolini and Filelfo in a job lot of carping philologists who were compared unfavourably with the friendly company of artists (1990, p.105). Yet it is only in recent decades that the central importance of philology in the development of humanist methodology has been emphasized, thanks in large part to the work of Garin. The extract indicates, however, that Garin does not systematically set out to dismantle Burckhardt's account of Renaissance humanism. Despite the fact that he has other preoccupations which were not shared by his precursor, notably the development of philosophy and the failure to advance scientifically (preoccupations which do not emerge in this extract), his view of the Renaissance, especially of the concern with antiquity and the development of the individual, is still very reliant on nineteenth-century historians such as Burckhardt. ❖

One of the main achievements of the Renaissance claimed by Burckhardt was 'the discovery of the individual'. This too has recently been subject to renewed attention in the debate surrounding the concept of 'self-fashioning', which was provoked by scholars such as Stephen Greenblatt (1980). Greenblatt associates this process of self-fashioning with the idea of the self as it was portrayed in sixteenth-century literature: the need to respond to social, religious and economic pressures by projecting an identity which would be acceptable to peers and superiors. It represents another modification of the view presented by Burckhardt, since it is at variance with his idea that the Renaissance emancipated people from the constraints of traditional learning, religion and social pressures.

So far our discussion of the phenomenon of humanism has been confined to the Italian peninsula, reflecting its concentration there in the fourteenth and fifteenth centuries. Connoisseurs of the arts such as Burckhardt and Symonds found little to attract them north of the Alps, but it had been implicit in histories of the Renaissance that the religious upheavals of the sixteenth century, the art of the Low Countries and the literature of the British Isles were, at least to some extent, influenced by humanism.

And what of France? The work of Franco Simone in the middle decades of the twentieth century calls into question the nineteenth-century view of the French reception of Italian humanism and art, which he characterizes as follows:

> The myth of the Italian wars is a dazzling product of Romantic historiography. We all remember those fanciful pages where Michelet delighted in describing the troops of Charles VIII [the French king who invaded Italy in 1494], barbarians in dress and behaviour suddenly transformed into perfect Renaissance men upon contact with Italian civilization: a miracle supposedly accomplished by the landscape, the classical remains and the new works of art ... a total surrender on the part of a culture which, after exhausting its Medieval energies, received the stimulus of original and reinvigorating ideas through contact with a country virtually unknown before.
>
> (1969, p.39)

Simone, basing his conclusions on modern scholarship, suggests a very different model. Italian humanism had been admired in France since the time of Petrarch; his residence in Avignon and visits to Paris facilitated the transfer of his ideas and methods. And for a later generation the work of Lorenzo Valla proved equally influential. A group of French scholars who Simone describes as 'humanists' were achieving standards of eloquence and literary ability in Latin which made them comparable to Italian contemporaries. Such men included Jean Gerson, Nicholas de Clamanges and the brothers Pierre and Gontier Col, who all flourished in the late fourteenth and early fifteenth centuries. It had been claimed that the resurgence of the Hundred Years War suspended innovative scholarly activity until the end of the century; again Simone draws on a variety of evidence to demonstrate continuity in the pursuit of the new learning as it was being developed by the humanists. French humanists themselves, men like Symphorien Champier (1472–1539) and Guillaume Budé (1467–1540) took up the cause early in the sixteenth century.

Figure 3.4 Jean Clouet, *Guillaume Budé*, *c.*1536, oil on wood, 39.7 x 34.3 cm. Metropolitan Museum of Art, Maria DeWitt Jessup Fund, 1946 (46.68)

> [Champier claimed] thus from the Romans we have seized both the glory of learning and the honour of teaching, so that we might legitimately claim to be the heirs to the Athenians.

(Simone, 1969, p.84)

Budé condemned the servile attitude French scholars adopted towards Italian culture and took delight in pointing out the errors in grammar and spelling that he found in Italian humanist authorities. This robustly independent attitude was also displayed by the French poets known as the **Pléiade**: Ronsard (1524–85), for example, preferred Greek to Latin models for his *Odes*. The solution to how French learning from the late fourteenth to the end of the fifteenth century should be described seems to depend to a large extent on whether one wants to characterize the work of its greatest exponents as 'humanist' or 'scholastic', but at least Simone has effectively seen off the myth of the culturally besotted soldiers of Charles VIII.

Figure 3.5 Hans Holbein the Younger, *Desiderius Erasmus*, 1530–32, varnished distemper on limewood, diameter 10 cm. Oeffentliche Kunstsammlung Basel, Kunstmuseum. Photo: Oeffentliche Kunstsammlung Basel, Martin Bühler

Until recently there has been a tendency to distinguish the work of scholars (initially mostly Italian) preoccupied with classical literature and philosophy (secular humanism) from the northerners who applied their knowledge and methodologies to the dilemmas facing the contemporary Catholic church (Christian humanism). It would, however, be a mistake to assume too great a divide between the preoccupations of northern and southern Europe. In his article, 'The spread of Italian humanism', Peter Burke (1990) demonstrates that from the Middle Ages Italian scholars travelled, studied and taught throughout Europe and that northerners were drawn to Italy. Early reformers such as Desiderius Erasmus (*c.*1466–1536) and Sir Thomas More (1478–1535), concentrated on establishing the most accurate texts of the scriptures and on attempting to remedy perceived shortcomings in personnel and organization from within the Catholic church. From the time of Martin Luther (1483–1546) the intensity of the intellectual and ideological debate led to a schism between those who remained within the church and the Protestants who broke away from it and formed separate churches. This led to changes, not only in the fabric and teaching of the Catholic church, but also in the

Figure 3.6 Hans Holbein the Younger, *Sir Thomas More*, 1527, oil on oak panel, 74.9 x 60.3 cm. The Frick Collection, New York, 12.1.77

character of the states which supported or rejected the Reformation (see Book 3 in this series, Chapters 1 and 2).

Exercise

In the late twentieth century Lisa Jardine's account in *Worldly Goods* of how humanism began to penetrate northern Europe represents a tendency amongst scholars (J. Hale, 1993; M. Baxandall, 1972) to explain the spread of humanism by economic as well as intellectual factors. Read the extract from *Worldly Goods* below. What does Jardine consider to be the principal reasons for the dissemination of humanism?

> The shift in scholarly humanistic activities out of Italy and into northern Europe in the 1520s was linked to a significant alteration in the goals and aspirations of humanism as an intellectual movement. Italian humanists like Petrarch had had a strong vested interest in retrieving their intellectual 'roots' in the culture of ancient Rome (and

their exiled Byzantine colleagues had had an equivalent interest in tracing their cultural heritage to the ancient Greeks). From the very outset, however, both these projects were underwritten by northern European financial backing. For the German merchants and bankers who invested in intellectual undertakings like Nicolas Jenson's printing press in Venice, the new learning was a status symbol and a potentially lucrative commercial undertaking ...

To the German merchant bankers the potential of the new technology to disseminate knowledge along the same routes they customarily used for other consumer commodities (including perishables like oranges) was immediately attractive. Around 1504 the German Johann Cuno, a friend of Reuchlin [German humanist], made the journey to Venice to study Greek with the circle of specialists associated with the editions of classical Greek works being produced by the Aldine printing press. In search of expertise in one of the ancient languages fundamental to the study of sacred scripture in the original, Cuno was drawn to Venice by its reputation as an international cosmopolitan trading centre (the same reputation which had encouraged Bessarion [a Greek cardinal of the Roman Church] to leave his Greek-dominated collection of manuscripts and books to Venice).

(1996, pp.223–5)

Discussion

While Italian humanists from Petrarch onwards were attempting to retrieve their cultural 'roots', Jardine believes that commercial interests were a prime motivator for northern entrepreneurs. The attractions of Venice, an accessible centre of excellence for the new technology of printing and for the scholarly expertise which went with it, the status conferred by the new learning and the key it provided to the study of the scriptures, are all presented as factors in the growing northern involvement in the Renaissance. Jardine's approach is characterized by her unapologetic presentation of knowledge as a commodity. ❖

As you progress with this study of the Renaissance you will find that humanism influenced not only the political and economic structures of Europe, but also its art, architecture, scientific enquiry, philosophy, religion, music and literature. According to Nicholas Mann, who was writing on the origins of humanism:

[it] involves above all the rediscovery and study of ancient Greek and Roman texts, the restoration and interpretation of them and the assimilation of the ideas and values they contain. It ranges from an archaeological interest in the remains of the past to a highly focused philological attention to the details of all manner of written records –

63

from inscriptions to epic poems – but comes to pervade ... almost all areas of post-medieval culture, including theology, philosophy, political thought, jurisprudence, medicine, mathematics and the creative arts.

(1996, p.2)

This is a more inclusive account than that implied by my working definition of humanism and sets the agenda for the topics we will consider below. Before you engage with these aspects, however, I will discuss the origins and development of humanism, concentrating on texts which illustrate the scholarly processes involved.[1]

The retrieval of the past

The humanists' admiration for classical antiquity, and their desire that it should be studied so that its best features could be incorporated into contemporary life, was stimulated by the surviving relics of Roman antiquity to be seen in Italy (Burckhardt, 1990, pp.123–9). From the early Middle Ages Romans prided themselves on what remained of their great city and various works were produced expatiating on its marvels with varying degrees of imagination. Yet this veneration was confined in practical terms to a small group of writers and visitors; most of the population considered that the best use for a sarcophagus was as an animal drinking trough, and, even worse, for marble ruins to be burnt down to produce lime. Paradoxically, whilst during the Middle Ages the remains had declined gently through neglect, the Renaissance urge to produce new buildings in the classical style, straight roads and triumphal monuments, led to the far more rapid destruction of Roman remains: humanist popes were among the most enthusiastic builders.

A few wealthy people did pay for the repair of some of the remains. For example, under Pope Paul II (1464–71):

the bronze equestrian statue of Marcus Aurelius ... was extensively restored [also] the arch of Titus, the two horse tamers of the Quirinal, as well as a column in the vicinity of the baths of Diocletian.

(Weiss, 1969, p.104)

An even better insurance for the survival of ancient buildings was their continued use, so the Pantheon (the church of Santa Maria ad Martyres), the Capitol (government offices) and the castle of San Angelo (a papal residence), formerly the mausoleum of Hadrian, continued to be well maintained. Some scholars and antiquaries did

---

[1] If you wish to read an up-to-date review of the subject of humanism, I recommend *The Cambridge Companion to Renaissance Humanism* (Kraye, 1996).

not simply confine themselves to lamenting the passing glories of
Rome; they collected statues, coins and jewels, drew surviving
aqueducts, temples, walls etc. and copied inscriptions. Not all were
humanists, yet their activities raised the consciousness of wealthy and
educated Italians about their classical heritage and reinforced the
desire to restore, through language, literature and public works, the
moral standards and material grandeur of ancient Rome. Giovanni
Francesco Poggio Bracciolini (1380–1459), a renowned member of
the 'first generation' of fifteenth-century humanists, gave an eloquent
account of what remained of ancient Rome in the first book of his *On
the Inconstancy of Fortune* (*c.*1448). You can read an extract from this
account in the Anthology (no. 1)and refer to Figures 3.7 and 3.9 and
Plate 13 which show some of the ancient sites mentioned by Poggio.

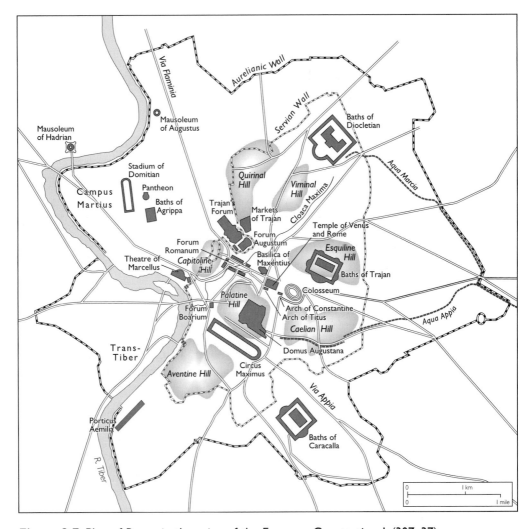

Figure 3.7 Plan of Rome in the reign of the Emperor Constantine I (307–37)

Figure 3.8
Giovanni Francesco
Poggio Bracciolini,
portrait in an initial
letter, mid fifteenth
century. Biblioteca
Apostolica Vaticana,
MS Urb. Lat. 224, fol.
2 recto

Figure 3.9 Engraving of
view of Rome, from Jacopo
Filippo Foresti da Bergamo,
*Supplementum. Supplementi
de le chronice vulgare*, 1520,
Venice (sig. 75v). You can
see the statues of the horse
tamers and the recumbant
figure of a river god in the
lower left of the engraving,
the Colosseum in the upper
left, the domed Pantheon in
the centre and the castle of
San Angelo surmounted by
the figure of an angel in the
upper right. Photograph
reproduced by permission
of the Warburg Institute,
University of London

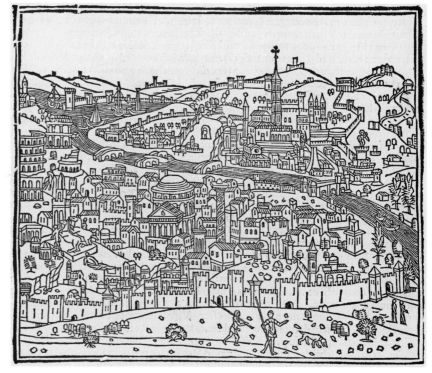

Ciriaco of Ancona (*c.*1390–*c.*1455) was the friend of many humanists and devoted much of his life to recording inscriptions and monuments throughout Italy and in the eastern Mediterranean. His career did not follow the conventional pattern for a humanist; his business as a merchant and activities as a diplomat afforded him excellent opportunities to travel extensively and combined with his keen interest in classical remains to make him an assiduous and successful antiquarian. His education seems to have been initially rudimentary, although he did eventually learn Latin and some Greek. Jean Colin, his biographer, considers his Latin style to have been no more than adequate, although it was sufficient for the task of making copies of classical inscriptions (1981, p.509). Ciriaco was by no means unique in recording and collecting antiquities; others, including a number of scholars, were active in the fourteenth, fifteenth and sixteenth centuries. What makes him particularly interesting is the scale of his achievement and the voluminous correspondence by which he reported his finds to humanists and political leaders. In some cases he even sold his finds and thus enjoyed a multiple status as an entrepreneur, antiquarian and diplomat.

Ciriaco never worked as a teacher or an orator and, apart from the *Itinerary* and the *Commentaries* (his records of the monuments and texts he encountered on his travels), his literary output was confined to a few poems and a large correspondence. The *Itinerary* dealt with his Italian journeys up to 1435 and was printed in the mid eighteenth century. The *Commentaries* were almost certainly destroyed in a fire at the library at Pesaro in the early sixteenth century. They can, however, be largely reconstructed from surviving copies of fragments and from the many letters and reports Ciriaco sent to his friends and fellow enthusiasts. These contained not only his accounts of what he had seen on his later journeys but many transcriptions and pictures of buildings and statues. In some cases the originals have disappeared since the fifteenth century and modern scholars depend on his accounts for their knowledge of them. His activities coincided with the period immediately preceding the fall of Constantinople to the Ottoman Turks in 1453; after that time it was more difficult for westerners to visit the area of the former eastern empire, and the Turks' Islamic religion predisposed them to destroy those classical remains which incorporated representations of the human body.

Ciriaco may not have been a conventional humanist, yet this does not detract from the importance of his antiquarian activities. Their significance for his own time, however, can only be assessed if the process of their transmission is considered. He had a wide circle of friends, including humanists like Poggio Bracciolini and Leonardo Bruni, which also extended to Pope Eugenius IV (1431–47) and a number of influential diplomats (including some Turks) and merchants, who eased his access to remote areas in the Aegean and facilitated his purchases of antiquities.

Examine the following evidence for Ciriaco's activities, May to September 1444, and then answer the questions below.

- A map of Asia Minor and Greece showing sites visited by Ciriaco (Figure 3.10)

- An extract from the record of his travels and contacts (p.69)

- His record of visits to Cyzicus, July/August 1444 (Anthology, no. 2i)

- Copies of an inscription and drawings of the temple of Hadrian at Cyzicus (Figures 3.11–13)

- The second letter sent by Ciriaco to John Hunyadi on 24 June 1444 (Anthology, no. 2ii) (note that the first letter was sent on 12 June 1444)

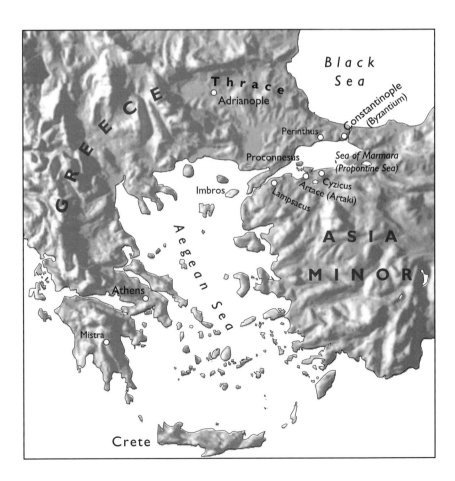

Figure 3.10 Map of Asia Minor and Greece showing sites visited by Ciriaco of Ancona

1 Comment on Ciriaco's travels, May to September 1444. What did he do while he was in the eastern Mediterranean, and what role did he play in political negotiations there? You might also suggest how his visit to Cyzicus may have been linked in his mind to the intense negotiations in which he was involved.

2 What appears to have motivated Ciriaco in his roles as an antiquarian and a diplomat?

Ciriaco of Ancona's travels and contacts, May to September, 1444

May: With Francesco Drapperio, the Genoese ambassador, observed the Turkish–Hungarian negotiations.

22 May: At **Adrianople** accompanied Drapperio to a public audience given by Sultan Murad II.

12 June: Sent first letter to John Hunyadi (a Hungarian general fighting offensive war against the Turks).

18 June: Left Adrianople on horse and travelled to Byzantium (**Constantinople**).

24 June: Second letter to John Hunyadi.

15 July: Took part in a hunt arranged by the Greek emperor, John VIII Palaeologus, and his brother, the despot, Theodore Porphyrogenitus.

21 July: Sent a letter to his friend Andreolo Giustiniani, the Genoese governor of Chios.

24 July: Left Byzantium for **Perinthus** and **Cyzicus**.

25 July: At Selymbria, Perinthus.

31 July: Arrived at **Artaki**, west of Cyzicus.

12 August: Returned to Perinthus after his visit to Cyzicus.

14 August: At city of **Mistra**, offered a silver coin of Vespasian to a friend.

19 September: Sent a letter to Cardinal Cesarini reporting on the military and diplomatic situation.

20 September: Left Byzantium in a galley of the emperor and went to the pontifical fleet.

27 September: Went to **Imbros**.

29 September: At **Lampsacus**. Sent a letter to George Scolarios, an expert in western theology at the imperial court at Byzantium.

(Source: Colin, 1981, pp.580–83; translated by L. Kekewich, 1999, places in bold are shown on map in Figure 3.10)

Figure 3.11 Bartolomeus Fontius, after Ciriaco of Ancona, drawing of main doorway of the temple of Hadrian at Cyzicus, late fifteenth century. The Bodleian Library, Oxford MS Lat. misc.d.85, fol. 133 verso

Figure 3.12 Bartolomeus Fontius, after Ciriaco of Ancona, drawing of vine-wreathed column with frieze and entablature, and Gorgoneion, temple of Hadrian at Cyzicus, late fifteenth century. The Bodleian Library, Oxford MS Lat. misc.d.85, fol. 134 recto

Figure 3.13 Bartolomeus Fontius, after Ciriaco of Ancona, drawings of Corinthian columns with architrave and portico, from temple at Cyzicus, late fifteenth century. The Bodleian Library, Oxford MS Lat. misc.d.85, fols 132 verso–133 recto

Discussion

1 As Ciriaco was a merchant he may have done some trading during his sojourn in the eastern Mediterranean, although this is not apparent from the evidence provided above. During the five months of 1444 under consideration he was, in any case, employed in other activities. In addition to social pursuits like attendance at the imperial hunting party, he was deeply involved in the negotiations between the Sultan and Christian powers such as the eastern emperor, the papacy, Venice and Hungary. His voluminous correspondence, his ability to read and write Latin and some Greek and the fact that he knew practically all the participants in the complex hostilities and negotiations which are known as the 'crusade of Varna', made him a key player in this important episode. Despite the delicacy of the situation, Ciriaco took time out for nearly three weeks to pay a second visit to the ruined temple of Hadrian at Cyzicus (his first visit had been fourteen years earlier). We could suggest that there was a link in the minds of Italians such as Ciriaco, who saw themselves as the heirs of ancient Rome, between the huge temple of one of the greatest of Rome's emperors and the intense negotiations of 1444. These culminated in the arrival of the Venetian-papal fleet and the brief hope that it might mark a triumph of the Christian west, led by the Roman pontiff, over the expanding power of Islam.

2 The standard of Ciriaco's drawings and epigraphy at Cyzicus was high and the originals from which the surviving versions were copied were probably even more accurate. His motivation to recover and record antiquity was strong despite the difficult circumstances. The stream of information which he sent back to his many humanist friends and their patrons could only nourish the enthusiasm for antiquity in the early Renaissance and improve the knowledge available to historians, rhetoricians, teachers and artists. Ciriaco was also playing an accepted classical role: the private citizen, without thought of personal profit, devoting himself to the public good, in this case the supreme task of rescuing Christendom from the infidel. Ciriaco's use of such terms as 'barbarians', 'proud tyrant' and 'Pannonia' (the classical name for Hungary), in his letter to John Hunyadi, indicates that he was operating within a rhetorical convention that would have been familiar to all readers of ancient history. The parallel of the Greeks quelling the might of the Trojans would have come readily to the minds of educated contemporaries. This would have been regarded as an example of the application of the knowledge of antiquity to acts of civic virtue: an ideal Baron (1966) attributed to early humanism. ❖

The activities of Ciriaco, his contemporaries, and immediate successors were instrumental in establishing antiquarianism as an important pursuit for humanists. From this in turn arose the systematic study of ancient remains, coins and inscriptions – archaeology, numismatics and epigraphy – which fed the development of the discipline of history. In the course of the next two hundred years, the combination of printing with ever more exacting standards of scholarship led to the production of great collections of written and monumental data drawn from classical antiquity. Their dissemination throughout Europe provided the essential tools with which historians could reconstruct and interpret the past. Eric Cochrane gives a good picture of the diversity of such activities once these collections and the methodologies with which to use them became available (note the classical, non-Christian first names such as 'Scipione' and 'Enea' which were in vogue):

> the real novelty of the antiquarians was that they elevated to the rank of historical documents wholly non literary remains of the past. Giovanni Giovane searched for traces of the Hellenic origins of Taranto not only in the well-known passages of Livy and Dionysius of Halicarnasus but also in the remnants of Greek still present in the local dialect. Giovan Francesco Lombardi, Scipione Mazella, and many others surveyed the ruins at Pozzuoli and lined up the visible remains with corresponding passages in scores of ancient and modern authors – from Tacitus and the Acts of the Apostles to Panormita and

Pontano. Antonio Ferri identified, with the help of many other authors, the statues recently discovered at Cuma. Alessandro Canobbio reconstructed on paper the original appearance of the amphitheater at Verona from the decorative fragments then scattered among the private collections of the city. Vincenzo Mirabella spent over ten years comparing what Thucydides and Plutarch had said about ancient Syracuse with those of its remains that were still visible. Enea Vico discovered in late imperial coins the names of emperors who were not mentioned in the written sources. And Sebastiano Erizzo discovered in late republican medals many new details concerning the shape of military insignia, the manner in which military captains took oaths of allegiance, and the way in which captives and spoils of war were exposed in triumphal processions.

(1981, p.425)

A further aspect of the growth of antiquarianism should not be neglected. As commodities, classical artefacts (ancient jewels, vases and coins, for example) had been highly valued throughout the Middle Ages. The work of antiquarians such as Ciriaco of Ancona and Felice Feliciano enhanced their value and added statuary and inscriptions to the objects eagerly sought by collectors such as Pope Paul II, Lorenzo de' Medici 'the magnificent' (1449–92) and Cardinal Francesco Gonzaga (1444–83). Artefacts which could be connected with a famous classical personage or text were particularly valuable, so a monetary as well as an intellectual incentive was given to antiquarianism and its attendant disciplines. This modifies, although by no means contradicts, Burckhardt's claim that the latter was not financially motivated but the result of a surge of interest arising from the spirit of the time.

The recording and acquisition of classical texts was, on the whole, a rather less arduous pursuit than the fieldwork undertaken by antiquarians like Ciriaco of Ancona. In the past it was often suggested that the former activity was promoted by the 1453 Turkish conquest of Constantinople which sent many clerics scurrying to the west, in some cases taking expertise in classical Greek and/or Greek manuscripts with them (see Burckhardt, 1990, pp.133–4 for a version of this view). More recently there has been a tendency to stress the political, commercial and diplomatic links which existed between the Greek empire and the west during the Middle Ages. These were by no means all positive – in the notorious Fourth Crusade (1204), for example, the Christian knights turned on the Greeks and looted Constantinople, causing a great deal of destruction. There also seems to have been an important connection between the interests and methods of Greek scholars such as Manuel Chrysoloras (*c.*1350–1415), who first introduced Greek scholarship into Italy, and the achievements of their Italian pupils, such as Bruni and Guarino (1370–1460) (Fryde, 1983, p.23).

From the time of Petrarch humanists had been attempting to recover as much as possible of the intellectual heritage of Rome, and a universal fluency in Latin among scholars greatly assisted this process. In undertaking a similar enterprise for Greece, most were incapacitated by their ignorance of the language, the lack of good grammar books and the paucity of suitable teachers. Throughout the fifteenth century more scholars did acquire an effective knowledge of Greek and the process received impetus during the council of Ferrara/Florence (1438–9) when, under increasing pressure from Islam, Catholic and Greek Orthodox theologians debated the possibility of achieving a union between the churches. Before and after the fall of Constantinople it was possible to acquire Greek texts, both through normal commercial channels and from Greeks, such as Cardinal Bessarion (c.1403–72), who travelled to the west. Yet, in comparison with the universal scholarly knowledge of Latin, 'Greek ended the Renaissance in the position in which it had first entered Italy; as a new subject, something on the margins of the curriculum' (Grafton and Jardine, 1986, p.119).

While there is little doubt that the study of Greek represented a new departure for Renaissance scholars, the question of how widely knowledge of the Latin classics was disseminated before 1500 is much more controversial. Grafton and Jardine maintain that the moral and civic values which humanists derived from Latin texts gradually replaced the traditional scholastic system of education; but Robert Black's study of the curricula and teaching methods in several Italian towns has led to the opposite conclusion:

> in Italy at least, grammatical education – in the fourteenth as well as the fifteenth centuries – always had pronounced moral and civic goals, and ... vice versa, grammar education continued to maintain its practical claim to prepare professionals and specialists even in the later fifteenth and sixteenth centuries, when most Italian grammar teachers were full-fledged, if not always distinguished humanists.

(1991, p.139)

What could be achieved for Latin scholarship by a humanist who knew how to search and what to look for, is illustrated by two letters concerning the activities of Poggio Bracciolini.

Exercise

Read Burckhardt, pages 131–3 and Poggio's two letters (Anthology, no. 3). What specialized skills did Poggio use to acquire classical texts and how was he able to spread information about them?

Discussion

The first letter to Guarino describes a visit to the monastery of St Gall in search of new texts and the treasures that Poggio and his associates found, as well as the deplorable condition in which they were kept. The greatest prize was a complete Quintilian (*c*.35–*c*.100), the *Training in Oratory* (which had not been known before except in a fragmentary version). Poggio's skill and fluency in Latin enabled him to make copies of the new texts very quickly and he set about distributing them to his friends. In the second letter to Niccolò Niccoli, written later from Rome, he said that he hoped to purchase copies of a number of books which a monk claimed to have in his possession. Poggio had to practise considerable forbearance to persuade monks, such as this one, to do what he wanted. Even when the texts were already known, they were worth pursuing in case they contained versions which were closer to the original. His letters to bibliophiles, like Niccoli and Guarino, ensured that news of his finds would be rapidly disseminated throughout humanist circles. ❖

The high profile activities of Poggio and his associates, and their capacity to report them widely, motivated scholars throughout the next centuries to continue the search for classical texts. Even today different versions of known texts and fragments of new ones can still be found. The account of the rediscovery and dissemination of classical texts given above has recently been further modified; writing in 1990 John Stephens suggests that the humanists were not so much innovators in the pursuit of antiquity as more expert than their predecessors in publicizing their activities.

> classical texts did not reach the *Quattrocento* by leaping across chasms represented by the tenth, eleventh and thirteenth centuries, or the Dark Ages. Manuscripts did not survive hundreds of years through ignorance or neglect. Classical texts crossed the Dark Ages because they were conserved; they reached 1300 because they were copied *and* conserved. There was a more general and refined interest in pagan classical texts in late antiquity, in the ninth century, in the twelfth and in the fourteenth centuries than in the intervening epochs. One reason, however, that fewer of them were copied in those intervals must have been because so many were available ...

> The staple diet of the Italian humanists remained that which they had inherited: Cicero, Seneca, Virgil, Livy, Horace, Ovid and Sallust. However, after 1500 Tacitus and Lucretius were to influence European ideas deeply.

> A novelty was the appreciation of little-known works by well-known authors. A great number of Cicero's speeches and letters became generally known. More works were unearthed of Livy, Ovid, Horace and Quintilian ...

These discoveries were the fruit of conscious and sustained effort. Petrarch searched for manuscripts with extraordinary enterprise and zeal. He found them in places as far apart as Verona, Avignon, Paris and Liège, and in libraries as little alike as the papal library, the Chapter library at Verona and the library of the Sorbonne. Moreover, these discoveries were the outcome of thirty years of labour, from 1333 to the 1360s. This was a pattern which Poggio imitated in the fifteenth century in Germany and France, and Aurispa and Guarino did the same in the Greek monasteries of the east.

(1990, pp.160–61)

Textual criticism

The growth of antiquarianism and the search for new or better versions of classical texts were part of the humanist attempt to recover as much of the learning of antiquity as possible. Another aspect of this process was the development of philology, the critical analysis of ancient texts in respect of both their content and the language in which they were expressed. Lorenzo Valla (*c*.1405–57) was a Roman humanist who challenged traditional scholastic thought by advancing the study of rhetoric and subverting the accommodation of pagan ethics to Christianity (see Chapter 5). He also used his wide reading and formidable grasp of the Latin language for the practical purposes both of advancing his career and establishing more rigorous standards of textual criticism. Valla was employed by Alfonso I of Naples during the late 1430s while the king was involved in a dispute with the papacy, and this was the context for his composition of the treatise *On the Donation of Constantine*.

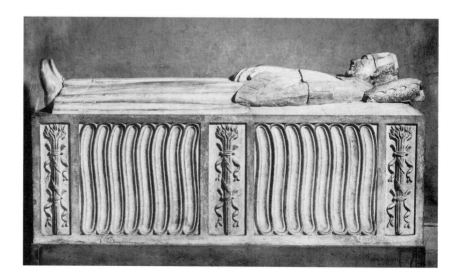

Figure 3.14 Tomb of Lorenzo Valla, d.1457, Basilica of St John Lateran, Rome. Photo: Scala

Exercise

In the Anthology read the extract from the *Donation* (no. 4i) and the four extracts from Valla's treatise against it (no. 4ii). In the first extract from Valla's treatise the Latin original of the first paragraph has been included so that you can get a feel for the rhetorical rhythms he employs. Comment on:

1 The rhetorical style of Valla's treatise.

2 The arguments he uses to undermine the credibility of the *Donation.*

Discussion

1 Notice how the introductory passage to the first extract from the treatise is measured and formal: Valla uses the favourite Ciceronian device of repetition to good effect. 'Dishonouring' (*dedecorantes*) occurs three times in one sentence.

His style changes in the second extract starting with the arresting vocative address: 'O avarice, ever blind and ill-advised', a characteristic classical oratorical flourish. What follows is a series of rhetorical questions, heavy with irony, which ends by Valla offering the solution to the ever more unlikely scenarios that his questions have postulated.

The third extract, which is devoted to the analysis of the language used in the *Donation,* employs the questioning technique more sparingly as Valla wishes to show, by discussing and criticizing the terms used, that his knowledge is superior to that of those who had made the forgery: for this he employs a less spectacular, more didactic tone.

In the final extract, Valla returns to his favoured style of elegant vituperation. 'Crimes', 'evils', 'wickedness' are imputed to the papacy, whose greed and luxury are compared in a graphic metaphor with 'Christ dying of hunger and nakedness in so many thousands of paupers'. Although it was written rather than spoken, the treatise belongs to a tradition which derives from the speeches delivered by classical orators such as Cicero.

2 In the first extract Valla begins by stating the ridiculous and unreasonable claims to overall power made in the *Donation.* He then outlines the seven arguments he will use to refute it:

- the psychological and legal barriers;

- that the donation never, in fact, took place;

- that although Sylvester received nothing, an earlier pope was given a modest grant for his subsistence;

- that no copy of the *Donation* was to be found in the *Decretum* or in the *History of Sylvester* (Valla was mistaken in this);

- that it was full of contradictions and linguistic barbarities;
- that even if an earlier pope had received it, it had been ineffectual for such a long time that it could not be legally reinstated;
- and finally, that claims made through the *Donation* could not be validated by prescription (long enjoyment of a right).

The second extract deals with the historical facts of the claim. With a devastating series of questions, Valla demonstrates that no record existed of any donation having been made or received. He then promises to cite a number of Latin and Greek histories which state that Constantine, his sons and successors continued to enjoy possession of the whole Roman empire.

The third extract concentrates on the linguistic barbarities of which the authors stood accused. Some of them are rather arcane, but the accusation that the forgers mistakenly used the word 'harlots' can be appreciated: Valla is again asserting the superiority of his learning and holding up the forgers to ridicule.

The final extract contains the last part of the treatise: Valla has presented all his arguments that the *Donation* was a forgery, so he chooses a different approach for his peroration or conclusion. The wickedness of many popes, who had brought strife and devastation to Italy instead of being a force for Christian virtue, is condemned. Pope Eugenius IV is dismissed by the Homeric phrase 'a people-devouring king' and this is followed by unflattering classical parallels. It was the moral stature of the early popes which gave them strength, not material possessions. Valla ends with a threat: he does not urge that the papacy should be put in tutelage but that it should stop promoting conflict. If it fails to do so, he will write another, bolder discourse. ❖

Although Valla's powerful intelligence and his facility with the Latin language enabled him to establish new standards of textual criticism and historical expertise, his insights depended on his personal capacities rather than on a systematic approach to the study of ancient texts. (You probably noticed the 'saturation bombing' approach he adopted in the preceding exercise.) A systematic methodology was being developed, however, and foremost among those who initiated it was Politian (Angelo Poliziano, 1454–94), a member of the circle of Lorenzo de' Medici in Florence. His comparative approach instituted practices that have since been incorporated into historical and philological studies which are still in use today:

Figure 3.15 Obverse: Politian (Angelo Poliziano), reverse: Constantia and Concordia (Constancy and Concord), medal attributed to Niccolò Fiorentino, before 1500, bronze. Kunsthistorisches Museum, Vienna MK 12919 bss

> His guiding principle was that the oldest available manuscript was the most likely to be close to the original wording. Even its errors would be closer to the correct wording than the accumulated guesses and scribal errors of many generations of copyists. He demonstrated a practical way of examining a group of manuscripts and establishing their relationships. Poliziano [Politian] also realized the need to consult collateral sources, especially inscriptions and laws, and to seek out Greek parallels since many Latin authors had followed Greek models. His knowledge not only of Greek language but also of its literature was so thorough that he was able to uncover the correct wording and meaning of many passages that had puzzled all predecessors.
>
> (Nauert, 1995, p.41)

Burckhardt treated Politian primarily as a poet, but he did recount an incident when he exhorted John of Portugal to send him the accounts of his discoveries in Africa so that they could be incorporated into a systematic narrative and escape the terrible fate of obscurity (1990, p.109). Another example of Politian's grasp of the importance of establishing accurate records, written in good prose, can be derived from the preface to his translation of Herodian's third-century CE *History of the Empire after Marcus Aurelius,* which he dedicated to Pope Innocent VIII (1484–92). The Pope instigated this work when Politian was visiting Rome as part of an embassy in 1484. Innocent VIII suggested that he should make a collection of the testimonies about Roman emperors to be found in Greek historians. Politian linked this enterprise to the emergence of a new and better political order which could be introduced into Italy under papal patronage:

> As you have raised a sign of good hope for us from the eminence of your pontificate, proceed I beg most Holy Father, proceed I say to favour good Arts and make them famous, they come as suppliants before your most holy feet. Use your power against uncultivated ignorance, which fosters barbarism, so that there may be peace in Italy, which will be restored throughout the world, and obviously by the same peace letters will be nourished and saved from harm.

(*Herodiani Historiae de Imperio post Marcum*, 1493, Bologna, f.2v; translated by P. Fawcett, 1999)

By the end of the fifteenth century humanists were well-established in the bureaucracies of the princely courts of Italy, including the papal chancery. Even conservative scholars had been obliged to adopt the critical apparatus that had been developed from the time of Petrarch onwards, and to use classical as well as Christian authorities in their writings and speeches. Highly competent humanists continued to be active in Italy in the later Renaissance, when the standards of scholarship they had established were generally accepted throughout Europe. The new styles of writing, which were mentioned in Chapter 2, were also developed and were enormously influential on modern handwriting and printing; the cursive was the basis for the development of italic script.

The early sixteenth century saw the initiative in textual studies passing to northern Europe and to Spain: much of the impetus for this change of focus came from religious conflicts, many of them centred on the interpretation of religious texts. In some cases, however, engagement with textual criticism and the urge to produce more accurate versions of Christian authorities preceded the religious controversies in which they were to become embroiled. Other factors which promoted the activities of this later generation of humanists and motivated the patrons, on whose support they depended, were the successful establishment of printing with movable type as a cheap and profitable means of distributing texts for which there was a high demand, and the increase in literacy amongst the laity (although it is hard to quantify the extent to which this occurred).

Elizabeth Eisenstein provides invaluable insights into the problems and opportunities which faced the early printers (Reader, no. 4). Please read the extract now and refer to what Burckhardt has to say about the formation of libraries and the impact of printing (1990, pp.129–33). Printing, Eisenstein suggests, was not initially received with uncritical enthusiasm. She concludes with an important reservation about assuming too facile a connection between new technology and the Renaissance:

It makes sense to employ the term 'Renaissance' when referring to a two-phased cultural movement which was initiated by Italian literati and artists in the age of scribes and expanded to encompass many regions and fields of study in the age of print. But needless confusion is engendered when the same term is also used to cover the ensemble of changes which were ushered in by print.

Not only is a major communications revolution obscured by this practice, but so, too, is the reorientation of the cultural movement. It becomes difficult to guard against prematurely endowing the Petrarchan revival with the attributes of print culture. Our modern sense of antiquity 'as a totality cut off from the present' gets confusingly coupled with the quattrocento sense of antiquity on the verge of being reborn.

(1993, pp.145–6)

Despite Eisenstein's caveat about imputing to the Renaissance characteristics which were specifically produced by printing and which led to a separate sequence of events, it is still important to decide what opportunities printing could offer to humanists.

Exercise

What advantages did sixteenth-century humanists possess as a result of the introduction of printing, which were not available to their predecessors?

Discussion

Probably the greatest advantage brought about by printing was access to well-stocked shelves, since plentiful and relatively cheap printed books enabled both individuals and institutions to own a far greater number and variety of works than had previously been possible. Among the resources now available to scholars were grammars, dictionaries, collections of inscriptions, woodcuts of historical monuments, botanical specimens and maps: some of these reference works simply did not exist until the advent of print made it worthwhile to compile them.

The trade of printing could make a good profit (Jardine, 1997, pp.179–80), and this gradually liberated scholars from dependence on one patron for a living and enabled them to follow more innovative and sometimes subversive lines of thought. Printers like Aldus Manutius in Venice, the Frobens in Basle and Christopher Plantin in Antwerp were able to combine successful commercial careers with the production of some of the greatest works written and edited by the humanists of their time. Scholars could also gain a European reputation more easily when their works enjoyed print runs of up to a thousand at one time and could, if there was a demand, be quickly reprinted. Once they could refer to the same books and even exchange precise page references, it was easier for scholars to communicate with each other and develop new ideas and practices. ❖

Generalizations about the nature of humanist activity in the later phases of the Renaissance usually begin with a consideration of the work of Desiderius Erasmus. His open approach to new ideas and methods, his wide circle of friends and acquaintances, his travels, his relative financial independence and, most of all, his consummate scholarship, made him the focus of northern humanism in the early decades of the sixteenth century. This period coincided with the first phases of the Catholic and Protestant Reformations and the time when the technique of printing was sufficiently advanced to guarantee the rapid and widespread dissemination of popular texts. The humanist background of Erasmus informed all his works (although he also owed a debt to scholasticism) including the *Adages, Colloquies* and *Praise of Folly* (see Chapter 5). His greatest achievement in the field of textual criticism, however, and the one that established his European reputation, was his Latin translation of the New Testament, printed by his friend and collaborator Johann Froben of Basle (*c.*1460–1527). This was accompanied by an edition of the Greek New Testament and a commentary or *Annotations* in which Erasmus explained and defended the decisions he had made in the preparation of the texts. This entailed proposing corrections and changes to the Greek and Latin[2] versions which had been venerated by Christians since antiquity. He dedicated the first edition in 1516 to Pope Leo X (1513–21) and brought out four subsequent versions, the final one in 1535.

Exercise

Read the Annotations on St Paul's Epistle to the Romans 1.1–3 by Erasmus (Anthology, no. 5). What do you think were his principal considerations in making a new translation and commentaries? Don't worry about the technical points he makes concerning the interpretation of Hebrew and Greek words, the main purpose here is to engage with the nature of his scholarship.

Discussion

I suggest that Erasmus had three main considerations in undertaking this onerous task. First he was establishing himself as a biblical scholar in a venerable Christian tradition which stretched back to saints Augustine, Ambrose, Chrysostom and Jerome, authorities whom he frequently quoted with respect. Despite the fact that he is often described as the prime exemplar of Christian humanism, he was also the product of the intellectual heritage of scholasticism, which gave the highest status to commentators on the scriptures. Second he was attempting to establish as accurate a working text as possible for the use of contemporaries. He was undoubtedly ambitious for the renown he would win by doing so, but we may also accept that for a genuinely devout Christian this was an act of piety. In his concern to help readers to appreciate the text fully he introduced some historical background: note his reference in the

[2] The Latin version of the Bible was called the **Vulgate**.

first paragraph of his commentary to 'Alexander the Great's empire etc.' Third he believed, rightly, that by proposing that changes should be made to the Latin and Greek texts he would bring down on his head criticisms from both traditionalists who disliked any change on principle and jealous humanists who were already working on the same project. Notice how careful he was to say 'I neither approve nor disapprove' of the opinion of Lorenzo Valla. ❖

There must always be a suspicion that British scholars attribute an unjustified significance to the Renaissance in these islands. The work of Roberto Weiss, especially his *Humanism in England during the Fifteenth Century* (1957), established that there had been some noble and scholarly interest in Italian learning in the middle decades of the fifteenth century; but beyond putting a few humanist texts into circulation it had little impact. It was the visits made to Italy by British scholars in the last years of the century which initiated reform in scholarship and education. Thomas Linacre (*c.*1460–1524) and William Grocyn (*c.*1446–1519) were representatives of the growing band who had embraced the new learning. They studied under Politian in Florence and also had dealings with Aldus Manutius in Venice. They returned to England well versed in Greek as well as Latin and were able to widen the curriculum for the children of monarchs as well as the sons of some of the nobility, gentry and merchants to include both classical languages taught to a decent standard.

John Colet (1467–1519), who refounded St Paul's school in London and went on to become dean of St Paul's Cathedral, has generally been hailed as another innovatory humanist. Recently, however, scholars have voiced doubts. J.B. Trapp, for example, in his 1990 Panizzi lectures, found him rather too traditionally pious to have given himself whole-heartedly to the new learning. His statutes for the school may be interpreted as an attempt to promote a humanist programme:

> As towchyng in this scole what shalbe taught of the Maisters and lernyd of the scolers it passith my wit to devyse and determyn in particuler but in generall to speke and sum what to saye my mynde, I wolde they were taught all way in good litterature both laten and greke, and good auctors suych as haue the veray Romayne eliquence joyned with wisdome specially Cristyn auctours that wrote theyre wysdome with clene and chaste laten other in verse or in prose, for my entent is by thys scole specially to increase knowledge and worshipping of god …

But, Trapp points out, Colet went on to recommend mainly early Christian writers such as Lactantius and Prudentius, who had also

Figure 3.16 Hans Holbein the Younger, an Ecclesiastic, unknown, sometimes identified as John Colet, 1530s. The Royal Collection © Her Majesty the Queen

been authorities for medieval thinkers, although he did include two works by Erasmus. This choice makes his next remarks sound rather less like a humanist programme. He condemned:

> all barbary all corrupcion all laten adulterate which ignorant blynde folis brought into this worlde and with the same hath distayned and poysenyd the olde laten spech and the varay Romayne tong which in the tyme of Tully [Cicero] and Salust and Virgill and Terence was vsid, whiche also seint Jerome and seint ambrose and seint Austen and many hooly doctors lernyd in theyr tymes. I say that ffylthynesse and all such abusyon which the later blynde worlde brought in which more ratheyr may be callid blotterature thenne litterature I vtterly abbanysh and exclude oute of this scole and charge the Maisters that they teche allway that is the best and instruct the chyldren in greke and laten ...

(1991, pp.114–6)

Yet Colet was an admirer and correspondent of the Florentine Neoplatonic philosopher Marsilio Ficino (1433–99), possessing and annotating several of his works. His classical curriculum at St Paul's was a model eventually adopted by all grammar schools and made an impression on British education which has lasted to the present day.

The friendship between Sir Thomas More and Erasmus was probably a major factor in encouraging the latter to make several

Figure 3.17 Andrea di Piero Ferrucci, *Marsilio Ficino*, 1521–2, from Florence Cathedral. Photo: Alinari

visits to England and to work there. More's reputation as a fearless defender of the Catholic faith (including some rather nasty propaganda he put out against Martin Luther) has probably surpassed for many people the recognition of his importance as a humanist. His *Utopia*, which will be discussed in Chapter 5 as a philosophical text, was arguably the most important prose work produced by an Englishman during the Renaissance. However, More was active well before the publication of *Utopia*, composing Latin poems, writing letters to fellow humanists and translating Gianfrancesco Pico della Mirandola's *Life* of his philosopher uncle, Giovanni. He also translated from Greek into Latin some of the witty and satirical *Dialogues* of Lucian of Samosata (*c*.120–*c*.180). He did this during 1505–6, and at the same time Erasmus, who was staying at his house, was also producing Latin versions of some of the *Dialogues*. The Latin translations were very popular and were to be influential on better-known books later produced by the friends, the *Praise of Folly* and *Utopia*. More's versions of the *Dialogues* were printed at least thirteen times during his lifetime, often accompanied by those of Erasmus, whilst *Utopia* only appeared five or six times before 1535. *Utopia* was not translated into English until 1551, when it became accessible to a much wider audience; the *Dialogues* remained in Latin. Together More and Erasmus developed a sense of irony, which was to become typical of later Renaissance humour and would culminate in the *Essays* of Montaigne.

Read the extract from the letter which More addressed to Thomas Ruthall, a learned cleric, to accompany his translation of three of Lucian's *Dialogues* (Anthology, no. 6). How does he justify Christians reading pagan works?

Lucian 'combined delight with instruction', censuring in an honest and amusing fashion the 'shortcomings of mortals'. In the first dialogue, the 'Cynicus', 'the simplicity, temperance and frugality of the Christian life, and finally that straight and narrow way that leads to life are commended'. More claimed that these qualities led St John Chrysostom to incorporate part of the first dialogue into his commentary on St John's Gospel (the idea that pagan ethics could lead Christians to virtue as surely as the scriptures was shared by Erasmus). The second dialogue, the 'Necromantia', castigated the falsity and frivolity of magicians, poets and philosophers. The third, the 'Philopseudes', rejected superstition and lies told under the guise of religion. More went on to associate these with mendacious elements in certain lives of saints and martyrs which brought the whole Christian religion into disrepute. It did not trouble him that Lucian also called the possibility of immortality into doubt: 'why should it concern me what a pagan thinks about those matters?' ❖

This letter illustrates how, early in his career, the intensely orthodox More connected the reform of learning through humanist scholarship with the reform of the church. By the sixteenth century English humanists benefited from the prosperity of the country, their contacts on the Continent and the support of well-educated Tudor princes. Similar feats of scholarship were achieved in many other parts of northern and eastern Europe as well as in Italy and the Iberian peninsula. This brief consideration of the transmission of humanism to England can be taken to be representative of much that was going on in the sixteenth century, despite significant national variations.

Please read now the section in Burckhardt entitled 'Fall of the humanists in the sixteenth century' (1990, pp.177–84). Here he states that humanists lost credibility because of the arrogance and licence with which they expressed their ideas. Certainly few figures in the later stages of the Renaissance achieved the status of Bruni, Politian, Ficino or Erasmus, but this could be explained by the fact that by then much of their work had been accepted as part of the mainstream of education and scholarship. The nature of humanism changed: Aristotelianism and Neoplatonism were both challenged by scepticism, which questioned the possibility of achieving any kind of certainty in human affairs. It is also suggested below (pp.100–1) that the Italian veneration for antiquity was subverted by northern European historians, who used humanist methodologies to reject the notion that classical Rome was the founder of their nations, and substituted accounts of ancient German and Celtic tribes.

John Barclay (1582–1621), a French-born, Scottish Catholic who was educated by **Jesuits** in Lorraine, but gained employment at the English court of James I (1603–25), typified the ironic, eclectic spirit of late humanism. He wrote *Euphormio's Satyricon* (1605–7) inspired by the *Satyricon* which the Roman writer Petronius Arbiter composed during the reign of Emperor Nero (54–68). Barclay used the voyage of his hero, Euphormio, as a vehicle to expose the folly and corruption of contemporary European society, subjecting Jesuits, Puritans and the act of smoking to particularly harsh censure. He ensured, however, that his hero finished up in England where the country and its king were treated to fulsome praise. (See the extract from Barclay in the Anthology, no. 7).

Barclay typifies several of the traits displayed by later humanists: his Scottish background and European education gave him a cosmopolitan view of society and its follies, which distanced him from the relatively narrow, national pieties of writers such as Bruni and Budé. As a member of a generation which had witnessed the terrible results of the religious conflicts in Britain, France, the Low Countries and Germany, he voiced his scepticism in the *Satyricon* about the Christian religion when taken to extremes, both by the Jesuits and the Puritans.

Women humanists

If you look back to this chapter's introduction you will recall that humanists were generally members of professions with access to education, resources and scholarship. These, however, were closed to women and those who wanted to pursue humanist studies encountered enormous difficulties. Even educated women with financial resources who could, and did, study the classics using the new methodologies were absolutely excluded from all the professions through which they could communicate their knowledge and contribute to further advances in scholarship. A few women were members of academies and informal bodies, but they could not teach in the schools for older boys or the universities, where the reform of education had to be achieved. A certain number of nuns were learned women who corresponded with humanists, but their influence was slight and there is little evidence that the teaching they offered was much affected by humanist studies. To give any account at all of women humanists, therefore, reference has to be made to particular studies and individuals. At the end of this section I will ask whether this has been worth doing beyond some sort of tokenism.

Now read what Burckhardt said about the 'Equality of men and women' (1990, pp.250–53). He was more interested in establishing that women could have strong personalities, as part of his thesis about the development of the individual, than in their humanist activities. Yet what he said, especially about their educational attainments, anticipated later scholarship in this area. Margaret King (1991) suggests that only a few women were sufficiently notable to have left records, while others may have existed whose identities have not survived (this would also be the case with men, of course). Those we know about were all drawn from the governing classes and most lived in the princely states of northern Italy or in Venice. Their active careers as humanists tended to be terminated if they chose to marry, though those who remained celibate or entered convents sometimes continued with their studies. A history course would find surviving records of such women interesting, irrespective of the impact they had on the development of humanism. In this case, it is only in that last respect that we are pursuing this line of enquiry, so we will look at a few examples of the public recognition of, and reaction to, women humanists.

In his book on the French Renaissance, Simone (1969) mentioned the Italian scholar, courtier and poetess Christine de Pisan (*c*.1363–1431) (Plate 8), but did not specifically include her among the French humanists of the fourteenth and fifteenth centuries. While de Pisan certainly tended to work within the conventions of scholasticism so also did many other humanists and she could be claimed, at least in some respects, for the new learning. She was an accomplished writer in French and Latin who was acquainted with classical literature. She argued with a group of misogynist male writers on behalf of the moral and intellectual qualities of women in a literary dispute called 'the Debate of the Rose' (after some derogatory remarks made about women in a poem, *The Romance of the Rose*):

> As in ancient times the Romans in their triumphal marches allowed no praise or honor to such things as did not serve the good of the republic, let us look to their example in determining whether or not this romance is deserving of a crown ... despite your [Jean de Montreuil, one of her adversaries] proclaiming it a 'mirror for right conduct, a model for all walks of life in public affairs or in living religiously or prudently', I hold on the contrary that it is, with all due respect, an exhortation to vice giving comfort to dissolute ways, an indoctrination in deceit, a road to damnation, a universal libel, a cause for suspicion and mistrust, of disgrace to sundry individuals, and perhaps of heresy ... And may it not be laid to folly, arrogance, or presumption that I, a woman, do upbraid and refute so difficult an

author, diminishing the good fame of his work, when he, a sole and solitary man, dared to take it upon himself to defame and condemn without exception an entire sex?

(Willard, 1993, pp.158–9)

Women humanists in Italy sometimes encountered a negative response from contemporaries: Isotta Nogarola of Verona (1418–66) was slighted by her compatriot, the great teacher Guarino. When he did not reply to a letter she sent him, she claimed his neglect had exposed her to ridicule on all sides. She also annoyed one writer so much by daring to claim that women could acquire and practise humanist learning that he accused her, quite without evidence, of incest. This was very damaging, since, as she was unmarried, her best chance of retaining her respectability and hence the sympathy of fellow humanists was by her blameless life. Now read an extract from Isotta's best-known work, *Of the Equal or Unequal Sin of Adam and Eve* (Anthology, no. 8). Isotta conceded that 'women's natures were weaker than males', but this made Adam more blameworthy for the Fall since God had endowed him with superior merits. Indeed she apologized in this work for being a woman and writing of such matters. This automatic acceptance of an inferior status to male humanists runs through nearly all transactions involving learned women in fifteenth-century Italy. For example, Cassandra Fedele, addressing the doctors of the University of Padua, stated:

I shall contain my timidity – although I know it might seem to many of you audacious that I, a virgin too young to be learned, ignoring my sex and exceeding my talent, should propose to speak before such a body of learned men, and especially in this city where today (as once in Athens) the study of the liberal arts flourishes.

(King and Rabil, 1983, p.70)

Did she really mean all this (see Anthology, no. 9) or was it just an extreme example of a conventional scholastic formula of humility, given more emphasis because of her youth and gender? Leonardo Bruni certainly meant it when he advised the mother of a member of the Montefeltro family against allowing her daughter to learn rhetoric:

To her neither the intricacies of debate nor the oratorical artifices of action and delivery are of the least practical use, if indeed they are not positively unbecoming. Rhetoric in all its forms ... lies absolutely outside the province of women.

(King, 1991, p.443)

The spread of humanism, however, did improve the educational opportunities and broaden the horizons of those women who had access to some form of education in the humanities. There were instances in Italy and elsewhere of such women arranging for similar opportunities to be made available to their daughters. By the sixteenth century it was proving possible for some of them to achieve a standing independent of their immediate male circle and, in a few cases, to gain a wider reputation for learning.

In England throughout the sixteenth century the predisposition of the Tudor monarchs towards the new learning encompassed their womenfolk. Henry VII (1485–1509), the son of the pious and well-read Margaret Beaufort, Countess of Richmond, extended modest amounts of patronage to Italian humanists. His son, Henry VIII (1509–47), was well versed in humanist studies and allowed his first wife, Catherine of Aragon, to employ a fellow Spaniard, Juan Luis Vives (1492–1540), to tutor their daughter Mary. His other daughter, Elizabeth, later had the humanist Roger Ascham (1515–68) as her tutor, and both she and Mary were adept at reading, writing and translating Latin and Greek. Retha Warnicke (1991) has shown that the household of Sir Thomas More was like a small humanist academy and that in addition to his daughter, the learned Margaret Roper (Plate 9), its influence extended to the education of several other women in their circle. But whereas the English Renaissance led to the reform of grammar school curricula for boys, its impact on women was mostly confined to those who could afford a tutor competent in the new learning.

In France a succession of learned queens not only assisted in the process of the dissemination of humanist studies but, in one case, helped determine their direction. Marguerite of Navarre (1492–1549), the sister of Francis I, was a woman of considerable charm, intelligence and strength of character. She extended her patronage to many scholars and clerics, including some, like François Rabelais (?1494–?1553) and Jacques Lefèvre d'Etaples (c.1455–1536), who were critical of aspects of the Catholic church. Such writers were to prepare the way for the Protestant reform movement in France. Marguerite, like many humanists, maintained a wide correspondence and one of her warmest connections was with Vittoria Colonna (1490–1547), Marchioness of Pescara, who was equally renowned for her learning. Marguerite's humanism expressed itself not only through patronage but also by the composition of a number of works, some of them pious, although the best known, the *Heptameron*, has much in common with the collection of bawdy tales, the *Decameron*, by Giovanni Boccaccio (1313–75).

Figure 3.18 Attributed to Jean Clouet, *Marguerite of Navarre*, c.1544, oil on wood, 31 x 24 cm. Musée Condé, Chantilly, inv. 262. Photo: Giraudon

Exercise

In the Anthology (no. 10) read the story from the *Heptameron* by Marguerite of Navarre, with the accompanying commentary by the storytellers. (Note that Hircan is probably Henry of Navarre, second husband of Marguerite, who is usually portrayed in the stories as regarding women as the inferior sex whose role was to satisfy male passion.)

1　How positive is the account of women that emerges from this tale?

2　What attitude to the clergy emerges in the commentary?

Discussion

1　The psychology of the lady is complex and something of her anguish communicates itself to the reader and arouses sympathy. Her piety and chastity are proper for a young widow, but she expects more than was reasonable of herself and others with terrible results: 'this poor lady placed all her pride in the restraint she put upon her body'. In consequence she has to seek the assistance of the papal legate whose wise and worldly advice enables her to make the best of a bad job. Here is a rich, independent woman who thinks that she can control her life, but who actually causes a series of calamities which are only brought to an end by male intervention. So ultimately the account given of this woman is negative.

2　Hircan draws the moral: 'This is what happens, ladies, to those of your sex who think they can vanquish love and nature, and all the faculties which God has given them, by their own strength and virtue.' Most of the others are shocked by the story and agree with him, although two of the courtiers take the opportunity to blame such vainglorious conduct on the preaching of those who encourage the laity to believe that they can resist sin by their own efforts. Such clergy also test themselves by taking sexual liberties which often result in sinful behaviour. Hircan reminds the company that the monks who had been given permission to listen to the stories from behind a hedge, hearing the conversation turning to religion, were ringing the bell for vespers. The only cleric who emerges with any credit is the nobly born papal legate. This humanist circle displays some of the critical attitudes which were to lead to large scale conversions to Protestantism in France in the following decades. ❖

The sixteenth century in France saw the emergence of two institutions which were to be characteristic of its civilization: the **academy** and the *salon*. The informality of the latter and the need for it to be located in congenial surroundings, offered opportunities for witty and intelligent women. An example of a provincial *salon* at Poitiers held by a mother and daughter, members of the minor nobility, has been described by L. Clark Keating (1941). A great deal is known about this particular *salon* because the humanist Étienne Pasquier (1529–1615) was one of a number of lawyers sent to Poitiers in 1579 to conduct legal business which would relieve pressure on the Parisian courts. He was delighted to find a cultivated *salon* there. On his first visit, after a conversation on current affairs and philosophy, he glimpsed a flea on the breast of the daughter, Catherine des Roches. This led to a poem (which was strongly influenced by a similarly ironic piece by the greek satirist Lucian of Samosata). Catherine responded and soon a collection of 91 folios of flea poems had been made by humanists eager to display their talents to the ladies and to Pasquier, including the following by Barnabé Brisson (1531–91):

Vous grenouilles et souris	*You mice, and you, little frogs,*
Animees des escris	*Brought to life in hymns and in eclogues*
Du grand Prince des Poetes	*By Homer, prince of poets and the best,*
Heurreuses vrayment vous estes;	*How happy you are, how truly blest!*
Toy Passereau fretillard	*And you, sparrow, sprightly little thing,*
Caresse de vers mignard	*Whose pretty ways Catullus sings*
De Catulle, o que ta vie	*In dainty verse, oh how your days*
Est a jamais ennoblie	*Are ennobled by his praise!*
En cas semblable voit-on,	*So, too, little cousin, your name*
Petit cousin, ton renom	*Will forever be crowned with fame,*
Eternise par le stile	*Immortalized by the skill*
Du grave docte Virgile.	*Of the learned, grave Virgil.*

(Clark Keating, 1941, p.57; translated by A. Scholar, 1999)

Had women brought about such a trivialization of learning that poetry could be produced in such quantities to celebrate a flea on a bosom? Or did such episodes illustrate perhaps that women humanists by the later sixteenth century had sufficient confidence to participate in playful exchanges as well as in learned projects? Joan Kelly, in her seminal article 'Did women have a Renaissance?', takes issue with Burckhardt's positive account of the possibilities for well-to-do women in Italy. While conceding that some became highly educated, she considers that their intellectual integrity declined from the high courtly prestige they had enjoyed in the Middle Ages:

> In a sense, humanism represented an advance for women as well as for the culture at large. It brought Latin literacy and classical learning to daughters as well as sons of the nobility. But this very development, usually taken as an index of the equality of Renaissance (noble) women with men, spelled a further decline in the lady's influence over courtly society. It placed her as well as her brothers under male cultural authority ... The humanistic education of the Renaissance noblewoman helps explain why she cannot compare with her medieval predecessors in shaping a culture responsive to her own interests. In accordance with the new cultural values, the patronage of the Este, Sforza, Gonzaga and Montefeltro women extended far beyond the literature and art of love and manners, but the works they commissioned, bought, or had dedicated to them do not show any consistent correspondence to their concerns as women.
>
> (1984, pp.35–6)

A whole philosophy of life and education is at issue here: if you believe that gender differences should determine the nature and content of an academic curriculum for men and women you will agree with Kelly. Personally I believe that their participation in medieval courtly love literature and practice was a pleasant but essentially marginal game for a few elite women which confined them to a narrow, sexually defined role. Renaissance humanism transformed learning and education so that, by the time of the Enlightenment, bourgeois as well as noble women could benefit from it, and from the nineteenth century onwards it was gradually extended to the common people. It is suggested here that the main reason for studying women humanists is that while there were no female Vallas or Erasmuses, scholars like Isotta Nogarola and Marguerite of Navarre could hold their own among clever men, contribute to the sum total of knowledge and thought, and demonstrate, to all but the most extreme misogynist, that their sex was equally capable of intellectual attainments.

Humanists and the writing of history

History as a discipline only existed in the Middle Ages in the sense that the books by ancient writers like Plutarch, Sallust and Livy were known and read. When contemporaries set out to record the events of the past or their own times they usually produced chronicles. There is frankly not as much difference between a good chronicle and a poor history as some modern commentators would have us believe; the essential distinction is one of intention. A chronicler's main purpose was to recount what had happened in the past in an orderly sequence, which showed little recognition that it could be divided into periods with distinctive cultural and political characteristics. (Historians may or may not do this, but they will provide some explanation and analysis of the past.) Moreover, the chroniclers often gave credence to semi-mythical elements in the past, a reading which owed more to their Christian faith than it did to other criteria.

Exercise

In the Anthology (no. 11), read the extract from the *Florentine Chronicle* of the popular writer Giovanni Villani (*c.*1275–1348).

1 What characteristics of the account would cause it to be classified as a chronicle?

2 Are there any features which the account shares with history writing as we would understand it today?

Discussion

1 The approach of the writer is essentially linear: he recounts events as they occurred giving equal weight to all the incidents in the growing emnity between the pope and the king of France. Villani is very free with value judgements: the pope was 'disdainful and bold in all great things, of high purposes and powerful'. A historian might have explained the conflict in terms of ecclesiastical jurisdiction and threats to papal authority in France and Italy. Villani also wrote that 'much evil followed' from the strife. This seems again to be a verdict on the moral rather than the political and economic impact of the conflict. The story in the final paragraph, although the author concedes that the ass could simply have been frightened by the lion, attributes a supernatural significance to the incident and then links it to a prophecy by a **sibyl** (although they had been pagans, the sibyls were taken seriously in the Middle Ages because one was thought to have predicted the birth of Christ).

2 There are some features of the account which anticipate a more objective approach to the past. Before entertaining his readers with the tale of the ass and the lion, Villani had stuck closely to the actual political causes of the dispute. He also, in the first sentence, offered a

fairly convincing explanation of its origin, something which many early chroniclers would not have done. ❖

By the later part of the fourteenth century the admiration for classical historians such as Sallust and Livy was intense, but Cochrane suggests that this could have been an impediment to the emergence of history as a discipline:

> The early humanists lacked neither the ability nor the desire to write history. What they lacked was the recognition that other times and other places than those of the ancient Greeks and Romans were worth writing about. That defect could not be remedied until humanism, which had resurrected ancient historiography, could be brought together with communal patriotism, which had engendered the chronicle. And that was the work of Leonardo Bruni ...

> (1981, p.17)

Hans Baron, Paul Oskar Kristeller, Donald Wilcox and other post-war scholars, have been responsible for the growth in the reputation of Leonardo Bruni as the leading exponent of the 'new' history which was promoted by 'civic humanism':

> both the republican interpretation of Roman history and the view of Florence as the physical descendant, and heir to the political mission, of the *Respublica Romana* were novel elements in the historical thought of the Renaissance ...

> (Baron, 1966, p.64)

Bruni began the *History of Florence* in about 1415 and it was not finished at the time of his death; he had in the meantime become chancellor (the chief civil servant) of Florence.

Exercise

Read Bruni's *Preface* to the *History of Florence* (Anthology, no. 12).

1   Why did Bruni decide to write the *History*?

2   Compare the *History* with Villani's *Chronicle*, on which Bruni was reliant for many of his facts. How does it represent an advance in historical method?

Discussion

1   Despite the formidable task Bruni faced, he decided to undertake the *History* because of the impressive achievements of the Florentines in peace and war, involving 'deeds that are so worthy of memory that they appear in no way inferior to the greatest deeds of the ancients that we read about'. Knowledge of these would be of great profit to both private citizens and public servants and the wisdom they teach should lead to virtue. This is an important conclusion since the 'virtue' referred to here is not of a specifically Christian kind but rather the

classical conception of good citizenship. Contemporary history should be recorded for the characteristically humanistic purpose of trying to 'rescue it from oblivion and consecrate it to immortality'.

2 Bruni was clearly thinking of chronicles when he condemned the kinds of record which consisted merely of lists of names and dates 'whose harshness makes it hard to introduce any kind of stylistic elegance'. For him the main purpose of history was to persuade readers to emulate the civic virtue of their ancestors, so it was an essential part of the process that it should be cast in a rhetorical form. The scope of his work must include the whole of Italy so that events could be explained as well as recorded. In the same quest for intelligibility he used the chroniclers for accounts of the origins of Florence, 'but rejecting common and fabulous interpretations': tales of asses and lions would get short shrift. So while admitting his reliance on the chroniclers, Bruni conceived the purpose and method of historical writing to be entirely different from the motives which influenced their work. It should be eloquent, persuasive and selective, and offer a general overview of events so that rational explanations could be offered. ❖

Powerful material like Bruni's *History*, which enjoyed the additional prestige of being written by a Florentine chancellor and explicitly modelled on admired classical writers like Livy and Sallust, was bound to be emulated. Two humanists who held the post of chancellor later in the century, Poggio Bracciolini and Bartolomeo Scala (1430–97), wrote histories of Florence which were intended to bring Bruni's account up to their own times. Poggio lived long enough to do so but when Scala died he still had more than two hundred years to record. Both adopted Bruni's style and methodology and accepted his view of the connection between morality and civic virtue. Other contemporaries both in Florence and elsewhere in Italy continued to write in the traditional chronicle style throughout the fifteenth century. Yet the advantages of humanist historiography were obvious, and not just to republics like Florence. In Rome the papacy adopted it with enthusiasm. Flavio Biondo's (1392–1463) *History from the Decline of the Roman Empire* suggested that Rome's power came to an end with the sack of the city by the Goths. It did not, as was believed in the Middle Ages, continue under later emperors in Constantinople and northern Europe: the new nations were held together by the common heritage of Christianity rather than by force. This side-lined the whole issue of the *Donation of Constantine*, for if continuity with the Roman empire had been broken, modern princes had no obligation to pay it any regard. Such use of periodization to define distinctive stages in the historic past was one of the features of the new approach to history, as was Biondo's critical analysis of his sources.

Figure 3.19 Pinturicchio, *Pope Pius II (Aeneas Sylvius Piccolomini)*, detail from a fresco of his enthroned entry into St John Lateran, begun 1502. Piccolomini Library, Siena Cathedral. Photo: Scala. Reproduced by permission of the Opera della Metropolitana di Siena

Pope Nicholas V (1447–55) ensured that the works of the major classical Greek historians would be made available by commissioning Latin translations from humanists such as Poggio and Valla. Edmund Fryde describes Poggio's translation of the first five books of Diodorus Siculus as 'disasters' but thinks that Valla did a good job with the complexities of Thucydides (1983, p.27). Aeneas Sylvius Piccolomini wrote histories both before and after he became pope as Pius II (1458–64). The rhetorical thrust of his work, particularly the *Commentaries*, was to promote the project of a crusade against the Turk. It only took a few decades, therefore, for the original motivation of civic humanism in Bruni's history of republican Florence to be appropriated by ecclesiastical and secular princes. Not surprisingly, the historians they employed could be prevented from writing truly objective accounts by fear of annoying their patrons.

Now read Burckhardt on the subject of the traditional and new history (1990, pp.159–63). He voiced the opinion, shared by a modern historian of the Renaissance, John Stephens (1990, pp.176–201), that the slavish emulation of classical authors like Livy and the preoccupation with fine rhetorical phrases led to an arid, uninteresting sort of writing, 'insipid and conventional'. Burckhardt did not identify the strong theme of civic consciousness which historians such as Baron, Kristeller and Wilcox discerned in Bruni and his followers. For him such work was not produced until the sixteenth century when Niccolò Machiavelli and Francesco Guicciardini started to write in the vernacular (see below, Chapter 6). Moreover, critics of the Baron thesis of 'civic humanism', such as Jerrold Seigel, have queried whether it really provided the principal motivation for Bruni's writings:

> Civic sentiment and direct political involvement were not the determining elements in early humanism. Rather Bruni's writings, like the programme of Renaissance humanism in general, must be approached as the products of a particular kind of culture: a culture which centred on rhetoric and eloquence.

(1966, p.10)

Like many other twentieth-century interpreters Seigel saw far more continuity between the Middle Ages and the Renaissance than had previously been conceded. The stress he laid on the importance of rhetoric was determined by his view that it was an essentially public art (*negotium*), as opposed to philosophical speculation, which was best practised by those who had no official duties (*otium*). Seigel and Baron at least agreed that fifteenth-century humanists were characteristically professional and occupied a variety of public posts, where their ability as rhetoricians was of importance. Now read Albert Rabil's article 'The significance of "Civic Humanism"' in the Reader (no. 3) which gives a more detailed account of these issues.

A good example of the rapid dissemination of the humanist, Latin history which disgusted Burckhardt is to be found in the work of Antonio Bonfini (*c.*1427–*c.*1502), a minor north Italian writer. In 1491 the queen of Hungary, formerly an Italian princess, advised her husband, Matthias Corvinus (1458–90), to offer him a post as royal historian. He spent the rest of his life working on a *History of Hungary* which is heavily reliant in its rhetorical style and classical imagery on the work of his Florentine, Roman and Venetian predecessors as well as dependant on contemporary Hungarian chronicles, state papers, inscriptions and coins (Mitchell, 1994, pp.82–117).

Exercise

Read the following extracts from Bonfini's *History of Hungary* (3rd decade, book 7) in which John Hunyadi, father of Matthias Corvinus, delivers a speech to his troops before a battle with the

Turks. What features indicate that it could be a rhetorical composition rather than a report of words actually spoken?

> My loyal soldiers and good friends, now is the time for you to wipe out all stain of infamy, if you incurred any in that calamitous defeat of Varna [1444]. Now is the time for you to recover your reputation for loyalty and valour, and to avenge yourselves for so many wrongs and injuries received at the hands of these cursed Turks and unbelieving Mohammedans. If you wish to show yourselves as brave as usual, you must know that, having the right on our side, although we are much less numerous than the enemy, we will make him feel that in valour, spirits and generosity we have the advantage. For the soldiers of the Turk fight for the benefit of another, and for the advancement of a man who will not be grateful for their efforts. Even if they are victorious, they can hope for no more than slavery for their whole lives, and the loss of their souls after death, because they have served the most powerful and detestable tyrant on earth. My friends and faithful companions, whether fortune follows you or turns her back on you, you are fighting for our kingdom, for the safety of your wives and children, for your temples and altars, for your homes, and in order to enjoy eternal happiness after death. This is what moves you to fight so fiercely: the knowledge that if you do not win, what happens to your goods, your wives and children, and to the whole realm happens by your own acts ...

> Let us deliver Hungary from fear, in order that it may enjoy peace and live happily henceforward in a lasting tranquillity. My comrades, you must fight with all your strength, since necessity requires it, honour demands it, and our own interest advises it: for however fortune treats us, we cannot be otherwise than happy. If we are victorious, we have won the safety, peace and happiness of our country, and imperishable praise of ourselves: if we die, it is on the bed of honour and in a holy war that we leave this world, in order to enjoy a more happy life in the next. For this reason my friends, let us go and fight so well and bravely that whether we conquer or die, posterity will remember us with praise, and we will win the immortal crown or glory.

> (Burke, 1969, pp.117–19)

Discussion

The language is elevated and eloquent: the repetition of 'now is the time' in the first two sentences would signal to readers that the speech is cast in the classical tradition of oratory. Stereotypes are used which would be immediately recognized: 'cursed Turks', 'detestable tyrant', 'safety of your wives and children'. Despite the strongly Christian message there is also an underlying recognition of the importance of Fortune in human affairs: 'she' occurs in both paragraphs enjoying the power to grant or withhold success. The final sentence, promising the soldiers 'an immortal crown or glory' if they fight well, is consistent with the classification of the work as a piece of humanist rhetoric. Bonfini could have written it without any precise knowledge of the circumstances he purported to describe, as it is devoid of any detailed information. It is unlikely that a commander who wished to win a battle, if he addressed his troops at all, would omit any reference to strategy (humanist historians deliberately avoided such 'low' subjects). Of course all this is really beside the point, for the king was not paying Bonfini to provide him with the sordid minutiae of Hungary's long resistance to the Turk. He wanted instead an elevating and inspiring account to encourage his people and enhance the prestige of his newly established dynasty. The evidence of passages like this supports the objection raised by Stephens that the kind of history introduced by Bruni and his followers subordinated factual accuracy and pragmatic analysis to the writing of eloquent passages of rhetoric. ❖

When Stephan Brodaric, chancellor of Hungary, wrote his account of the Turkish victory in 1526 which destroyed the old kingdom he adopted a very different tone (*The Conflict of the Hungarians with the Turks at Mohacs*). He avoided the artifice and rhetorical flourishes with which Italian humanists adorned their history and instead wrote in a sombre, restrained style, concentrating on an analysis of the causes of the disaster (Birnbaum, 1991, pp.306–7).

Humanists in northern Europe experienced greater problems in absorbing the new approach to history than was the case in other branches of the humanities. While their Italian counterparts could claim that they were the moral and intellectual heirs to Rome (which itself had inherited much from classical Greece), no such prestigious tradition was available to English, German or French writers. Rather pathetic attempts had been made from the time of Geoffrey of Monmouth in the twelfth century to fabricate Trojan ancestors for these northern states; thus Britain was founded by 'Brut' and France by 'Francus'. Burckhardt ridiculed such national fables as 'fantastic rubbish', not appreciating that they can be very enlightening about the values of the past. Yet practitioners of the new history were sceptical about legends which could not be supported with firm evidence. Polydore Vergil (*c*.1470–*c*.1555), a humanist from Urbino, who wrote a *History of England* for the early Tudor monarchs, was influential in setting such standards as well as demonstrating the merits of clear, concise narrative expressed in classical Latin. He had been hired by Henry VII to give a good account of the new dynasty; similarly Sir Thomas More wrote his *History of Richard III* to discredit the last Plantagenet king.

Northern writers who emulated humanist history, however, soon diverged from their models in their attitude towards the Middle Ages. Paradoxically it was the Roman writer Tacitus, whose works only became widely known and used in the course of the fifteenth century, who provided an excellent justification for their gradual emancipation from the domination of classical antiquity. He had compared the Germans of his time favourably with the Romans, whom he thought had become corrupt and effeminate. Conrad Celtis (1459–1508) was professor of rhetoric at the university of Vienna and belonged to a group of scholars at the court of the Emperor Maximilian who were anxious to promote the national pride and identity of Germany. He brought out an edition of the *Germania* of Tacitus and published a collection of medieval source material but died before he could complete his project of writing a history based on it. Similarly John Major (1469–1550) in Scotland and William Camden (1551–1623) in England felt no need to rely on foundation myths which linked their countries to ancient Greece or Rome. The latter combined, in the *Britannia* (1586), what he perceived to be the best aspects of the humanist approach to history with his own particular mission: the glorification of Britain (that is, from 1603, Scotland, Ireland and Wales ruled from England) as an empire, owing no allegiance to an external power.

Figure 3.20 R. White, *William Camden*, engraving, from Camden's *Britannia*, 1695 edition. British Museum 1258.d.18 © British Museum

The strongest reaction against the kind of history writing introduced by humanists like Bruni was to be found amongst the French writers of the sixteenth century. Guillaume Budé was in the service of Francis I (1515–47) and on account of his immense learning was often compared, with an element of national pride, to Erasmus. In his legal, biblical and antiquarian studies he employed much humanist historical methodology, but refused to regard antiquity as the source of all wisdom and fine culture: the contribution of the Middle Ages had been essential to the emergence of the French state. For example, his *From Hellenism to Christianity* (1535) presented a critique of classical philosophy from a Christian perspective. He was the first of a school of legal historians who used temporal and cultural relativism to dissipate the distortions and inaccuracies which pervaded the study of both history and law in France. Whilst Budé put his scholarship at the service of the monarchy, François Hotman (1524–90), one of the next generation of writers, was a Protestant activist whose work was considered by the Catholic government to be extremely subversive. His *Franco-Gallia* (1573) rejected the legacy of the Roman empire, especially its laws and institutions, in favour of those of the Frankish kingdoms. He believed that they had enjoyed a mixed monarchy which ruled by customary law, rather than the Roman civil code, and which consulted an assembly of its subjects: the precursor to the **Estates General**. Writing in 1573 after the massacre of

French **Calvinists** on St Bartholomew's day [3] (Plate 10), for which he blamed Queen Catherine de' Medici, he claimed that feudal custom (not the **Salic law**) excluded women from the throne, and threw in some choice episodes from the past to demonstrate the awfulness of women rulers.

Figure 3.21 François Hotman, from Pierre de l'Estoile, *Les Belles Figures et drolleries de la Ligue*, 1589, Paris. Bibliothèque Nationale de France. Rés. Gr. fol. La25.6

[3] Civil unrest in France reached its climax in six days of communal violence in Paris with many thousands of people losing their lives. The massacre began on 24 August 1572, immediately after the wedding of the Protestant Henri of Navarre to Catherine de' Medici's daughter, Marguerite of Valois.

Donald Kelley has suggested that in its form, self-consciousness and critical spirit the *Researches on France* by Étienne Pasquier should be compared to the *Essays* of his friend Michel de Montaigne (1970, pp.271–2). Sharing the **Gallican** (the belief that government of the French church should be largely free from papal control) loyalties of his predecessors and contemporaries he chose to write in the vernacular – a brave decision in a period when scholars were expected to use Latin if they wished to be taken seriously. He set about a long-term project to record the language, laws and institutions of France. His Gallican view of these was coloured by the wars of religion which formed a background to his work and he developed an antipathy towards the Jesuits, who he saw as agents of **ultramontanism** (that is papal interference in French affairs).

Apart from being politically undesirable, deference to Rome, even for orthodox Catholics like Pasquier, seemed to be yet another manifestation of the cultural dominance which Italy had enjoyed for too long. For example, he rejected the canonist (church law) formulas justifying arbitrary rule, which were an Italian not a French, invention, made by Italian officials of the papal court (Kelley, 1970, p.286). The attribution of a recent origin to a legal development is characteristic of Pasquier and his circle, reacting against the 'Trojan founders' school of history, which they believed was offensive to national integrity. Indeed he took this view to its logical conclusion in his third book of *Researches*, which was a systematic defence of the Gallican liberties of the French church. This was based on three main premises: that the pope had no power to excommunicate French subjects, no right to intervene in temporal matters in France, and that he was subordinate to general councils of the church. Pasquier was able to produce plenty of evidence to justify these claims from the last few centuries when the French monarchy had invariably bested the papacy in encounters over jurisdiction. It was ironic that humanist history, which began with the praise of Florentine republican institutions (thought to be based on classical models), should end with confident assertions of the independence of the greatest of the 'new' nation states from the tutelage of Rome, both ancient and modern.

Conclusion

Does the working definition of humanism offered in the introduction to this chapter still stand up after further reading and reflection? While the 'spirit of enquiry' seems a reasonable description of the approach of those considered, many would query whether it really entailed 'little respect for traditional authority'. The tendency of many of the twentieth-century writers whose work has been mentioned has been to stress continuities with the past, particularly with scholasticism. The eloquent and defiant words of a few polemicists such as Valla and Poggio were not typical of the majority of humanists who had been educated traditionally.

While little that has been discussed above would call in question the humanists' 'veneration for classical antiquity', the way in which it could be applied to the society and political structures of the fifteenth and sixteenth centuries has been debated ever since. Exactly how and to what extent did commentators from Bruni to Machiavelli envisage the revival of classical forms of republican government? Perhaps Baron overstates the case but even critics such as Seigel are prepared to find some element of 'civic humanism' in the writings of Italian humanists. Hankins (1995), however, has recently suggested that Bruni's work was little more than a front for the oligarchical control of Florence by a few rich families rather than an expression of true republican sentiment. A later generation of northern writers, most notably Hotman, had reservations about the contemporary application of classical models of law and government. It did not seem reasonable that areas such as northern France and Germany, in the late sixteenth century, should slavishly emulate systems which had been developed nearly two thousand years earlier south of the Alps.

The improvement in texts and other scholarly resources during the Renaissance is not a subject which provokes much contemporary debate, but the way in which those texts and resources were received and transmitted, especially in schools and universities, does. These are areas where the non-specialist must tread with care, since views can only be formed on the basis of a great quantity of well-researched information. We have seen, however that those who possess such information, for example, Grafton and Jardine (1986), differ from Black (1991) over the question of how far the curriculum in Italian schools really was affected by humanist methods, invoking again the wider issue of how much continuity there was with the learning of the Middle Ages (see above, p.74).

Florence and Florentines may seem to play a disproportionate part in this account of humanism, as they do for Burckhardt who was in no doubt they were 'the pattern and the earliest type of Italians and modern Europeans generally' (1990, p.71). However, many humanists usually identified as Florentine actually originated from other parts of Italy; they were mobile professionals who would go wherever they saw the best prospects of employment. This very mobility implies a common culture and value system which, to some extent, negates

Burckhardt's claims for Florence. However, as in many parts of his still-influential work, his extravagance and enthusiasm, so different from the measured analyses of modern historians, can still be a useful guide to our interpretation.

Bibliography

ASHMOLE, B. (1956) 'Cyriac of Ancona and the temple of Hadrian at Cyzicus', *Journal of the Warburg and Courtauld Institutes*, vol. 19, pp.179–91.

BARON, H. (1966, rev. edn) *The Crisis of the Early Italian Renaissance: Civic Humanism and Republican Liberty in an Age of Classicism and Tyranny*, Princeton, NJ, Princeton University Press; first published 1955.

BAXANDALL, M. (1972) *Painting and Experience in Fifteenth-Century Italy: A Primer in the Social History of Pictorial Style*, Oxford, Oxford University Press.

BORSOOK, E. (1973) *The Companion Guide to Florence*, London, Collins.

BIRNBAUM, M.D. (1991) 'Humanism in Hungary' in A. Rabil (ed.) *Renaissance Humanism: Foundations, Forms and Legacy*, vol. 2, 'Humanism beyond Italy', Philadelphia, University of Pennsylvania Press.

BLACK, R. (1991) 'The curriculum of Italian elementary and grammar schools, 1350–1500' in D.R. Kelley and R.H. Popkin (eds) *The Shapes of Knowledge from the Renaissance to the Enlightenment*, Dordrecht and London, Kluwer Academic.

BURCKHARDT, J. (1990) *The Civilization of The Renaissance in Italy*, trans. S.G.C. Middlemore, Harmondsworth, Penguin; first published 1858.

BURKE, P. (1969) *The Renaissance Sense of the Past*, Documents of Modern History Series, eds A.G. Dickens and A. Davies, London, Edward Arnold.

BURKE, P. (1990) 'The spread of Italian humanism' in A. Goodman and A. MacKay (eds) *The Impact of Humanism in Western Europe*, London and New York, Longman.

CLARK KEATING, L. (1941) *Studies on the Literary Salon in France, 1550–1615*, Harvard Studies in Romance Language Series, vol. 16, Cambridge, Mass., Harvard University Press.

COCHRANE, E. (1981) *Historians and Historiography in the Italian Renaissance*, Chicago and London, University of Chicago Press.

COLIN, J. (1981) *Cyriaque d'Ancône, le voyageur, le marchand, l'humaniste*, Paris, Maloine.

EISENSTEIN, E.L. (1993) *The Printing Revolution in Early Modern Europe*, Cambridge, Cambridge University Press.

FRYDE, E.B. (1983) *Humanism and Renaissance Historiography*, London, Hambledon Press.

GARIN, E. (1965) *Italian Humanism: Philosophy and Civic Life in the Renaissance*, trans. P. Munz, Oxford, Blackwell.

GRAFTON, A. and JARDINE, L. (1986) *From Humanism to the Humanities: Education and the Liberal Arts in Fifteenth and Sixteenth Century Europe*, London, Duckworth.

GREENBLATT, S.J. (1980) *Renaissance Self-fashioning: From More to Shakespeare*, Chicago, University of Chicago Press.

HALE, J. (1993) *The Civilization of Europe in the Renaissance*, London, Harper Collins.

HANKINS, J. (1995) 'The "Baron thesis" after forty years and some recent studies of Leonardo Bruni', *Journal of the History of Ideas*, vol. 56, pp.309–38.

JARDINE, L. (1996) *Worldly Goods*, London and Basingstoke, Macmillan.

KELLEY, D.R. (1970) *Foundations of Modern Historical Scholarship: Language, Law and History in the French Renaissance*, New York and London, Columbia University Press.

KELLY, J. (1984) *Women, History and Theory: Essays*, Chicago and London, University of Chicago Press.

KING, M.L. (1991) 'Book-lined cells: women and humanism in the early Italian Renaissance' in A. Rabil (ed.) *Renaissance Humanism: Foundations, Forms and Legacy*, vol. 1, 'Humanism in Italy', Philadelphia, University of Pennsylvania Press.

KING, M.L. and RABIL, A. (eds) (1983) *Her Immaculate Hand: Selected Works by and about the Women Humanists of Quattrocento Italy*, New York, Binghamton.

KRAYE, J. (ed.) (1996) *The Cambridge Companion to Renaissance Humanism*, Cambridge, Cambridge University Press.

KRISTELLER, P.O. (1988) 'Humanism' in C.B. Schmitt (ed.) *Cambridge History of Renaissance Philosophy*, Cambridge, Cambridge University Press.

MANN, N. (1996) 'The origins of humanism' in Kraye, J. (ed.) *The Cambridge Companion to Renaissance Humanism*, Cambridge, Cambridge University Press.

MITCHELL, S. (1994) 'The image of Hungary and Hungarians in Italy, 1437–1526', Ph.D. thesis, Warburg Institute, University of London.

NAUERT, C.G., JR (1995) *Humanism and the Culture of Renaissance Europe*, New Approaches to European History Series, Cambridge, Cambridge University Press.

SEIGEL, J.E. (1966) 'Civic humanism or Ciceronian rhetoric?', *Past and Present*, vol. 34, pp.3–48.

SIMONE, F. (1969) *The French Renaissance: Medieval Tradition and Italian Influence in Shaping the Renaissance in France*, trans. H. Gaston Hall, London, Macmillan.

STEPHENS, J. (1990) *The Italian Renaissance: The Origins of Intellectual and Artistic Change before the Reformation*, Harlow, Longman.

SYMONDS, J.A. (1937 edn) *Renaissance in Italy: The Revival of Learning*, London, John Murray; first published 1877.

TRAPP, J.B. (1991) *Erasmus, Colet and More: The Early Tudor Humanists and their Books*, The Panizzi Lectures 1990, London, The British Library.

WARNICKE, R.M. (1991) 'Women and humanism in England' in A. Rabil (ed.) *Renaissance Humanism: Foundations, Forms and Legacy*, vol. 2, 'Humanism beyond Italy', Philadelphia, University of Pennsylvania Press.

WEISS, R. (1957) *Humanism in England during the Fifteenth Century*, Oxford, Blackwell.

WEISS, R. (1969) *The Renaissance Discovery of Classical Antiquity*, Oxford, Blackwell.

WILCOX, D.J. (1969) *The Development of Florentine Humanist Historiography*, Harvard Historical Studies, vol. 82, Cambridge, Mass., Harvard University Press.

WILLARD, C.C. (ed.) (1993) *The Writings of Christine de Pizan*, New York, Persea Books.

Anthology and Reader sources

Giovanni Francesco Poggio Bracciolini, from *On the Inconstancy of Fortune*: *De Varietate Fortunae*, 1, ed. O. Merisalo, Suomorlainen Tiedeakatemia toimituksia, *Annales Academiae Scientiarum Fennicae*, Sar B, nide 265, Helsinki, 1993, pp.91–7, translated for this edition by Caryll Green. (Anthology, no. 1)

Ciriaco of Ancona, Journeys in the Propontis: (i) The ruins of Cyzicus, *Cyriacus of Ancona's Journeys in the Propontis and the Northern Aegean*, ed. E.W. Bodnar and C. Mitchell, American Philosophical Society, Philadelphia, 1976, pp.27–31, trans. Chris Emlyn-Jones. (ii) Letter to John Hunyadi, J. Colin, *Cyriaque d'Ancone: le voyageur, le marchand, l'humaniste*, Maloine, Paris, 1981, pp.358–9, trans. Lucille Kekewich. (Anthology, no. 2)

Giovanni Francesco Poggio Bracciolini, Two letters about classical manuscripts: (i) and (ii) *Two Renaissance Book Hunters: The letters of Poggius Bracciolini to Nicolaus Niccolis*, ed. and trans. W.G. Gordon, Records of Civilization: sources and studies, 91, Columbia University Press, New York and London, 1974, Appendix: Letter III, pp.193–6, Letter XL, pp.99–100. (Anthology, no. 3)

Lorenzo Valla, from *The Treatise of Lorenzo Valla on the Donation of Constantine*: (i) and (ii) *The Treatise of Lorenzo Valla on the Donation of Constantine*, ed. and trans. C.B. Coleman, Yale University Press, New Haven, 1922, pp.11–19, 24–9, 63–7, 115–17, 177–83. (Anthology, no. 4)

Elizabeth L. Eisenstein, 'The emergence of print culture in the west: defining the initial shift': *The Printing Revolution in Early Modern Europe*, Cambridge University Press, Cambridge, 1983, pp.12–41. (Reader, no. 4)

Desiderius Erasmus, Annotations on St Paul's Epistle to the Romans 1.1–3: (i) St Paul's Epistle to the Romans, The Authorised Version of the Bible, British and Foreign Bible Society, London, 1.1–3. (ii) *Collected Works of Erasmus*, 56, *Annotations on the Epistle to the Romans*, ed. R.D. Sider, trans. and annotated J.B. Payne, A. Rabil, R.D. Sider, W.S. Smith, New Testament Scholarship, University of Toronto Press, Toronto, London, 1994, pp.3–8. (Anthology, no. 5)

Thomas More, Dedicatory letter to Thomas Ruthall on his translation of the Dialogues of Lucian of Samosata: *The Translations of Lucian by Erasmus and St Thomas More*, C.R. Thompson, Ithaca, New York, 1940, pp.24–7. (Anthology, no. 6)

John Barclay from *Euphormio's Satyricon*: *Euphormio's Satyricon*, ed. and trans. D.A. Fleming, Nieuwkoop, B. de Graef, 1973, pp.339–47, 349–51. (Anthology, no. 7)

Isotta Nogarola, *Of the Equal or Unequal Sin of Adam and Eve*: *Her Immaculate Hand: Selected Works By and About Women Humanists of Quattrocento Italy*, ed. and trans. M. L. King and A. Rabil, Binghamton, 1983, pp.59–67, 69. (Anthology, no. 8)

Cassandra Fedele, Oration to the University of Padua: *Her Immaculate Hand: Selected Works By and About Women Humanists of Quattrocento Italy*, ed. and trans. M.L. King and A. Rabil, Binghamton, 1983, pp.70–73. (Anthology, no. 9)

Marguerite of Navarre, Novel XXX from the *Heptameron*: *The Heptameron: Tales of Marguerite, Queen of Navarre*, trans. W.M. Thompson, London, The Temple Company, 1896, pp.190–95. (Anthology, no. 10)

Giovanni Villani, from *The Florentine Chronicles*: *Villani's Chronicle: being selections from the first nine books of the 'Chroniche Fiorentine' of Giovanni Villani*, trans. R.E. Selfe and P.H. Wicksteed, Archibald Constable and Co. Ltd., London, 1906, pp.344–6. (Anthology, no. 11)

Leonardo Bruni, Preface to *The History of the Florentine People*: *The Humanism of Leonardo Bruni, Selected Texts*, ed. and trans. G. Griffiths, J. Hankins, D. Thompson, Medieval and Renaissance Texts and Studies, 46, New York, 1987, pp.190–92. (Anthology, no. 12)

Albert Rabil Jr., 'The significance of "civic humanism" in the interpretation of the Italian Renaissance': *Renaissance Humanism: Foundations, Forms and Legacy*, vol. 1, *Humanism in Italy*, ed. Albert J. Rabil Jr., University of Pennsylvania Press, Philadelphia, 1988, pp.141–79. (Reader, no. 3)

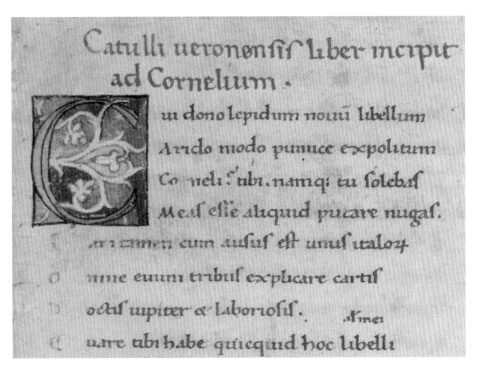

Plate 3 Workshop of Sandro Botticelli, *The Wedding Feast*, oil on canvas. Private collection. The Bridgeman Art Library, London/New York

Plate 4 Workshop of Apollonio di Giovanni, *Dido's Banquet* (detail), *c.*1460, oil on wood, 67 x 188 cm, central *cassone* panel. Niedersachsisches Landesmuseum, Landesgalerie, Hanover

Plate 5 Anthonis Mor, *Portrait of a Gentleman*, 1569, oil on canvas, 119.7 x 88.3 cm. National Gallery of Art Washington, Andrew W. Mellon Collection. Photo: Richard Carafelli

Plate 6 Anthonis Mor, *Portrait of an Artist*, after 1569, oil on canvas. Galleria degli Uffizi, Florence. Photo: Scala

Plate 7 Isaac Oliver, *Portrait of a Melancholy Young Man*, c.1590–95, oil on wood, 11.68 x 8.25 cm. The Royal Collection © Her Majesty the Queen

Plate 8 Christine de Pisan writing in her study. The British Library, MSS Harleian 4431, fol. 4 recto. Reproduced by permission of the British Library

Plate 9 Hans Holbein, *Thomas More and his family*, 1527, ink and pencil over chalk drawing, 38.9 x 52.4 cm. Margaret Roper is seated on the floor in the right-hand corner of the drawing. Oeffentliche Kunstsammlung Basel Kupferstichkabinett Basel, Inv. 1662.31 Kat. 1988 Nr. 65

Plate 10 François Dubois, *St Bartholomew's Day Massacre*, 1572–84, oil on wood, 93 x 154 cm. Musée Cantonal des Beaux-Arts, Lausanne. Photo: J-C Ducret, Musée des Beaux-Arts

Plate 11 *Execution of Savonarola*, by unknown artist, oil on canvas. Museo di S. Marco, Florence. Photo: Scala

Plate 12 Muziano Giovanni Girolamo (1528–92), view of the Villa d'Este and of the gardens in the original plan, oil on canvas. Villa d'Este, Tivoli. Photo: Scala

Plate 13 View of Rome, by unknown artist, oil on canvas. Palazzo Ducale Mantova. Photo: Scala

CHAPTER FOUR

Music and humanism

BY FIONA RICHARDS

Objectives

The objectives for this chapter are that you should:

- relate developments in music during the Renaissance to the discussion of humanism in Chapter 3;
- listen to representative examples of music from the period *c.*1350–1630;
- focus on the composer Josquin Desprez, and gain some understanding of how his music reflects the impact of humanism.

Even if you have no prior musical experience you should still be able to enjoy and learn from this chapter. Technical discussion has been kept to a minimum. There are listening exercises throughout the chapter, and sources for all of the music tracks referred to can be found on page 129. A few musical scores have been included, but they are not essential to your work. They are also of uneven quality and include a mixture of good and not-so-good editions with wording in both modernized and unmodernized French.

Introduction

The composition and reception of music in the Renaissance was profoundly affected by humanist thought. The full impact of humanist ideals, however, spread only very slowly from Italy across Europe. This chapter will focus mainly on Italian composers and on composers working in Italy, and will be based on the evidence of surviving manuscripts and printed editions.

In Chapter 3 the following distinctive features of the Renaissance were highlighted:

- a move away from the culture of the Middle Ages;
- a spirit of enquiry and criticism, and a desire to communicate new and revived knowledge;
- 'pagan', i.e. secular, tendencies and the importance of the individual;
- an engagement in the humanities, i.e. grammar, poetry, history, etc.;

- commercial interests and new technologies, especially printing;
- a veneration for classical antiquity and an attempt to retrieve the past.

These characteristics are reflected in music of this period in the following ways:

- a move away from the musical techniques of the Middle Ages;
- a spectacular increase in the composition and performance of music;
- a growth in secular music;
- the dominance of the word (i.e. text above music);
- the rise of printed music, and therefore a much greater dissemination of musical works;
- a veneration for classical antiquity, seen particularly towards the latter part of the sixteenth century.

Figure 4.1 *Josquin Desprez,* woodcut, from Petrus Opmeer, 1611, *Opus Chronographicum.* Bibliothèque Nationale de France, G719

While you will be listening to a number of pieces by various musicians, the figure who has been chosen as the main focus of this chapter is Josquin Desprez (*c.*1440–1521). The reason for this is that Josquin, perhaps more than any other composer, stands at the border between the Middle Ages and the Renaissance. Josquin enjoyed high renown during his lifetime and was tremendously influential well into the sixteenth century. His works gradually spread throughout western Europe and were regarded as models of musical composition by many composers and musical theorists, and by literary figures including Baldassare Castiglione and François Rabelais.

Recent scholarship disputes the date and place of Josquin's birth, and it is unclear whether he was born in France or in modern-day Belgium. He died in 1521 in Condé-sur-l'Escaut, which was at that time in the imperial county of Hainaut, now the Franco-Belgian border. Music in the second half of the fifteenth century was dominated by the styles of the Franco-Flemish school, which included the composers Johannes Ockeghem (*c.*1425–97) and Jacob Obrecht (*c.*1450–1505), and, although he was resident in Italy for much of his life, Josquin's musical heritage and background belong to this school. His works include about eighteen **Masses** (musical settings of the 'Ordinary' service of the Roman Catholic church, comprising the Kyrie, Gloria, Credo, Sanctus, Benedictus and Agnus Dei), 100 **motets** (vocal settings of Latin sacred text), and 70 **chansons** (French songs) and other secular vocal works.

The earliest known archival evidence concerning Josquin dates from about 1459 and refers to him working as a singer at Milan Cathedral from about 1459–72. After this period of employment, he entered the chapel of Galeazzo Maria Sforza, along with the composer Loyset Compère (*c.*1450–1518). Josquin then went into the service of Cardinal Ascanio Sforza, from about 1479–89 (for discussion of Josquin's associations with the Sforzas, see Book 2 in this series). According to Edward Lowinsky, who has studied the relationship between Ascanio and Josquin:

> Ascanio's life, with its ups and downs, with its phases of triumph and despair, with the brightness of its feasts and the gloom of its crises, culminating in the final tragedy of the Sforzas' downfall and the imprisonment in France – this colourful, dramatic and eventually tragic life is the background against which Josquin evolved as a composer, commanding from the beginning a stupendous technique, but developing in slow stages, each one of which holds its own fascination and its own masterworks, a musical language of ever growing expressivity.

> Josquin loosened the musical tongue of his age, and all who listened felt touched and addressed in ways they had not known or felt before. We can understand him better if we study his long connection with an Italian Renaissance prince, a man of intense passions, fierce pride, great culture, and infinite artistic sensibilities. For it is with Ascanio that he learned of human passions and developed the musical language expressing them. And it is in liberating himself from Ascanio – he left Italy before Ascanio's death – that he arrived at his own, deeply felt religious views, and composed works so strongly rooted in the Christian tradition that they were capable of inspiring Catholics and Protestants alike.

> (1976, p.75)

After leaving Ascanio's service, Josquin went to France, and it is possible that he worked at the French court under Louis XII (1499–1515). From about 1503 he was *maestro di cappella* (musical director of the chapel) at the court of Ferrara, though he was there for only a very short time and his activity is little documented. It is probable that he left for Condé some time later in the same year.

Exercise

One of the pieces that we will study later in this chapter is the motet 'Absalon fili mi' (Track 1).[1] A musical score of the motet is in Appendix 1, and the words are shown below. Listen to it now before you read on. ❖

Absalon fili mi

Absalon fili mi,
quis det ut moriar pro te,
fili mi Absalon.
non vivam ultra,
sed descendam in infernum plorans.

Absalom my son

Absalom my son,
would that I might die for you,
my son Absalom.
Let me live no longer,
but descend into hell weeping.

Musical developments

The acceptance of humanism represented a move away from the culture of the Middle Ages. However, any attempt to pinpoint this process with precision is difficult to establish since radical changes coexisted with a continuation of the old styles. One such change was a gradual shift away from the complex **polyphony** (many voices) of the late fifteenth century towards a homogenous style in which **counterpoint** (weaving together of independent melodic lines) and **homophony** (parts moving together in **chords**) were carefully balanced. The function of sacred music in the medieval period was to encourage spiritual contemplation through sound, with the words of the Mass (which was the dominant vehicle for composers) subordinate to the music. What this meant in practice was that syllables were broken down into **melismatic** (one syllable sung over more than one note) musings. The words could therefore be difficult to follow. Voice parts were written successively: one part was written first and then others were constructed around it, creating a **contrapuntal** web of sound. Technical virtuosity was expected of the singers, and there were often concealed meanings and numerical symbolism in the music. Generally speaking, melodic lines were rhythmically complex. The great polyphonic works of composers such as Guillaume Dufay (*c*.1400–74) and Ockeghem used words primarily

---

[1] The provenance of this work is unclear, and although it is purportedly by Josquin, it has also been ascribed to another composer, Pierre de la Rue (*c*.1460–1518).

as a means to an end. They were a hook on which to hang interweaving melodic lines. The music was pure and unsullied by the words which were broken up and dissolved in it.

The new style, as exemplified in the works of Giovanni Palestrina (*c*.1525–94), ensured that the words were both heard and understood. This meant that the former complex melodic mesh developed into a

Figure 4.2 Johannes Ockeghem (in glasses) with Nicole Levestu and his royal singers at Puys de Rouen, 1523, miniature. Bibliothèque Nationale de France, Fonds Fr.1537, fol. 58 verso

more homophonic style, with many note-against-note, syllabic passages. Instead of composing a work around a melodic line, all the parts were conceived together. Nevertheless, the great polyphony of the past did continue to exert a powerful attraction.

Exercise

Listen now to two settings of the 'Gloria' for an illustration of the points made above. The first is from a Mass by Ockeghem, *Missa 'Mi-mi'*, and is an example of the 'old', essentially contrapuntal style (Track 2a). In this work the overall effect is to produce a mesh of interweaving melodies. The music example in Figure 4.3 is taken from the last few bars of Ockeghem's 'Gloria', and is included to show you the complex melismas. Notice how the 'A' of 'Amen' is stretched out over many notes. The second setting of the 'Gloria' is from a Mass by Palestrina, *Missa 'Papae Marcelli'*, and is an example of the 'new', more homophonic style (Track 2b). Here there are many more passages of chordal writing. The words of the 'Gloria' are shown below. ❖

Gloria

Gloria in excelsis Deo.
Et in terra pax hominibus bonae voluntatis.
Laudamus te, benedicimus te,
adoramus te, glorificamus te.
Gratias agimus tibi
propter magnam gloriam tuam.
Domine Deus, Rex coelestis.
Deus Pater omnipotens.
Domine Fili unigenite, Jesus Christe.
Domine Deus, Agnus Dei, Filius Patris.
Qui tollis peccata mundi,
miserere nobis.
Qui tollis peccata mundi,
suscipe deprecationem nostram.
Qui sedes ad dexteram Patris,
miserere nobis.
Quoniam tu solus Sanctus.
Tu solus Dominus.
Tu solus Altissimus, Jesu Christe,
Cum Sancto Spiritu in gloria Dei Patris.
Amen.

Gloria

Glory be to God on high,
and on earth peace to men of goodwill.
We praise Thee, we bless Thee,
we worship Thee, we glorify Thee.
We give thanks to Thee
for Thy great glory.
O Lord God, heavenly King,
God the Father almighty.
Lord, the only-begotten Son, Jesus Christ.
O Lord God, Lamb of God, Son of the Father.
Who takest away the sins of the world,
have mercy upon us.
Who takest away the sins of the world,
receive our prayer.
Who sittest at the right hand of the Father,
have mercy upon us.
For Thou alone art holy.
Thou alone art Lord.
Thou alone art most high, O Jesus Christ,
with the Holy Spirit, in the glory of God the Father.
Amen.

Figure 4.3 Extract from Ockeghem, 'Gloria'. From: F. Blume (ed.) (1930) *Johannes Ockeghem: Missa 'Mi-mi'*, Das Chorwerk, Wolfenbüttel, Karl Heinrich Möseler Verlag

Josquin's work stands between the old and the new styles. There are some problems establishing a distinct chronology, but generally his early works can be identified by their contrapuntal style; the works of the middle period can be seen as a synthesis of the earlier northern polyphony of Dufay, Antoine Busnois (d.1492) and Ockeghem and the more chordal, harmonically orientated practice of Italy; and, on account of their more homophonic style, his late works point firmly forward into the sixteenth century. His Masses are more conservative than his motets, and some of these maintain the features of the medieval Mass. The *Missa 'Faisant regretz'*, for example, which is believed to be one of Josquin's earlier Masses, is based on a **rondeau** (type of medieval French song with refrain) by the English composer Walter Frye (d. before 1475) and has the long drawn-out melodic lines of the medieval Mass. Later works, such as the *Missa 'Pange lingua'*, contain more chordal writing, such as that in the 'Gloria' by Palestrina (Track 2b).'

Exercise

Now listen to the 'Credo' from Josquin's *Missa 'Pange lingua'* (Track 3). This is a fine example of a work in which words and music are woven together. The score of this piece is in Appendix 2. Listen for the following points, all of which are marked on the score:

- The first words you hear are 'Patrem omnipotentem, factorem coeli et terrae'. The two lower voice parts (tenor and bass) start the work. Listen to the way in which the bass imitates the tenor.

The same words are then sung by the top two voice parts, also using imitation.

- There is then an extended section (starting at bar 30) in which all four voices weave round one another in imitation. Sometimes two of the voice parts move together, for example in bar 70, where the tenor and bass sing the words 'Deum verum'.

- At the words 'Genitum, non factum' (bar 73) the **texture** (ways in which voices and instruments can be combined) thins once more.

- There is a clear **cadence** (end of a **phrase**) at the word 'coelis' (bar 90).

- A new section of music begins at the words 'Et incarnatus est' (bar 91). Note the very different texture here. This is a section of chordal composition in which the simple syllabic writing allows these important words to be heard clearly.

- At bar 111 a new imitative section begins.

- The final section begins at bar 151, with the words 'Et in Spiritum'. This section is a good example of the perfect balance between chordal and contrapuntal writing, and between two-part and four-part textures. ❖

In Josquin's day, the Mass was still the traditional vehicle for a composer, but, because of its unvarying text and liturgical formality, it was limiting. The motet, however, offered greater scope for expression, as a wide range of texts was available with fewer performance restrictions. Josquin's motets are generally speaking more innovatory than his Masses.

Although the developments discussed so far illustrate one way in which humanist ideals affected the composition of music, perhaps even more significant was the shift in emphasis away from the divine to the human. While there had been secular music in the Middle Ages, it had always been subordinate to sacred music and few scores survive. Sacred music was recorded by hand in tomes of great beauty. During the Renaissance there was a tremendous flowering of secular works, including the French chanson and the Italian **frottola** (generally speaking a simple song in several verses which had a distinct tune and accompaniment), and in particular the **madrigal** (a setting of a short poem for voices of equal importance). By the end of the sixteenth century the first operas were being produced, works in which composers turned to Greek legends for their subject-matter. The increase in secular music went hand-in-hand with the increasing importance of the word. Words were to be heard and understood rather than used as tools of the music. At the same time there was a growth in instrumental music which was independent of vocal music. Josquin holds a special place in this transitional era, contributing to both the French chanson and the frottola repertories.

The French chanson of the Renaissance was a new and original secular genre, though the term 'chanson' had a long history. In French-speaking countries the word had for several centuries been used in a general way to describe any kind of song based on a vernacular text, and there were a number of poetic *formes fixes* (fixed forms). These fixed forms had a limited number of rhyming lines, which we might label 'A', 'B' etc. When these poems were set to music the musical form was always determined by the poetic form. The musical structure of the rondeau, for example, consisted of two melodic lines repeated and alternated. One of the most common patterns was ABaAabAB, i.e. two different rhyming lines. The capital letters indicate textual refrain and the lower-case letters indicate new sections of text. Other fixed forms included the *virelai* (type of medieval French song with the usual structure AbbaA), and the *ballade* (type of medieval French song with the usual structure aab). The master of the early chanson was Guillaume de Machaut (*c.*1300–77).

Figure 4.4 *Guillaume de Machaut visited by Nature and her children*, miniature, Bibliothèque de France. Fonds Fr.1584, fol. E

Exercise

Listen now to a recording of Machaut's rondeau 'Quant je ne voy' (Track 4). The words are shown below with the distinct rhyming pattern marked alongside. 'A' and 'B' are the recurring refrains. Those labelled 'a' and 'b' are new lines of text, but rhyme with 'A' and 'B' respectively. In order to match this in music Machaut produced only two different lines of music, which correspond with the A and B of the poetry. Bear this in mind as you listen to the song, and pay particular attention to its very formalized construction. In particular, try to detect the repeating 'A' refrain, the music and words of which are shown in Figure 4.5. ❖

Quant je ne voy

A Quant je ne voy ma dame n'oy,
B Je ne voy riens qui ne m'annoye.

a Mes cuers font en moy comme noy,
A Quant je ne voy ma dame n'oy,

a N'onques tel mal, par m'ame, n'oy,
b Pour mon oueil qui en plour me noie.

A Quant je ne voy ma dame n'oy,
B Je ne voy riens qui ne m'annoye.

When I cannot see

*When I cannot see or hear my lady
everything I see is a burden to me.*

*My heart melts in my breast like snow
when I cannot see or hear my lady;*

*never, I swear, did I suffer so much grief,
on account of my eyes which drown me in tears.*

*When I cannot see or hear my lady
everything I see is a burden to me.*

Figure 4.5

Josquin made a significant contribution to the development of the French chanson, and produced a wide variety of works in this genre. In the early part of his career some of the poems he set to music were still in rondeau form, and the chansons were correspondingly old-fashioned in form and content. Gradually composers abandoned the rondeau in favour of **strophic** (repeating verses) poems with more vivid imagery. Here again Josquin marks the division between the old and the new: whereas his predecessor Ockeghem set mainly *formes fixes*, Josquin set a wide variety of texts, ranging from complex, skilfully constructed examples to simple songs in which the lucidity of the text is matched in the music.

Exercise

Listen to a recording of Josquin's chanson 'Mille regrets' (Track 5). The words are shown below and the score is in Appendix 3. How are the sentiments of the words matched in the music?

Discussion

The prevailing mood of the words is one of grief and sorrow. Josquin therefore chooses predominantly and appropriately languid, drawn-out **durations** (note lengths). The opening words, 'Mille regrets', are clear to the listener. There are a number of drooping phrases (short, distinct part of a **melody**), for example, 'face amoureuse' (amorous anger) and 'peine douloureuse' (sorrowful anguish) to emulate the sadness in the words. And at moments of intensity, such as 'j'ai si grand deuil' (I have such great grief), the voices move together to emphasize the words. The overall effect, with the variations of texture and the prevailing sense of melancholy, is one of great expressivity. ❖

Mille regrets	*A thousand regrets*
Mille regrets de vous abandonner	*A thousand regrets to forsake you*
Et d'élonger votre face amoureuse;	*And to escape your amorous anger;*
J'ai si grand dueil et peine douloureuse	*I have such great grief and sorrowful anguish*
Qu'on me verra brief mes jours déffiner.	*That one will see me shortly end my days.*

In Italy some of the earliest contributions to the new secular music were the *canti carnascialeschi* (carnival songs) of Florence. These were strophic, generally homophonic songs in which the words were important. For an example of this listen to Alexander Coppinus, 'Canto de' Giudei' (Track 6). In Mantua the new secular song was the frottola, which soon became popular and spread to other Italian centres. Two of the leading composers were Marchetto Cara (d. after 1525) and Bartolomeo Tromboncino (*c.*1470–after 1535). For examples of works by both these musicians listen to Cara, 'Bona dies, bona sera' (Track 7) and Tromboncino, 'Ostinato vo' seguire' (Track 8). By about 1535 the frottola was losing popularity and the madrigal took over as the most important type of secular vocal music, continuing to flourish into the seventeenth century.

Exercise

Josquin wrote only three frottole, each very different in style. His 'El grillo', described by Lowinsky (1976, p.453) as a 'humanistic **scherzo**' (lively movement), is a vivid attempt to mimic the sound of the cricket in music. Now listen to 'El grillo' (Track 9). The words are shown below (note that some are repeated). ❖

El grillo	*The cricket*
El grillo è buon cantore	*The cricket is a good singer*
Che tiene longo verso.	*Who holds a long note.*
Dale, beve grillo, canta,	*Go ahead, drink and sing, cricket.*
Ma non fa come gli altri uccelli,	*But he is not like the other birds,*
Come li han canto un poco,	*Who sing a little*
Van'de fatto in alto loco,	*And then go elsewhere.*
Sempre el grillo sta pur saldo.	*The cricket always stands firm.*
Quando la maggior el caldo	*When it is hottest,*
Alhor canto sol per amore.	*He sings alone for love.*

From about 1530 to the end of the sixteenth century the madrigal was the most important form of secular vocal music. The creation of the madrigal went hand-in-hand with a literary movement in Italy in which Pietro Bembo promoted the fourteenth-century poet Petrarch as the model of introspection and sensibility in verse. The Italian madrigal was equally expressive. While occasionally written for ceremonial occasions, it was primarily an intimate genre in which words and music were perfectly combined. The earliest composers of madrigals, such as Costanzo Festa (*c.*1480–1545), Philippe Verdelot (d. before 1552) and Jacob Arcadelt (*c.*1500–68), wrote in a fairly simple, often chordal style in which the words were clearly declaimed. As the madrigal developed in the hands of Luca Marenzio (*c.*1553–99) and Don Carlo Gesualdo, Prince of Venosa (*c.*1560–1613), the desire for greater expressivity led to vocal writing of increasing virtuosity and moments of **dissonance** (jarring sound). Listen to Gesualdo, 'Mercè grido piangendo' (Track 10) for an example of this.

One of the characteristics of the Italian madrigal was **word-painting** (the 'painting' of words with a suitable musical sound, such as a falling pattern for a sigh). This technique continued throughout the sixteenth century and reached its peak with Claudio Monteverdi (1567–1643), whose books of madrigals contain many examples of elaborate word-painting. Developments along similar lines were late to reach other European countries – in England, for example, madrigals were not composed until after 1588.

Figure 4.6 Bernardo Strozzi, *Claudio Monteverdi*, c.1630. Tiroler Landesmuseum Ferdinandeum, Innsbruck

Now listen to the madrigal 'Zefiro torna' by Monteverdi (Track 11). While this is a very late work by the composer (1632), and therefore a **Baroque** rather than a Renaissance piece, it has been included as it exemplifies the overt manner of word-painting used by composers of the Italian madrigal. While listening to this madrigal, concentrate on the ways in which the words are 'painted' in the music. The words are shown overleaf and are followed by a listening guide to help you. The guide includes extracts from the score (Figures 4.7–9) and you should also be aware that many of the words are repeated. ❖

Zefiro torna

Zefiro torna e di soavi accenti
l'aer fa grato e'il pié discioglie a l'onde
e, mormorando tra le verdi fronde,
fa danzar al bel suon su'l prato i fiori.

Inghirlandato il crin Fillide e Clori
note temprando lor care e gioconde;
e da monti e da valli ime e profonde
raddoppian l'armonia gli antri canori.

Sorge più vaga in ciel l'aurora, e'l sole,
sparge più luci d'or; più puro argento
fregia di Teti il bel ceruleo manto.

Sol io, per selve abbandonate e sole,
l'ardor di due begli occhi e'l mio tormento
come vuol mia ventura, hor piango hor canto

Zephyr returns

Zephyr returns and with his sweet breath
freshens the air and ruffles the waters,
and, murmuring through the green branches,
makes the flowers in the field dance to his music.

Phyllida and Cloris, garlands decking
their hair, sound sweet and joyous notes;
and from mountains and from valleys, high and deep,
re-echoes the harmony from the sonorous caverns.

Dawn rises more lovely in the heavens,
and the sun spreads more golden rays;
purer silver decks Thetis's fair cerulean mantle

Only I, through desolate and lonely woods,
as my fate decrees, now weep, now sing
of the brightness of two lovely eyes and of my torment

'Zefiro torna' listening guide

Zefiro torna e di soavi accenti
l'aer fa grato e'il pié discioglie a l'onde

Zephyr returns and with his sweet breath
freshens the air and ruffles the waters,

Two voices imitate one another, singing short musical phrases. At the words 'ruffles the waters' they have long drawn-out melismas, adding to the image of lapping water.

e, mormorando tra le verdi fronde,

and, murmuring through the green branches,

The voices 'murmur'.

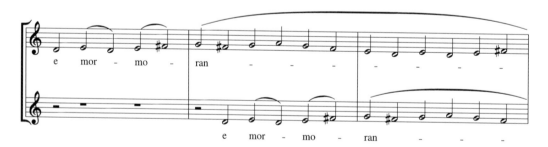

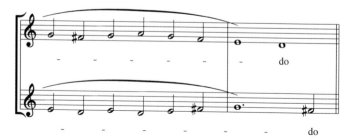

Figure 4.7

fa danzar al bel suon su'l prato i fiori.   *makes the flowers in the field dance to his music.*

The music is livelier to give the impression of 'dancing'.

Inghirlandato il crin Fillide e Clori   *Phyllida and Cloris, garlands decking*
note temprando lor care e gioconde;   *their hair, sound sweet and joyous notes;*

The singers emphasize the word 'notes'.

e da monti e da valli ime e profonde   *and from mountains and from valleys, high and deep,*

The music moves up for 'mountains' and down for 'valleys'.

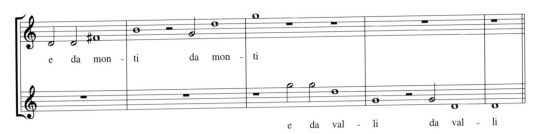

Figure 4.8

raddoppian l'armonia gli antri canori.   *re-echoes the harmony from the sonorous caverns.*

The voices echo one another.

Sorge più vaga in ciel l'aurora, e'l sole,   *Dawn rises more lovely in the heavens,*

There is a sense of the sun rising, with rising music.

sparge più luci d'or; più puro argento   *and the sun spreads more golden rays;*
fregia di Teti il bel ceruleo manto.   *purer silver decks Thetis's fair cerulean mantle*

The voices sing in harmony.

Sol io, per selve abbandonate e sole,   *Only I, through desolate and lonely woods,*

There is a dramatic change: the music slows, and one voice declaims the words 'Only I'.

Figure 4.9

l'ardor di due begli occhi e'l mio tormento   *as my fate decrees, now weep, now sing*
come vuol mia ventura, hor piango hor canto   *of the brightness of two lovely eyes and of my torment*

There are clashing notes for 'torment', before the piece comes to a close.

Music printing

One of the most significant factors in the growth of music at this time was the development of music printing. Before the advent of a means of printing music it was preserved and circulated in manuscript form. The problem with this method was that it was difficult to make works widely available. While the printing of books was soon a successful, thriving business, with the appearance of many beautiful examples, an equally sophisticated and accurate standard of music printing was slower to emerge. Music did appear in a printed format as early as about 1473 (the *Constance Gradual*), but the music printing industry took some years to become established. The main reason for this was the complex problem of producing and combining a series of diverse symbols. In the case of vocal music (the predominant type of music in the early stages of music printing) three different elements – **staves** (lines and spaces on to which music is written), notes and words – had to be aligned accurately in order for the music to make sense. Early attempts to do this were often clumsy and error-ridden.

The figure that revolutionized music printing was Ottaviano dei Petrucci (1466–1539), who was born in Fossombrone, near Pesaro. He is thought to have received a humanistic education at the court of Guidobaldo I, Duke of Urbino (where Castiglione wrote his *Book of the Courtier*, see below, Chapter 5), from whence he travelled to Venice in about 1490 in order to learn the art of painting. In 1498 he obtained an exclusive 20-year privilege to print music in the Venetian Republic – an accessible and cosmopolitan trading centre.

Petrucci's contribution to the development of the music printing industry was significant. His first book of music, the *Harmonice Musices Odhecaton A* (the *Odhecaton*), appeared in 1501. By 1520 he had published 61 volumes of music (the later ones appearing in Fossombrone), ranging from works by composers writing in the latter part of the fifteenth century to contemporary pieces. Thus he began to make available a huge corpus of music. His editions included music by composers of the Franco-Flemish school, books devoted exclusively to the music of Josquin, and frottole by Italians including Cara and Tromboncino. His technical skills were vastly superior to those of other printers of his time, and he succeeded in producing texts of great beauty as well as accuracy.

Petrucci used movable type and employed triple impression. This meant that the staves were printed first, and then two separate impressions were used: one for the text, initial letters, signatures and page numbers, and the other for notes and other musical symbols. This was an accurate and artistically satisfying process, but time-consuming and expensive. Triple impression was rarely used elsewhere, and printers after Petrucci used double rather than triple impression.

Look at Figure 4.10. This is a section of music from one of Petrucci's early volumes of motets, printed by triple impression. The lines (the staves) would have been printed first: note that they are smooth and unbroken. A separate impression would have covered any text, the decorative initial letter and the **signatures** (these are the symbols which, along with the stave and the initial letter, are labelled on Figure 4.10). All the musical symbols would have been printed in a third impression. ❖

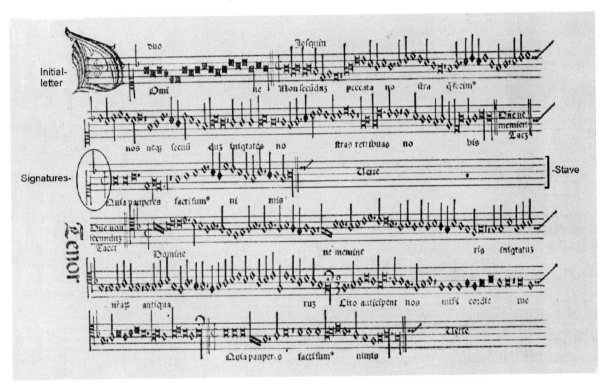

Figure 4.10 Early mensural music printed from type by triple impression, *Motetti de passione, de cruce, de sacramento*, Ottaviano dei Petrucci: Venice, 1503; fol. 27 verso. The British Library k.1.d.2

Petrucci's seminal *Odhecaton A* was a collection of 96 items, mainly French chansons. In this volume Petrucci included works by Heinrich Isaac (*c*.1450–1517), Alexander Agricola (*c*.1446–1506), Compère and Josquin. B and C volumes of the *Odhecaton* followed in 1501/2 and 1503/4. The *Odhecaton* is significant not only for its technical ingenuity, but also for the type of music it contained. As mentioned earlier, the French chanson was a new genre, and the *Odhecaton* contains some of the first examples using four voices, as opposed to the older three-voice format. A move away from triple to **duple metre** (two or four beats in a bar of music) can also be seen in a number of chansons.

Exercise

Now look at Appendix 4 which is taken from Petrucci's *Odhecaton A.* This is a printed version of Josquin's chanson 'Adieu mes amours'. Note that there are four voices – two to a page. You can see where each voice starts, as indicated either by a decorative initial or by the labelling of the voice part (tenor, altus, bassus). The symbol that indicates duple metre is labelled. ❖

In addition to his vocal music, Petrucci was the first printer to attempt to use movable type (this time by double impression) to produce **tablature,** a form of notation for **lute** and keyboard players whereby the notes were intabulated using either letters or numbers. Here, too, his attempts were highly successful and the first printed lute tablature

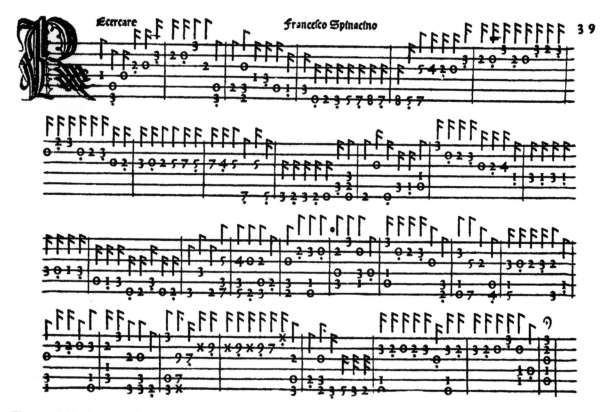

Figure 4.11 Petrucci, *Intabolatura de lauto, libro primo,* 1507, Venice, p.39. Facsimile 19, reproduced from W. Apel, *The Notation of Polyphonic Music, 900–1600.* (Medieval Academy Books, 38.) Fifth edition, revised. Cambridge, Mass., Medieval Academy of America, 1961. Reproduced by permission of the publishers

was published in 1507. This was *Intabolatura de lauto, libro primo*, containing transcriptions and some original compositions by Francesco Spinacino (late fifteenth century–after 1507), an Italian lutenist. For an example of Spinacino's work listen to 'Ricercare' (Track 12). Figure 4.11 shows an example taken from Petrucci's 1507 publication, where again the perfection of his methods can be seen.

Petrucci was followed by printers who made their own innovations. Pierre Attaingnant (*c.*1494–1551/2) in Paris was the first to use the technique of printing music from a single impression, with the appearance of his *Chansons nouvelles en musique à quatre parties* (1527) (Figure 4.12). Instead of cutting separate pieces for staves and notes, Attaingnant cut single blocks, each of which contained a portion of the staff along with a note. This was a more economical method, which corresponded with the flowering of the new French chanson.

Figure 4.12 Pierre Attaingnant, *Chansons nouvelles en musique à quatre parties*, Paris, 1527, fol. 22 recto. Koninklijke Bibliotheek, Hague 1D16

Conclusion

This chapter has focused on the humanist characteristics listed on pages 109–10. I'd like you now to go back to this list to see if you have been able to detect these characteristics in the work of musicians of this period. You should then return to Track 1, Josquin's motet 'Absalon fili mi' (words, p.112, score, Appendix 1), and listen once again with these characteristics in mind. As you do this, jot down the ways in which you think this motet can be said to be a 'Renaissance' rather than a 'medieval' work.

In terms of its musical style this work clearly belongs to the Renaissance – to the 'new' rather than the 'old'. Its simple, clean textures and smooth vocal lines allow the words to be heard and understood, and there are none of the complex medieval melismas. The importance of the words is acknowledged and highlighted in the music. ❖

From this motet, and the other works you've heard in this chapter, you should now have some understanding of the way in which musical developments mirror humanist influences, in that there was a great increase in the writing of musical works and a gradual change of style. You've heard examples of the 'old' style by Ockeghem and Machaut in which the words are subservient to the music and in which structures are strictly determined. And you've heard examples of the 'new' style by Palestrina and Monteverdi in which the meaning of the words shapes the music. You've heard a variety of pieces of music from the Renaissance period, in particular those of Josquin, including a motet, a chanson, a frottola and part of a Mass. Finally, you've looked at some examples of music printing, and seen how the development of the printing industry played a significant role in the growth and dissemination of music in this period.

Bibliography

LOWINSKY, E. (ed.) (1976) *Josquin Desprez: Proceedings of the International Josquin Festival–Conference held at the Juilliard School at the Lincoln Center in New York City, 21–25 June 1971*, London, Oxford University Press.

Music sources

Note: the following sources were used in preparing this chapter, but other sources or versions of the music would be acceptable for your study.

Track 1: Josquin Desprez, 'Absalon fili mi', from *Motets et Chansons*, performed by The Hilliard Ensemble, EMI CDC 7 49209 2 (1987) Track 2 (4'27)

Track 2a: Johannes Ockeghem, *Missa 'Mi-mi'*, 'Gloria', performed by The Hilliard Ensemble, Virgin Veritas 7243 (1995) Track 11 (5'06)

Track 2b: Giovanni Palestrina, *Missa 'Papae Marcelli'*, 'Gloria', performed by The Tallis Scholars/Peter Phillips, Gimell CDGIM 994 (1994) Track 4 (5'36)

Track 3: Josquin Desprez, *Missa 'Pange lingua'*, 'Credo', performed by The Tallis Scholars/Peter Phillips, Gimell CDGIM 009 (1986) Track 4 (7'03)

Track 4: Guillaume de Machaut, 'Quant je ne voy', from *Lancaster and Valois French and English Music, c.1350–1420*, performed by Gothic Voices/Christopher Page, Hyperion CDA 66588 (1992) Track 6 (5'20)

Track 5: Josquin Desprez, 'Milles regretz' from *Motets et Chansons*, performed by The Hilliard Ensemble, EMI CDC 7 49209 2 (1987) Track 8 (2'03)

Track 6: Alexander Coppinus, 'Canto de' Giudei' from *Canti carnascialeschi: Karnevalslieder der Italienischen Renaissance*, performed by Josquin-Ensemble Wien, Christophorus CD 74538 (1988) Track 6 (1'39)

Track 7: Marchetto Cara, 'Bona dies, bona sera' from *Renaissance Music from the Courts of Mantua and Ferrara*, performed by Circa 1500, Chandos CHAN 0524 (1991/1983) Track 4 (1'10)

Track 8: Bartolomeo Tromboncino, 'Ostinato vo' seguire' from *Renaissance Music from the Courts of Mantua and Ferrara*, performed by Circa 1500, Chandos CHAN 0524 (1991/1983) Track 16 (2'42)

Track 9: Josquin Desprez, 'El grillo' from *Motets et Chansons*, performed by The Hilliard Ensemble, EMI CDC 7 49209 2 (1987) Track 7 (1'50)

Track 10: Don Carlo Gesualdo, 'Mercè grido piangendo' from *Quinto libro dei madrigali*, peformed by The Consort of Musicke/Anthony Rooley, L'Oiseau-Lyre 410 128-2 (1983) Track 11 (3'36)

Track 11: Claudio Monteverdi, 'Zefiro torna' from *Canti amorosi*, performed by Nigel Rogers/Ian Partridge (tenors) and instrumentalists under the direction of Jürgen Jürgens, Archiv 437075–2 (1993/1972) Track 5 (5'37)

Track 12: Francesco Spinacino, 'Ricercare' from *Renaissance Music from the Courts of Mantua and Ferrara*, performed by Circa 1500, Chandos CHAN 0524 (1991/1983) Track 5 (1'17)

Appendix 1

Josquin Desprez: Absalon fili mi
(transcribed and edited by John Milsom)

From: B. Turner (ed.) (1979) *Renaissance Performing Scores, Josquin Desprez: Absalon fili mi*, Series B: Franco–Flemish Church Music, no. 7, London.

Editorial note

This edition is based on the earliest and most authoritative source for the motet: London, British Library, Ms. Royal 8. G. vii, ff. 56v–58. The complex key-signature of the original has been taken to imply (in terms of the original pitch) a B flat and an E flat signature in all voices. All other pitches which are unequivocally altered in the source, whether by partial signature or by accidental, are shown in the edition by an accidental on the stave. Accidentals above the stave are editorial suggestions; those in brackets are cautionary and editorial. All accidentals apply throughout the bar unless otherwise cancelled. The text underlay of the source is often clearly inexact, and was intended only as a basic guide for performance; in the edition it has been freely modified without further note.

Appendix 2

Josquin Desprez: Credo from *Missa 'Pange lingua'*

From: F. Blume (ed.) (1929) *Josquin Desprez: Missa 'Pange lingua'*, Das Chorwerk, Wolfenbüttel, Möseler.

Tenor and bass moving together

Appendix 3

Josquin Desprez: Mille regrets

From: F. Dobbins (ed.) (1987) *The Oxford Book of French Chansons*, Oxford and New York, Oxford University Press Music Department. pp.1–3.

Appendix 4

Josquin Desprez: Adieu mes amours

Reproduced from: Petrucci, *Harmonice musices Odhecaton A*, 1501, Venice, fol. 16 verso–17 recto. Civico Museo Bibliografico Musicale, Bologna. Photo: Fornasini.

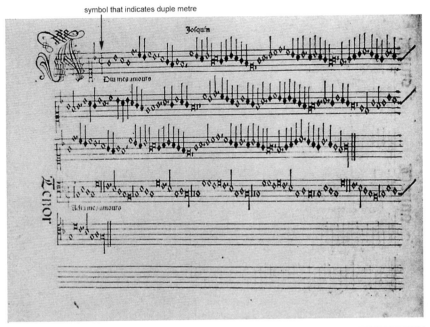

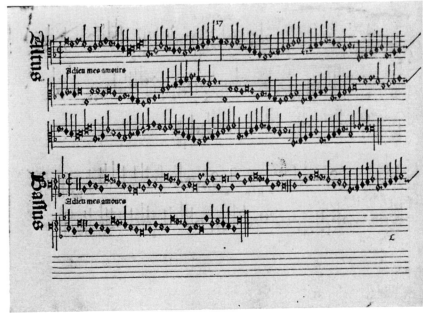

The humanists and ancient philosophy

BY SUSAN KHIN ZAW AND LUCILLE KEKEWICH

Objectives

When you have completed this chapter you should be able to:

- identify the principal features of ancient ethics and the schools of thought associated with them;
- define the main concerns of moral philosophy during the Renaissance;
- explain the contribution to moral philosophy made by the four texts selected for study;
- assess the validity of Burckhardt's view of Renaissance philosophy.

Introduction

The focus of this chapter is the humanist revival of ancient ethics and its interpretation in the context of **moral philosophy**, which, during the Renaissance, was central to the work of humanists. In order that you may identify the main concerns of moral philosophy, which included political philosophy and economics (household management), extracts from texts by four humanists, including north European writers, will be studied. The texts are: *Of the True and the False Good* (1431), by Lorenzo Valla (*c*.1405–57); *The Courtier* (1528), by Baldassare Castiglione (1478–1529); *Praise of Folly* (1511), by Desiderius Erasmus (*c*.1466–1536); and *Utopia* (1516), by Thomas More (1478–1535). Castiglione's work was written in Italian and the works by Valla, Erasmus and More were written in Latin. To get a sense of the nature of moral philosophy you need first to acquaint yourself with the basic ideas of ancient ethics.

Ancient ethics

The main pagan religions of classical antiquity were not primarily concerned with ethics – ethical ideals were instead associated with several schools of philosophy, which differed over what was the supreme good for man, that is, the purpose of human life. The most important of these schools for Renaissance philosophy were Platonism, Aristotelianism, Stoicism and Epicureanism, all of which were of Greek origin, but were taken up by the Roman world.

Platonism

Platonism is the school of thought which developed from the teaching of the ancient Greek philosopher Plato (*c*.429–347 BCE). He believed that virtue is knowledge of the true good, and that no one behaves knowingly in a morally corrupt manner, for even those who commit vices do what seems good to them. Vice is therefore a kind of mistake about what is good. The supreme attainment for man is contemplation of 'goodness itself' (i.e. the abstract idea of good). These ethical ideas are connected to Plato's **metaphysics**. He distinguished three parts to the soul: reason, appetite and spirit. Reason is the faculty of understanding and knowledge. Appetite and spirit are both motivational faculties: appetite covering physical drives such as hunger and sex, and spirit covering mental drives such as anger (think of 'spirit' not as in, say, 'spirituality' but as in a 'spirited horse'). The function of reason is to control motivation so that action is directed towards the true good (i.e. the knowledge of goodness). Vice results from preferring physical forms of good such as sensual pleasure to mental forms of good such as knowledge. This is to mistake the false for the true good.

All this is a spin-off from Plato's 'Theory of forms or ideas', which was devised to account for the fact that we apply the same general word, or universal, for example 'justice', to a number of very different cases, but do not as a result suppose that justice itself changes. What then is the meaning of 'justice', since the idea or form of justice can't be identified with the changing cases to which we apply the word? Plato believed that different cases in the changing physical world of the senses were like shadows or imperfect copies of the unchanging form of justice in the immaterial world of ideas, which constituted true reality. This is expressed by him in the myth of the cave, in which prisoners in a cave mistakenly assume that the shadows of objects invisible to them, cast by a fire behind them, are the only real objects present. Here the light of the fire represents the false light of empirical knowledge which is acquired by the senses. This is contrasted with the light of the sun outside the cave, which represents true knowledge obtained by pure intellectual intuition (for example, knowledge of the truths of mathematics). The more one is able to dissociate oneself from the senses and the physical world, the closer one gets to the true good. Thus, the most direct route to virtue and the true end of life is mathematics, the form of knowledge which is least dependent on the senses. According to Plato, the best rulers are philosophers, since they get closest to comprehending the true good for man through their understanding of the forms or universals. Plato also believed in the immortality, immateriality and transmigration of souls, and in one of his works appears to describe the creation of the world by a divine being (though not the supreme divine being). Apart from the idea of transmigration of souls, Renaissance Christian Platonists could accept most of this. Inconveniently, however, Plato takes homosexual love for granted, and in the *Republic,* his description of an ideal polity, he advocates the holding of both property and wives in common.

Plato believed live argument (*dialectic*) to be superior to books but nevertheless left a number of written dialogues in which his teacher Socrates is the main spokesman, presenting his ideas both through abstract logical argument and through poetic myth. His more poetic and mythical writings were admired for their literary qualities almost as much as for their content. One of these, the *Phaedrus,* starts with a discussion of whether a youth with two suitors, both attracted by his beauty, should prefer the man who is not in love with him to the one who is. Socrates defends the claims of the latter (because love is a form of divine madness) and recounts a myth expressing the moral value and power of love.

Exercise

Read the extract from the *Phaedrus* (Anthology, no. 13).

1 Do you recognize the philosophical views described above?

2 Do you find them more or less convincing in their mythological form?

Discussion

1 Using the myth of the human soul, which is partly a charioteer and partly a pair of horses (one horse representing the finer things of the spirit and the other sensual appetites), Plato explains how individuals can be trapped in the world of the senses. Those who have been able to suppress their lower instincts and concentrate on the pursuit of wisdom will have received some intimation of the immaterial world of ideas, which is the true 'reality with which true knowledge is concerned, a reality without colour or shape, intangible but utterly real, apprehensible only by intellect which is the pilot of the soul'. This is the world in which the universals are to be found. The sensual versions of these forms in the physical world are merely poor copies or shadows of reality.

2 You might say that the graphic account of reason in the soul trying to control the two horses, spirit and appetite, is effective in the way it

presents humanity striving after 'goodness itself', an ideal which few attain. You don't have to accept all the implications of Plato's philosophy to find his myth persuasive. On the other hand, you might not find the metaphor of the charioteer a very compelling one for the twenty-first century and could go on to suggest that this kind of ethical system was attractive to the ancient and medieval world because it fed the self-esteem of the more educated and privileged orders and provided a rationale for keeping the lower orders in subservience. ❖

The school of philosophy founded by Plato was known as the Academy. In the third century BCE it adopted the philosophy of Scepticism, which doubts the possibility of the attainment of true knowledge. This may seem a surprising development in the light of the moral importance given to knowledge by Plato, but note that in the Phaedrus myth only the gods actually have knowledge. Mortals, with great difficulty, can only catch glimpses of it, which are forgotten when they are reborn into this world. True knowledge for humans in the world of the senses appears to be something to which they may only aspire rather than something which they might actually possess. Plato's revered teacher Socrates said that the only way in which his knowledge surpassed that of others was that he knew that he knew nothing. Various argumentative methods, known as sceptical techniques, were developed accordingly: for example, putting forward equally good arguments on either side of a question, which was initially convincing but ultimately self-contradictory.

During the Middle Ages Plato was principally known through the *Timaeus* (a dialogue which dealt with the creation of the world and had been translated into Latin) and through references to him by other classical authors. Greek manuscripts of other works of Plato began to reach the west in the fourteenth century and individual dialogues were translated into Latin in the following century (the Greek language was not widely known in Italy at the time). The complete works of Plato were not generally available until they were translated into Latin towards the end of the fifteenth century by Marsilio Ficino (1433–99), who published them in 1484. These translations are almost identical to modern complete editions.

Neoplatonism

Broadly speaking, Neoplatonism is the name now given to later philosophies imitating or interpreting Plato, but it is specifically applied to the Hellenistic school of philosophy which descended from Plato's Academy. This school flourished in Alexandria in Egypt in the third century. Its chief exponents were Plotinus (*c*.205–70), his student Porphyry (*c*.234–*c*.305), and Porphyry's student Iamblichus (*c*.245–*c*.325). Neoplatonism developed the mystical and religious aspects of Plato's thought, stressing the spiritual importance of escaping from the influence of the body and of quasi-mystical intellectual intuition as a direct path to divine truths. Later, with Iamblichus, Neoplatonism turned to demonology and developed a complete hierarchy of good and evil demons governing various aspects of the universe, which could be invoked by the appropriate rites.

In fifteenth-century Italy, Ficino revived Plato's school and philosophy by starting the 'Florentine Academy', a loose collection of students, scholars and amateur enthusiasts of learning who were devoted to the study and dissemination of Platonic philosophy (see Anthology, no. 14, for an extract from Ficino's commentary on the *Phaedrus*). Largely through Ficino's efforts, the works of Plato soon became more influential, although they never seriously rivalled the works of Aristotle. The doctrine expounded by Ficino's 'Academy' was derived to a great extent from the Hellenistic school of philosophy:

> [He constructed] a Platonist theology on the immortality of the soul. He was an ardent Christian apologist, convinced that the Neoplatonist authors had provided the most suitable philosophic sub-structure to mediate an understanding of the Christian revelation. His system is in fact generally based on that of ... Plotinus, and his most famous work, the commentary on Plato's *Symposium*[1] written in 1469, incorporates the Plotinian theory of the soul's alienation in space and time. The soul, in its quest for reunification, is stimulated by one or more of the four Platonist 'furies'[2] (the poetic fury, extended to include the effects of music, the religious, prophetic and erotic furies) and ascends through the four degrees of the universe (matter, nature, soul and mind) to achieve final reunification in the beautifying union with God.
>
> The commentary on the *Symposium* was an immensely influential work. It gave birth to a whole spate of treatises on love, and its doctrine was exploited by countless sixteenth-century authors. It was the first formal theory of love which allowed the compatibility of the love which is spiritually perfective with that which is instinctively based, and it was Ficino who coined the term 'Platonic love' to describe the spiritually perfective affection. But the facts that, in Ficino's Plotinian account of the soul's ascent to beatitude, there is no formal separation of natural and supernatural and that, in this system,

---

[1] A dialogue set at a drinking party where the main topic of conversation is love, both human and divine; the doctrine is similar to that of the *Phaedrus*.

[2] Forms of divine madness.

religious perfection therefore becomes clearly intrinsic to moral fulfilment, go a long way to explain how and why the commentary on the *Symposium* was so frequently exploited by the humanists of the sixteenth century.

(Levi, 1971, pp.21–2)

Aristotelianism

Aristotle (384–322 BCE) was tutor to Alexander the Great and, through Thomas Aquinas, to the whole of Christendom many centuries later. He was influenced by Plato, with whom he studied for 20 years, but came to disagree with his metaphysics, and developed an alternative school of philosophy. His best known and most influential work on morality is the *Nicomachean Ethics*.

In this work Aristotle argues that the purpose of human life is *eudaimonia*. This Greek word is usually translated as 'happiness' but it means something more like 'living well'. To the question 'what is *eudaimonia*?', that is, what sort of human life is the best, the most worthwhile and fulfilling, Aristotle proposed an objective answer. The answer applies to everybody, and follows from what it is to be human (in the same way that what makes a knife a good knife follows from what it is to be a knife – something that cuts). For Aristotle the essential human attribute is reason, since it is reason that distinguishes people from animals, and what makes a life a life is action. This can be compared with the modern admonition 'Get a life! – Do something!' To live well is therefore to act well and reasonably, and the best life is 'a life of excellent activity in accordance with reason' (Ackrill, 1981, p.136). Human beings, however, are complex creatures who can engage in various kinds of excellent activity and deploy reason in many ways. The different forms of excellence in action are the virtues, and the two main ways of using reason are by applying it either to the practical or to the contemplative life. So two kinds of 'best life' are possible: an active life of practical wisdom displaying moral virtues, and a life of philosophical contemplation displaying intellectual virtues. Of these, Aristotle, like Plato, believes the latter is preferable, but a life of pure contemplation is not humanly possible; it is the sort of life we may reasonably attribute to the gods, and belongs to man only in so far as he has a spark of the divine in him.

Most of the *Nicomachean Ethics* is taken up with description of the moral virtues that constitute the best practical life. This is the best life for humans, and the one appropriate to most of us most of the time. Aristotle offers both a general analysis of virtue and a list and description of particular virtues. The general analysis, the 'doctrine of the mean', proposes that the moral virtues are at the mid point between two vices, a vice of excess and a vice of insufficiency. Thus, fortitude (courage) lies at the mid point between having too much fear – cowardice – and having too little – rashness or recklessness. Similarly, generosity mediates too much possessiveness – miserliness or meanness – and too little – prodigality or wastefulness. Temperance, the virtue governing the impulse towards pleasure, is the mean between addiction or over-indulgence and insensitivity or coldness. Moral virtue must be combined with practical wisdom or prudence, which is defined as the ability to judge when and how one should act on any particular occasion (for example, being able to judge correctly that *now* is the time to speak up courageously to the prince against the new decree he is contemplating, and *this* is the thing not to mention, and *now* is the time to stop speaking). In another work, his *Politics*, Aristotle examined the forms of government which were most likely to enable citizens to achieve the 'best life'.

The moral virtues specifically listed and described by Aristotle are those belonging to his time, culture and class. They are fortitude, temperance, liberality (generosity), magnificence, greatness of soul or proper pride, ambition, good temper, friendliness, truthfulness, ready wit, shame and justice. All were still highly valued in the Renaissance and should be viewed within the context of that time. This applies particularly to magnificence – being able to spend large sums of money fittingly and tastefully – and greatness of soul or proper pride – thinking oneself worthy of great things when one actually is worthy of them. Magnificence was a virtue attainable only by the very rich, and one which needy humanists might well have thought particularly appropriate to Renaissance princes. Similarly, the high opinion of themselves that many humanists displayed reflected their conception of greatness of soul.

In the thirteenth century, Thomas Aquinas (1225–74) integrated Aristotelian philosophy (including Aristotle's logic, metaphysics and natural philosophy, as well as his moral philosophy) into Christian belief. He produced a complete system of Christian philosophy: a Christian interpretation of the works of Aristotle. The scholastics developed different branches of philosophy within this system, using Aristotelian logic as a universal method of reasoning, and coining a multitude of special terms to formulate and deal with the various philosophical problems that emerged. They taught logic, ethics, metaphysics and natural philosophy. The latter was considered a suitable preparation for a career in medicine, and knowledge of ethics could lead to a career in law. Philosophy became a highly technical subject conducted in a language intelligible only to experts, and it was bitterly attacked by some humanists for this reason.

> Because Aristotle was and remained [throughout the Renaissance] the chief basis of university instruction in the philosophical disciplines, many general treatises on ethics take the form of commentaries on Aristotle's *Nicomachean Ethics* and *Politics*, or of introductions, paraphrases and summaries of those works.
>
> (Kristeller, 1991, p.284)

The humanists are generally represented as reacting sharply against this scholastic philosophical tradition, and certainly firebrands such as Valla and Rabelais poked fun at it. But the more general tendency was for amalgamation rather than opposition: Leonardo Bruni, for instance, produced translations of Aristotle, and a number of other scholars, such as Ermolao Barbaro the younger (1454–93), produced commentaries on the philosopher's works. In the sixteenth century Jacques Lefèvre d'Étaples (1455–1536) wrote introductions to Aristotle's writings on moral philosophy and Philipp Melanchthon (1497–1560), a follower of Martin Luther, made a characteristically scholastic attempt to harmonize Aristotle's ethical system with Christianity. Johannes Eck (1486–1543), one of Luther's main Catholic opponents, produced for his students at Ingolstadt a complete commentary on Aristotle based on the humanist translations of Johannes Argyropoulos (1416–*c.*1486).

Lisa Jardine encapsulates the ambiguity of these studies for religious reformers and traditionalists alike:

> [Eck] ... despite his commitment to conventional scholastic logic, found himself led in the direction of revised readings and reconsidered interpretations of Aristotle's texts, even though he was not in general in sympathy with the 'grammatical' dialectic of the humanists.
>
> (1988, p.193)

Most influential of all for those who were challenging intellectual and ideological authority, was the Aristotelian account of the virtues. Whether they were theologians like Melanchthon, worried about what the characteristics of a good person should be, or political theorists like Machiavelli, weighing up alternative courses of effective action, their starting point was invariably the old Aristotelian virtues they had been taught at school. The four **cardinal virtues** (justice, prudence, temperance and fortitude) were particularly important and frequently occur in political treatises as the appropriate attributes of princes. Increasingly in the sixteenth century, however, though lip-service was still paid to the cardinal virtues, the influence of humanist methods led writers to interpret them in a more realistic or even hard-headed manner. You will see examples of this tendency below in the texts chosen for study.

Figure 5.1 Aristotle, *Organon*, 1605 edition by Julius Pacius, Greek and Latin text side by side with commentary. This illustrates the continuing popularity of Aristotle's works throughout the Renaissance. The British Library 8460.f.19, p.Aij

Stoicism

The Stoic school of philosophy was founded in Athens in the fourth century BCE, but proved congenial to Roman culture and was favoured by Roman philosophers such as Cicero (106–43 BCE) (although he was not a whole-hearted Stoic) and Seneca (*c.*4 BCE–*c.*65 CE). It was also congenial in many respects to Christianity, and Stoic ethics influenced Christian ethics (see Colish, 1985). Stoics believed that the natural world was orderly, and they sought to submit human life to the same order. The Stoic universe was a living rational being shaped and held together by a force which was a rational spirit, composed of a fiery substance, hence material in nature, and identified with God. Stoics believed in a form of divine and benevolent Providence that ruled the universe. Virtue was achieved by aligning oneself with the laws governing the universe, that is, with the will of divine Providence. Vice occurred when one followed the irrational impulses of the emotions. The result of virtue was happiness in the form of *apatheia,* emotional equilibrium. This was often misinterpreted as complete absence of emotion, but Stoics actually thought there were rational emotions consistent with virtue, such as caution. All other emotions were irrational and should be eradicated. For Stoics the true human good is thus virtue and its concomitant, unruffled calmness. Later, Stoics recognized that perfect virtue, including total eradication of irrational emotions, was not humanly possible, and the best one could hope for was cultivation of the four cardinal virtues – justice, prudence, temperance and fortitude.

Epicureanism

Epicureanism was founded by the Greek philosopher Epicurus (341–271 BCE). It was, and is, commonly associated with the belief that the only good is sensual pleasure. Epicurus himself, however, while he believed that pleasure was the only good and pain the only evil, also held that true pleasure was not a momentary thing, as is sensual pleasure, but a tranquil habit of mind enduring throughout one's life, and that pleasures which brought pain should be avoided. He did not believe in an afterlife or Providence. The highest human good was a life completely without mental or physical pain, and the only way to achieve this was through the pursuit of something very like the Aristotelian virtue of temperance. The only Epicurean virtue was prudence, which estimated how to maximize pleasure and minimize pain by deciding between possible pleasures. Virtue so defined, however, is not good in itself, but only good as a means to pleasure. Feeling is the only judge of pleasure, and sensation the only source of knowledge. Epicurus, who was known for the frugality and benevolence of his life, founded a philosophical community of men and women who lived according to sober Epicurean tenets. Rumour had it, however, that the community lived in riotous self-indulgence. In antiquity the defenders of Epicureanism said this was a slander put about by the Stoics, but an enduring false impression of Epicureanism was created. Some among the educated – such as Lucretius (*c.*99–55 BCE) and Seneca – appreciated its true nature, which was also known to a few scholars in the Middle Ages. Epicureanism, however, had a generally bad reputation among those Christians who were familiar with its tenets.

Renaissance humanism and moral philosophy

The summaries of ancient philosophy above are based on the interpretations of twentieth-century scholars. Modern scholarship aspires to represent what the ancient authors really meant, by working from the best possible texts which are read with historical sensitivity toward their intellectual context and the circumstances of their production. If modern beliefs about the subject-matter are at odds with those of the authors, this is regarded as irrelevant to interpretation of the ancient texts: the first effort is to understand the authors on their own terms. Such a reading was not possible for Renaissance scholars, who often worked from poor texts and were only just beginning to develop this kind of historical understanding:

> Renaissance hermeneutics [interpretation], like medieval hermeneutics, was orientated overwhelmingly to the tasks of edification, not of criticism. The famous examples of Renaissance criticism ... were all of them hardly more than isolated acts of virtuosity. They were not expressions of a culture of criticism. The aim of most scholarship was not to establish the original meaning of the author ... Renaissance humanists still, overwhelmingly, chose to take their historical truths from traditional authorities rather than relying on *wissenschaftlichen Methoden* [scholarly methods]. Like most men before and after them, they preferred edifying myths to the moral paralysis of the scientific and critical mind.

> (Hankins, 1990, pp.364–5)

Modern interpretation, however, does depend on developments which were rooted in humanist philological and textual criticism and arose out of the humanist obsession with the classical languages. Yet these critical efforts were not undertaken in the cause of pure scholarship in the modern sense, but usually because a particular humanist had an axe to grind and brought all the resources of his learning to bear on it.

Figure 5.2 Obverse: Marsilio Ficino, reverse: inscription 'PLATONE', medal in the style of Niccolò Fiorentino, c.1499, bronze, diameter 5.5 cm. Samuel H. Kress Collection. Photo © 1998 Board of Trustees, National Gallery of Art, Washington

Valla, for instance, used philological criticism to expose the *Donation of Constantine* as a forgery (see Chapter 3). Yet the philological arguments occur in the context of a vituperative attack on the venality, violence and worldliness of the papacy and were written by Valla under the patronage of the king of Naples, who was in dispute with the pope at the time. Ficino translated Plato's works and set up his Academy as a remedy for the religious and political upheavals besetting Florence. Through it he brought his version of Platonism to the sons of the aristocracy and to middle-class professionals active in the civic life of Florence. It also gave Ficino himself – a professional scholar and priest of humble origin – the opportunity to consort on equal terms with the gilded youth of Florence. Indeed, he was able to converse with them *de haut en bas* (authoritatively), as the purveyor of esoteric wisdom essential for future rulers.

> The idea that Platonic theology was a spiritual link necessary to the health of the individual soul and the body politic was the central motive, or justification, for Ficino's Platonic revival. The goal of the Platonic revival was not a 'retreat to metaphysics' or a 'flight from the city of men', but a more profound integration of the active and contemplative life whereby the latter could give health and wisdom to the former.
>
> (Hankins, 1990, p.296)

Thus, newly discovered ancient authors were not typically read in a spirit of disinterested enquiry, with the object of understanding as accurately as possible what they had meant to say, but in a thoroughly partisan spirit. Humanist readers still admired the ancients as authorities in the medieval sense: the Greek philosophical texts were regarded as new mines of wisdom and of examples for imitation. Their authority ensured that any apparent discrepancy between prevailing Christian values and the views of ancient authors was likely to be perceived as a sign of misunderstanding on the part of the reader, although even Ficino was prepared to admit that there were some issues on which Plato's paganism was not compatible with Christianity. Humanist interpreters usually exerted themselves to find edification even in those ancient pronouncements most shocking to Christian doctrine and morals – such as Plato's belief in the transmigration of souls and advocacy of communal wives – and usually succeeded, resorting to the imposition of allegorical intentions on the text when all else failed. This could on occasion produce bizarre interpretations which modern scholarship would regard as far from the original author's intention. If the ancient author was deemed to support the opposition in some struggle in which the humanist was engaged, the process went into reverse: the worst possible construction was put upon his text, that is, the interpretation most likely to tarnish his morals and damage his authority.

The same principle applied to humanist translations. These were the chief instruments of the wider dissemination of ancient philosophy among the educated, but they often spread very partisan versions of that philosophy. Plato was sometimes bowdlerized or his words 'tweaked' (though not by Ficino) to fit whatever purpose his humanist translator had in mind. This is not to say the humanist translator deliberately engaged in deception; he may have thought he was genuinely representing the essence of the original, making only necessary adjustments to prevent misunderstanding of a profound and difficult author by readers less learned than himself. This was part of the broad humanist campaign to rescue philosophy from scholasticism, which had made it barbarous and unintelligible, and make it useful again by enlisting it under the banner of rhetoric. Medieval Latin translation of Greek philosophical texts was *ad verbum* (word for word), not just literal translation in the modern sense but *absolutely* literal. Not only the meaning but the sentence structure of the Greek was adopted. Since Greek contains parts of speech for which there is no Latin equivalent, Latin counterparts had to be invented. Such Latin translations were unintelligible to ordinary Latin speakers without elaborate commentary and explanation. Humanists translated *ad sententiam* (according to the sense or meaning), and generally valued readability, intelligibility, correct style and persuasiveness above literal translation of the original.

The modern concern to establish the best text and the most accurate understanding derives from the humanist desire for a purification of the language inherited from antiquity, which in turn was connected to the general desire at the time for a purification of religion and morals. Both aims inspired a return *ad fontes* (to the original sources), whether of language or of religion. In both cases the pure sources were texts which had to be cleansed of the alien accretions brought about by the activities of copyists and commentators in the intervening centuries. Thus Erasmus, after discovering and publishing a manuscript of Valla's philological notes on the Vulgate New Testament, sought to aid the renewal of religion. He did this by completing the task Valla had started: comparing the Latin of the Vulgate with the Greek originals from which it had been translated and correcting it as necessary. The result was the first printing of his new Latin translation together with the Greek New Testament, which became the source for many vernacular versions of the Bible.

Humanist representations and discussions of ancient philosophy, then, need to be approached cautiously without modern preconceptions. We should bear in mind the context of their production or else we risk misunderstanding their content. The texts discussed below are contributions to humanist moral philosophy, and as such, were intended to have practical application. Humanists tried to draw on the philosophical resources of antiquity to find a solution to the moral difficulties and anxieties of their time. The enterprise, however, was not without its problems, and chief among them was the attempt to reconcile ancient pagan values with those of Christianity. Humanists may have succeeded in doing this to their own satisfaction, but their efforts have not endured. Humanism did play a limited role in the origins and spread of the Protestant Reformation (see Book 3 in this series, Chapter 1). It also informed and shaped the Catholic response to the Reformation. However, its most far-reaching effect may have been the impetus it gave to the secularization of moral discourse. Readers of ancient philosophy were exposed to non-Christian discussions of morality which opened up intellectual possibilities not formerly easily available to them.

The texts

Lorenzo Valla, *Of the True and the False Good*

Lorenzo Valla was born and brought up in Rome, where he received a humanist education from the best teachers and was influenced by the writings of Leonardo Bruni. He hoped for employment at the papal court but was excluded, he believed, by the dominant Florentines surrounding the pope. This gave him cause for resentment. In Piacenza in 1431 he published the first version of *Of the True and the False Good*, then called *On Pleasure* (*De voluptate*), which he continued

Figure 5.3 De Brij, *Lorenzo Valla*, 1648, engraving. Mary
Evans Picture Library

to revise throughout his life. In 1435 he moved to Naples to become
secretary to the king, Alfonso I. There he wrote a number of treatises
including *Of the Profession of the Religious Life*, in which he attacked
both the corruption of the mendicant (friars living on alms) religious
orders and the view that taking religious vows was superior to the
secular life, and the *Donation of Constantine*. He also produced an
enormously successful and influential guide to correct and clear Latin
expression based on classical usage, *Six Books of Good Latin Usage*
(*Elegantiae linguae latinae*). The philological notes on the New
Testament, *Collation of the New Testament*, were not published in Valla's
lifetime, but were later discovered and published by Erasmus. Valla's
philological criticisms of religious texts (for example, he denied that
the Apostle's Creed was in fact written by the Apostles) led to an
accusation of heresy in 1444, but he was saved from the **Inquisition** by
the intervention of King Alfonso. Towards the end of his life he
managed to establish his religious orthodoxy, and was finally invited
to Rome to work for the papal court (1448–57), where he died.

Valla was a renowned Latinist, a bitter critic of the state of the church, a philosophical innovator, a fierce opponent of scholasticism and devotee of rhetoric, which, following Quintilian, he regarded as the true vehicle of philosophy. He was also a combative controversialist and a master of **invective** (the art of insulting one's enemies, a distinct rhetorical literary genre, in which truth was not an object). His philosophical works make a point of opposing traditional views, but he was no friend to Greek philosophy either, which he regarded as unchristian. Indeed, he might almost be called a Christian fundamentalist – in *Of the Profession of the Religious Life* he prefers the authority of scripture to all others, and he eventually draws the same conclusion in the text we study below.

Of the True and the False Good discusses the question of humanity's true good, by means of a debate between a Stoic and an Epicurean. The Stoic claims that the only true good is virtue: in Roman times this had been identified as acting on behalf of the public interest. The Epicurean represents the view that the only true good is pleasure, which was interpreted by Valla as acting in one's own interest. The issue is resolved by a representative of Christianity, who says that the Stoic and Epicurean are both right and both wrong, but the Epicurean is more right than the Stoic. Pleasure is the only good, but there are two forms of pleasure: earthly and heavenly. The true good for man is heavenly pleasure, or the joys of Paradise. Virtue is not good in itself, as the Stoics say, but only instrumentally, as a means of reaching Paradise. Thus virtue, the 'good of the philosophers', is not the true good.

The discussion is divided into three books, each preceded by a short proem (introduction) in Valla's own voice summarizing the content and method of the book and pointing out how its style is fitted to its argument. The proem to Book 1 sets up the discussion by attacking the humanist propensity to deplore the exclusion of virtuous pagans from salvation (see Anthology, no. 15i). This is followed by a dialogue which runs continuously through the three books (with a break for a dinner given by the Epicurean). The participants are all real people, well-known humanist friends and acquaintances of Valla's, though Valla changed the characters in different versions of the treatise.

In Book 1, the Stoic Catone laments the difficulty of attaining virtue. He chides nature for stacking the deck against humanity by making it prefer vice to virtue, and also for making vice much harder to avoid than virtue, since according to the Aristotelian doctrine of the mean, there are two vices for every virtue. Doing the right thing thus becomes a narrow and unappealing track through a dense minefield of vices. The Stoic is answered by the Epicurean, Vegio, who argues that nature endows everyone with some inclination to virtue, and supplies us with many forms of an undeniable good, namely sensory pleasure, if we are wise enough to adjust our pursuit of it to our circumstances. The so-called virtues are good only instrumentally, as means to get us to natural, sensory pleasures. If they do not succeed in this there is no point in pursuing them. In Book 2, the Epicurean argues that Stoic virtue is not really a good, since rather than benefiting its practitioner, it assists others. Thus the most outstanding examples of Stoic virtue – various ancient Romans who sacrificed life, personal welfare or family members for glory or for the public good – failed to gain any advantage for their exertions. Glory is no good to you once you're dead, nor indeed is the 'security of the state', which is simply a disguise for the advantage of the rulers. A closer look at celebrated instances of classical virtue such as that of Lucretia[3] would reveal them to be powered by self-interest.

Exercise

Read Valla's condemnation of the virtue of fortitude spoken by Vegio, the Epicurean (Anthology, no. 15ii). Would you expect such arguments from a humanist?

Discussion

Valla's opening shot in his outrageous series of arguments is to describe fortitude scathingly as 'a kind of acknowledged opportunity for exercise against pleasures'. He then makes the shocking suggestion that those who die for the good of their country – the ultimate act of fortitude – are no more than fools. They will not enjoy the benefits of the 'safety', 'freedom' or even 'greatness' for which they have sacrificed their lives; those will accrue to the lesser people who were not prepared to take risks. This whole argument is diametrically opposed to the kind of polemic you have encountered in the work of Leonardo Bruni (see Anthology, no. 12, discussed in Chapter 3) which was full of praise for ancient Romans such as Curtius and Regulus who, he claimed, embodied the civic virtue that it was the duty of his contemporaries to emulate. Valla may have admired Bruni's knowledge of Latin and Greek, but in this treatise, he showed that he was prepared to extend the boundaries of humanist rhetoric by challenging the authority of even the widely accepted Aristotelian virtues. ❖

In Book 3, the Christian apologist rebukes the previous speakers for indulging in ancient role-playing instead of discussing the subject seriously as Christians (see Anthology, no. 15iii). He criticizes the Stoic for relying on the flawed doctrine of the mean and the Epicurean for considering only earthly virtue. He then tries to convey the nature of the true good by a rhapsodical description of the joys of Paradise.

[3] Lucretia was a virtuous matron who killed herself after she had been raped by Tarquin, the last king of Rome.

In downgrading the 'good of the philosophers', the work vindicates both Christian against pagan virtue, and rhetoric against philosophy (by which Valla means the logic-based dialectic of the scholastic philosophers). In fact it could be sub-titled 'Against the philosophers': in the proem to Book 1, Valla declares himself the enemy of philosophy. In demonstrating the superiority of rhetoric over philosophy in the ensuing dialogue, he shows that oratorical, not philosophical, debate is the path to truth. Howard Jones describes Valla's motives in these terms:

> it would be a mistake to regard the De voluptate as a serious exposition of historical Epicurean teaching, or to speak of Valla as a committed Epicurean advocate. Rather, in a manner quite in accord with humanist fashion, the ancient secular tradition is introduced into a topic of contemporary interest as a point of departure, and Valla's presentation of Epicurean, and for that matter Stoic, teaching is deliberately coloured, at times to the point of serious distortion, to serve strategic or rhetorical ends.
>
> (1992, p.148)

Valla's brand of reformist Christianity was not, however, always recognized as such by his readers. He was pursued by the Inquisition because of the philosophical views expressed in *Of the True and the False Good* as well as for his philological work. His advocacy of Christianity was obscured, not just by his apparent defence of outrageous moral views but also by his use of a humanist method of argument – the oratorical, as opposed to the philosophical – which Valla claims to have instituted. In a nutshell, the oratorical method entails changing our beliefs by the most effective means available, whatever these might be. The means certainly include philosophy – what is explicitly asserted and argued – but also and more importantly, they include rhetoric, or the way in which it is said and argued. Philosophy becomes the handmaid of oratory, a means to the end of producing true understanding. Because Valla believes (or says he believes) that as a Christian he knows the truth, so he also claims to be justified in putting it over as convincingly as possible by fair means or foul (such as misrepresenting the opposition). Sceptical techniques are also used. In the case of the dialogue's pagan apologists, for example, the stated intention is to discredit pagan views by having their advocates put them forward in a self-refuting way which cannot possibly convince, rather than representing them fairly and then destroying them by a philosophical argument, as the scholastics did. Stoic and Epicurean condemn their doctrines out of their own mouths, the Stoic by admitting its impracticability, the Epicurean by celebrating the extravagant immorality which is its consequence.

Valla's demotion of philosophy does not make it an optional extra: the whole discussion assumes an Aristotelian virtue-theory of ethics as its intellectual framework. Aristotle's own version of this, the doctrine of the mean, is, however, roundly criticized, by arguments of a surprisingly modern type. Valla preferred rhetoric to philosophy partly because he viewed language as the creator of the human world, of civility, morals and culture. He draws on the Ciceronian myth of society created by oratory, the mastery of language leading to wisdom: hence, his passionate dedication to philology. The dialogue takes place within an intellectual tradition drawing on both classical and Christian sources which associated pleasure with the body and the senses, and virtue with rejection of the material, particularly of physical pleasure (the moral view advocated in Plato's *Phaedrus*), thus making virtue and pleasure mutually exclusive. Valla's own response to this tradition remains in doubt. Here he seems to endorse it with one hand and attack it with the other, perhaps because he is in fact combining the two poles of the tradition in his version of the Christian true good.

Modern commentators seem to agree that the text contains many layers of elaborate **irony** and can hardly ever be taken at face value. Unfortunately, however, they tend to disagree over what is ironical and what is not, and hence over what the treatise really says, or the nature of Valla's own convictions (Knox, 1989). One possible source of Valla's irony is Plato – the text mentions the irony used by Socrates – but if so, he takes it to unclassical lengths. What Socrates/Plato means by an ironic speech is never as much in doubt as what Valla means. There seems to be some agreement, though, that far from endorsing the Epicurean's outrageous morals, Valla had intended these to discredit Epicureanism. The Epicurean of the dialogue denies the reality of such (humanist) goods as patriotism, honour, glory and fame, recommending instead adultery, the ravishing of dedicated virgins, and indeed any crime if successfully concealed. He praises immoderate drinking as the one pleasure which is completely harmless and can be enjoyed despite the physical deterioration of old age (conventional morality regarded elderly drunkenness as particularly disgraceful). Other suggested rhetorical techniques include the sceptical ones of discrediting a view by introducing deliberate contradictions into its exposition, and supporting it with absurdly strained or untenable interpretations of well-known passages in the classics – a characteristically humanist *jeu d'esprit* (witticism). Commentators have suggested that Valla intended both the Stoic and the Epicurean to destroy themselves in these ways. One could also add that rhetoric urges the adaptation of a speech to its audience; Valla's is of course addressed to an elite, learned humanist circle. The known public character of the various speakers may also have been intended to affect the interpretation of what they say. Above all, Valla was concerned to display his religious orthodoxy after allowing the pagan philosophies their space:

> I have now confuted or condemned both the Epicurean and Stoic dogmas, and have shown that the highest good, or the good that ought to be desired, is not found in either school or among any philosophers, but does exist in our religion, being attainable not on earth but in the heavens.

(Anthology, no. 15iii)

Baldassare Castiglione, *The Courtier*

Baldassare Castiglione was a member of a minor land-owning family. After finishing his education at the court of Ludovico Sforza in Milan, Baldassare entered the service of the princely rulers of Mantua (1500–4, 1516–24) and Urbino (1504–16) as a diplomat and military advisor. Finally, he was sent by Pope Clement VII (1523–34) as **papal nuncio** to Spain, where he died. Throughout his life he cultivated an interest in classical literature. He published poems in both Latin and Italian, but is now remembered for his handbook of courtly behaviour, *The Courtier* (*Il cortegiano*). It is a treatise in dialogue form

Figure 5.4 Raphael, *Baldassare Castiglione*, 1516, oil on canvas. Louvre. Photo: RMN – J.G. Berizzi

written in Italian and suffused with humanist influences both in style and content. Castiglione composed it over a long period. The first draft was probably prepared by 1516, but alterations were made before its publication by Aldus Manutius in Venice in 1528. It soon became very popular, was widely translated, and strongly influenced upper-class education throughout Europe, especially in England (some attribute the nineteenth-century ideal of the English gentleman to this source).

The dialogue is set in an idealized version of Guidobaldo da Montefeltro's court in Urbino.[4] A circle of courtiers and Renaissance notables in the presence of Guidobaldo's duchess, Elisabetta Gonzaga, discuss the qualities of an ideal courtier and court lady. The ideal courtier may be characterized as someone who is able to distinguish himself with grace and tact and without apparent effort (*sprezzatura*) in all the arts of war and peace, including letters and music. He is an unfailingly agreeable and amusing companion, just the sort of person, in fact, to attract the attention of a cultivated Renaissance prince and, having done so, to make himself indispensable to him. There is much talk throughout the dialogue of how one should conduct oneself in love, and it concludes with a long speech on the subject by the humanist poet Pietro Bembo (1470–1547). He promises an account of a kind of love which is both blameless and entirely delightful and seemly in old and young alike: Platonic love.

During the fifteenth century the Greek Aristotelian scholar George of Trebizond (1395–1486) had virulently attacked Plato for promoting homosexual love:

> Aristotle, whom George regarded as the bulwark of Western civilization, may have been over fond of women, but at least he had not indulged in unnatural vice.
>
> (Kraye, 1994, p.77)

Plato's reputation, however, was defended by another Greek scholar living in Italy, Cardinal Bessarion (*c.*1403–72), who claimed that the love described in works such as the *Symposium* and *Phaedrus* was pure and elevated. From that point humanists progressively described the homosexual love featured in Plato's works as heterosexual. Pietro Bembo's *The Lovers of Asolo* (1505) was the best-known example of this genre and presumably this was why Castiglione chose him as the spokesman for Platonic love in *The Courtier* (see Reader, no. 6, for a discussion of this by Jill Kraye).

---

[4] See Burckhardt, 1990, pages 46–8 on Urbino under Guidobaldo's father Federigo and on Guidobaldo himself – a description which testifies to the influence of Castiglione on Burckhardt. See also Book 2 in this series, Chapter 1.

Figure 5.5 Titian, *Cardinal Pietro Bembo*, c.1540, oil on canvas, 64.5 x 76.5 cm. Samuel H. Kress Collection. Photo © 1998 Board of Trustees, National Gallery of Art, Washington

The Courtier, recommending as it does an ideal of behaviour, can be considered a work on morals, though in its first three books relatively little space is devoted to discussion of virtue. This is reserved for the fourth and final book (see Anthology, no. 16), where the discussion presupposes the standard opening question of Aristotelian discussions of virtue, namely, 'What is the true end of man?' or, 'What is the purpose of human life?' Accordingly, Castiglione's discussion of courtly virtue starts with the question 'What is the true end of the courtier?' or, 'What is the purpose of the courtier's life?' It turns out that the courtier must do for his prince what Plato failed to do for the tyrant of Syracuse,[5] that is, turn him into an ideal philosopher–king, who will rule wisely and well. All the courtier's social graces have apparently been acquired to this end, for Castiglione recognizes that, unfortunately, all too many princes rule badly and do not react well to unwelcome advice or exhortations to virtue. The aspiring courtly Plato can only hope to win his tyrant's ear by first charming him with the pleasure of his company and the brilliance of his accomplishments. Moral re-education must be smuggled in, disguised as entertainment. The reforming courtier must never, on any account, become boring or disagreeable, for everything depends on

[5] Plato is reputed to have spent some time with Dionysius the Elder, tyrant of Syracuse in Sicily, but they soon fell out.

the favour of the prince. Moreover, earlier it is suggested that there is little point in displaying virtues like fortitude unless the prince is watching. Here, for example, is Castiglione's advice on the proper way to distinguish oneself in arms:

> when the courtier finds himself involved in a skirmish or pitched battle, or something of that nature, he should arrange to withdraw discreetly from the main body and accomplish the bold and notable exploits he has to perform in as small a company as possible and in view of all the noblest and most eminent men of the army, and, above all, in the presence, or if possible under the very eyes, of the prince he is serving. For it is certainly right to exploit the things one does well. And I believe that just as it is wrong to seek false glory or what is not deserved, so also it is wrong to cheat oneself of due honour and not to seek that praise which is the only true reward of prowess [greatness of soul]. And I recall in the past having known men who, though very able, were extremely stupid in this regard [i.e. lacking in practical wisdom] and would as soon risk their lives to capture a flock of sheep as in being the first to scale the walls of a besieged town; but this is not how our courtier will behave if he bears in mind the motive that leads him to war, which ought to be honour pure and simple. But, then, if he happens to engage in arms in some public spectacle, such as jousting, tourneying or volleying, or other kind of physical recreation, mindful of where and in whose presence he is, he will make sure that he is as elegant and attractive in the exercise of arms as he is competent, and that he feeds the eyes of those who are looking on with everything that can give him added grace. He will ensure that the horse he has is beautifully caparisoned, that he himself is suitably attired, with appropriate mottoes and ingenious devices to attract the eyes of the onlookers in his direction as surely as the loadstone [magnet] attracts iron.

(Bull, 1976, pp.115–16)

Castiglione's courtier, it seems, pursues virtue not for its own sake but for the sake of the beholder. Indeed, we seem to see in him exactly the same calculated pursuit of self-interest that Burckhardt describes in 'The state as a work of art' (1990, pp.19–97). It also accords with the suggestion of New Historicists such as Stephen Greenblatt (1980) that social and political pressures promoted 'self-fashioning' among ambitious individuals eager to gain power and status. Castiglione's book begins to appear more like a symptom of the moral disintegration Burckhardt describes than as a possible solution to it. In fact, Castiglione's proposed solution to the moral and political problems of the age amounts to making everyone good through humanist education and involving more people in government through representative advisory bodies for the different levels of society. But no details are provided as to how such a system of government might work or how humanist education is to be made generally available. To modern commentators Castiglione's humanist programme does not look like a serious attempt to tackle the problem.

Figure 5.6 Fra Simone Ferri da Urbino, an imaginary illustration of a meeting of Elisabetta Gonzaga, Castiglione and other courtiers in the Sala delle Veglie at the ducal palace, Urbino, for a manuscript of Castiglione's *The Courtier*, c.1605–17. Biblioteca Apostolica Vaticana MS Vatic. Urbin. 1767, fol. 2 verso

The philosophical discussions in Book 4 of *The Courtier* could be dismissed as merely a fashionable gloss upon humanist learning, and the work little more than a handbook on how to do well out of a tyrant without losing one's self-respect or the esteem of the world. The book begins to seem as hard-headed in its way as Machiavelli's *The Prince*, and less honest: such a prince deserves such a courtier. This point has been much debated by scholars, especially as Book 4 was written some time after the first three books (Woodhouse, 1979). An alternative possibility is that, in the grim political circumstances of the 1520s, Castiglione wanted to present a work which would be taken seriously, and it could be argued that in Book 4 he achieves this objective through the idealism of Bembo.

Exercise

Read the first extract from Book 4 of *The Courtier* (Anthology, no. 16i). Try to identify and distinguish the Aristotelian and Platonic arguments?

Discussion

Signor Ottaviano voices conventional sentiments about the virtues a prince should possess. These probably derive originally from Aristotle's *Nicomachean Ethics*. In the first paragraph he expresses the hope that the courtier will be able to encourage his prince to be good by being able to 'instil virtue into his mind, to teach him continence, fortitude, justice and temperance'. He later claims that the ability to distinguish good from evil can be learned. Signor Gasparo, however, suggests that some people have an inherent disposition towards evil. Pietro Bembo comes to Ottaviano's defence with a more specifically Platonic account of how a bad character is formed: 'eventually the desires prove too strong for reason, which abandons the struggle, like a ship which for a time resists the storm but finally, battered by the overwhelming fury of the winds, with anchor and rigging smashed, lets herself be driven by the tempest'. This passage will probably have reminded you of the metaphor of the charioteer which was used to describe the soul's struggle towards goodness in the *Phaedrus*. ❖

There is a certain lack of continuity between the broadly Aristotelian morality advocated in the first part of the extract and the Platonic flights of speech put into the mouth of Bembo at the end. This could, though, be an artful presentation of the rival claims of the active and contemplative life, and of Aristotelian and Platonic philosophy, with Castiglione deliberately making no attempt to adjudicate between them. It contains, however, a hint that Bembo's is the higher philosophy, though not one of this world. A cynic might say that, in the circumstances of the time, it was a very convenient philosophy for Castiglione's courtier, as it conferred high moral status while imposing few burdensome practical restraints on conduct in the world. In this connection it is revealing to compare Castiglione's version with Plato's original in the *Phaedrus*, and reflect on the reasons for the similarities and differences, and also how they escape notice in the glamour cast over it by Castiglione's literary skill. You will notice that even Plato's injunction to forgo physical pleasure is relaxed in the case of Castiglione's young lover – only the old man, who is supposed to be less desirous of physical enjoyment, is expected to give it up.

Exercise

Read the second extract from Book 4 (Anthology, no. 16ii) and refer back to the myth of the charioteer in the *Phaedrus* (Anthology, no. 13). In what ways are these extracts similar to and different from each other?

Discussion

Bembo is undoubtedly influenced by Plato in his praise of a love which, although inspired by beauty, transcends the need for physical expression. The soul of a man is able to take this path and 'ascends to its noblest part, which is the intellect; and there, no more overshadowed by the dark night of earthly things, it glimpses the divine beauty itself'. Yet he has also absorbed Ficino's Christian interpretation of these ideas, which accorded not only with his own position in the church but also with the Neoplatonism of the Hellenistic school of philosophers. While the *Phaedrus* postulated the enlightenment of the soul through the pursuit of universal truth – through some intimation of the immaterial world of ideas and the rejection of sensual pleasure – Bembo envisages a gradual ascent to this end: 'he will determine to make use of this love as a step by which to climb to another that is far more sublime'. The climax of this ascent is a vision of God. He also, like most contemporary Platonists, substitutes heterosexual love for the homosexual love praised by Plato. ❖

The Courtier was to prove enormously popular in Europe throughout the sixteenth century. J.H. Whitfield suggests this was due to the fact that it was 'the first attempt in the vernacular to cull the social wisdom of the ancients for the benefit of an elite' (Hoby, 1975, p.xv). By the end of the century nearly 60 Italian editions had been published and in 1561 Sir Thomas Hoby provided an English translation. Castiglione had visited England briefly in 1506 as a proxy for his master, Guidobaldo da Montefeltro, to receive the Order of the Garter from Henry VII. The popularity of the book in England, however, stems from the Hoby translation:

> he [*The Courtier*] shall get him the reputation now here in England which he hath had a good while since beyond the sea in Italy, Spaine and Fraunce ... ought this to be in estimation with all degrees of men:

For to princes and great men, it is a rule, to rule themselves that rule others ... To men growen in yeares, a pathway to the beholding and musing of the mind, to whatsoever else is meete for that age: To young Gentlemen, an encouraging to garnish their minds with morall vertues, and their bodies with comely exercises ... To Ladies and Gentlewomen, a mirrour to decke and trimme themselves with vertuous conditions, comely behaviours and honest entertainment toward all men: And to [them] all in generall, a storehouse of most necessarie implements for the conversation, use, and trayning up of mans life with Courtly demeaners.

(1975, pp.2–3)

Despite the influence that Castiglione was to exercise for centuries to come, he was in many ways the least innovative of our humanist thinkers. *The Courtier* was a manual of good conduct for the ruling classes and, although it was wittier and more cultivated than most of that popular genre, much of it was not particularly original. Even in Book 4, Bembo's great speech in favour of a Platonic, spiritual form of love was nothing more than a Christianized version of the *Phaedrus*. Burckhardt expressed admiration for the contribution made to 'the state as a work of art' by *The Courtier* but he did not explain how the treatise might be able to reconcile traditional Christian morality with personal and intellectual freedom.

Desiderius Erasmus, *Praise of Folly*

Desiderius Erasmus was born in the Low Countries, the illegitimate son of a man intended for the priesthood and a physician's daughter. He was initially brought up by his mother, briefly went to school at Gouda and spent a year as a chorister at Utrecht. From 1478 to 1483 he was at school at Deventer (the cradle of Dutch humanism) where he seems to have acquired his taste for 'good letters', or a love of classical literature. On the death of his parents, poverty obliged him and his brother to become monks. Erasmus wanted to continue his studies at university and seems to have entered the religious life unenthusiastically (although his Christian piety is not in doubt). In the monastery he wrote two humanist works, one on contempt for the world and the other entitled *Against the Barbarians* (*Anti-barbari*), a defence of the study of pagan literature. In about 1492 Erasmus entered the service of the bishop of Cambrai, Henry of Bergen. Three years later he was released to study at Paris, where he supported himself, with some financial help from the bishop, by taking pupils. From that time on Erasmus no longer lived the usual life of a monk, settled in a religious community. He obtained special permissions to avoid this obligation and earned his living as a professional humanist, depending on the financial support of patrons and the income from pupils and his writing. For his Paris pupils he wrote the *Colloquies* (examples of conversational Latin, consisting of mini-dialogues on various subjects) and the *Adages* (a collection of proverbs, sometimes with commentaries, from a variety of sources, Christian and classical). Both these educational works became enormously popular and were frequently reproduced in ever-enlarged editions throughout his life.

One of his pupils in Paris was William Blount, Lord Mountjoy (later tutor to Henry VIII), who invited Erasmus to England. Erasmus travelled there in 1499 and met English humanists, including William Grocyn, John Colet and Thomas More. More introduced Erasmus to the household of Henry VII, where he met the nine-year-old prince Henry, the future Henry VIII. Erasmus made his first acquaintance with Florentine Neoplatonism through Colet (who had corresponded with Ficino) and Grocyn, and perhaps it was their influence which led Erasmus to study Greek and theology, especially the writings of St Jerome. In 1500 he returned to Paris, where the *Adages* was being printed, and then to the Low Countries, where he discovered a manuscript of Valla's *Collation of the New Testament*, which he published in Paris in 1505 (he was already an admirer of Valla's *Good Latin Usage*). He also wrote the *Enchiridion militis christiani*,[6] a work which subsequently made him a principal spokesman for liberal Catholic reform. For Erasmus the battles of the Christian soldier are conducted internally, in the struggle between the spirit and the flesh. The flesh is interpreted widely, to cover not just physical appetites but also the external trappings of religion, such as rituals, shrines and images. Religion should be spiritual not carnal, and true Christianity lies in the imitation of Christ. The Christian must abandon worldly wisdom (prudence) for Christian folly. Erasmus concludes with the advice:

> Creep not upon the earth, my brother, like an animal. Put on those wings which Plato says are caused to grow on the soul by the ardour of love. Rise above the body to the spirit, from the visible to the invisible, from the letter to the mystical meaning, from the sensible to the intelligible, from the involved to the simple [i.e. from scholastic argument to simple faith/mystical communion]. Rise as by rungs until you scale the ladder of Jacob. As you draw nigh to the Lord, He will

---

[6] The Greek word *enchiridion* is ambiguous, so the title translates as 'The dagger/handbook of the Christian soldier', another humanist play on words – a book can indeed be a small but effective weapon.

draw nigh unto you. If with all your might you strive to rise above the cloud and clamour of the senses He will descend from light inaccessible and that silence which passes understanding in which not only the tumult of the senses is still, but the images of all intelligible things keep silence.

(Bainton, 1969, p.94)

In 1505 Erasmus returned to England where he stayed for a year. He renewed his earlier acquaintance with More and they became intimate friends. Together they began translating the Greek satirist Lucian (see Chapter 3). In 1506 Erasmus went to Italy and lived there for three years, receiving a doctorate of theology in Turin, and visiting Bologna, Venice (where the printer Aldus Manutius was bringing out a new, enlarged edition of the *Adages*), Padua and Rome. He made powerful friends in Rome, but was also depressed by the worldliness and corruption of the papal court and the Roman clergy – the pope at the time was the bellicose Julius II (1503–13). He was offered an appointment in Rome, but decided instead to return to England where Henry VIII had become king and had expressed a desire to gather together a collection of scholars. Back in England, he stayed first with More, then moved to Cambridge where he taught at the university.

Figure 5.7 Jodocus Badius, *Printer's shop*, engraving, from title page of *Hegesippus*. *c*.1500. An example of an early printing press. Mary Evans Picture Library

While staying with More, Erasmus wrote *Praise of Folly* (*Encomium moriae*), which he published in 1511. Its Latin title is a pun on More's name (*moria* is also Greek for folly). The **encomium** is a classical genre, a speech praising someone or something, its construction governed by rhetorical rules. Here the form is used ironically: Erasmus has Folly, in the person of a woman, praise herself, and he pays little regard to the rules. The work is a satire, no doubt inspired

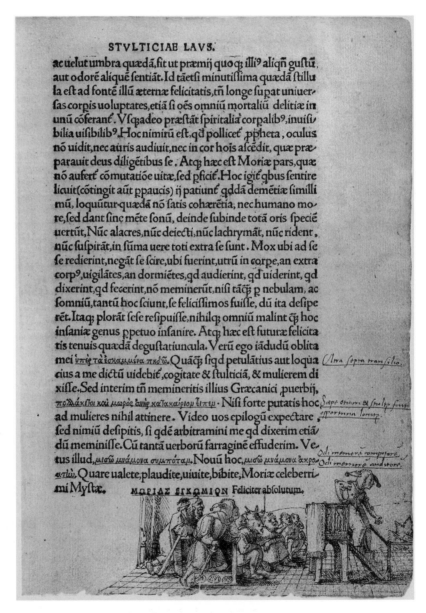

Figure 5.8 Hans Holbein the Younger, *Folly Descending from the Pulpit*, 1515, marginal pen drawing in Erasmus's *Praise of Folly*, Basle. Oeffentliche Kunstsammlung, Martin Bühler

by Erasmus's work on Lucian, in which Folly constantly changes sides and aspect, so that it is sometimes difficult to keep track of what is being praised and what is being mocked and where one's sympathies are supposed to lie. Along with the usual crop of human vanities, however, there are also some familiar humanist and religious reformist targets. The final shift is a sudden change of tone to serious praise of Christian folly.

The work recognizably has the same underlying moral and religious aims as the *Enchiridion*, despite the fact that the Platonism of Erasmus in this work is much more straightforward in its promotion of the good Christian life. In the *Praise of Folly* he uses the devious and contradictory means of the paradoxical encomium – a device he learned from Lucian. Another influence on the work could have been his experience of the English court and of popular revels in France. The Tudor monarchs (and Thomas More) kept fools, some of them women. And in France the mock sermon was a well-known festive event where a fool or group of fools would preach a 'sermon' in gibberish or rant about subjects such as 'Saint Onion', 'women' or 'taverns' (Miller, 1979, p.xviii). After pointing out that the targets of *Praise of Folly* are the same vanities listed by Erasmus when writing seriously on the Christian theme of contempt of the world, Roland Bainton suggests that *Praise of Folly* treats the same theme ironically:

> To say that it is ironic means, however, that it is not the medieval contempt of the world. Erasmus would not be willing, like Jerome and Colet, to see propagation cease that earth might be emptied and heaven filled. A more significant difference is the blending, everywhere to be found in Erasmus, of the Christian and classical themes. The Stoics distinguished the wise men and the fools, who because not governed by reason were both sots and knaves. The Neoplatonists deplored the servitude of man to the carnal. The first stage towards emancipation and self-mastery was self-knowledge – 'Know thyself'. The fool in the period of the Renaissance is consequently often portrayed eyeing himself quizzically in a mirror. He thus perceives that 'everyman' is a fool including himself. His very existence depends on that *élan vital* [vital spark] which is not amenable to reason. This insight enables him to smile at himself as Erasmus does on more than one occasion. The smile is not a laugh of scorn so much as of pity and of hope. For man, enthralled by the senses and spending himself for ephemeral goals, can be emancipated by Folly of another sort, that divine rapture of Plato transcending reason, and the divine self-emptying of the Christian, who pursues his earthly pilgrimage with fidelity and detachment.

(1969, pp.124–5)

Read the extract from *Praise of Folly* (Anthology, no. 17ii). What kind of theologians does Erasmus have Folly condemn, and on what grounds does she criticize them?

The theologians were the scholastics who had dominated all religious studies during the later Middle Ages. Folly starts her condemnation by exposing their arrogance and conceit. She then makes fun of the technical terms with which they hedge their debates so that they can always get the best of an argument. She lists the ludicrous subjects they have chosen to discuss (all were actually debated with the exception of the devil, ass, cucumber and piece of flint). The apostles, on the other hand, had celebrated their faith simply. Indeed they would seem quite unsophisticated in contrast to the scholastics, who spent years studying authorities such as Aristotle and the Scottish philosopher Duns Scotus (*c.*1265–1308). ❖

In 1514 Erasmus left England for Holland because of the threat of war between England and France, and was based there and in Louvain (in modern-day Belgium) till 1521, though he made occasional visits to England. Although these were lean years for him financially, he refused a bishopric in Sicily in order to continue his studies (he had been ordained by his first employer, Henry of Bergen). He was still working on Jerome and, inspired by Valla, was comparing the Latin of Jerome's Vulgate with the Greek New Testament and making his new Latin translation, as well as preparing editions of classical authors. The work on Jerome and the New Testament was published in 1516 under the title *Novum instrumentum* and included the Greek text side by side with Erasmus's translation. The English King James Bible, the Authorized Version of 1611, was partly based on this version. At the time, however, Erasmus was attacked for his temerity by, among others, the orthodox Louvain theologian Martin Dorp. He was defended by More.

You may now like to read the article on Valla and Erasmus by Letizia Panizza (Reader, no. 7). Both thinkers were prepared to use ancient ethics but only as a means to an end: to confirm and strengthen Christian morality. In 1523 Erasmus rather reluctantly engaged in public controversy with Luther. Initially he had been sympathetic to Luther's reforming zeal, but in the end deplored his contentiousness and intransigence. Erasmus urged the moral and human superiority of consensual reform and reconciliation over schism and confessional wars, but once the Reformation was under way his efforts to hold the middle ground only succeeded in drawing the attacks of both sides. In 1521 he left Louvain, whose orthodoxy had become uncongenial to him, and moved to Basle, where he remained until 1529. He then transferred to Freiburg im Bresgau, staying there until 1535, at which time he returned to Basle, where he died the following year.

In his introduction to the Penguin edition of *Praise of Folly*, A.H.T. Levi draws attention to its affinity with More's *Utopia*, written soon after:

> More, who had led Erasmus to Lucian, knew precisely how to understand the *Praise of Folly*. His reply was to be the similarly Lucianic *Utopia* which puts a serious exploration of advanced personal and social values into the mouth of Ralph Hythlodaeus or Ralph the fool. Like the *Praise of Folly*, *Utopia* is a fantasy, not a programme. Both have serious imaginative purposes, both explore seriously the compatibility and implications of the enlightened social and personal ideals which were the heritage of Colet. Needless to say, Erasmus and More are in total agreement.

(1971, p.39)

Thomas More, *Utopia*

Thomas More was a lawyer and the son of a lawyer, with entry to powerful and aristocratic circles. As a boy he was placed as a page in the household of John Morton (*c.*1420–1500), archbishop of Canterbury and Henry VII's lord chancellor. While training for the law More came into contact with English humanists, including William Grocyn and John Colet, who had both studied in Italy and fallen under the spell of Ficino's highly Christianized Neoplatonism. More learnt Greek and improved his Latin, acquired a love of literary scholarship, and seems to have spent as much time on it as on the law. He also considered a religious vocation. In 1499 he met Erasmus and they became close friends. A few years later More married and had four children by his first wife, who died in 1511. He subsequently married a middle-aged widow with a daughter. He rose rapidly in the legal profession and in 1517 entered Henry VIII's council. At first More was trusted and favoured by the king and became lord chancellor in 1529. In 1532 he resigned the chancellorship: the issue was the transfer of ecclesiastical authority in England to the king. In 1533 Henry VIII divorced his wife, Catherine of Aragon, without papal authorization, and married Anne Boleyn for which he was excommunicated. In 1534 the devout Catholic More refused to swear allegiance to the Act of Succession, which acknowledged the children of the king's new marriage as legitimate heirs to the throne. He was imprisoned, convicted of treason, and beheaded in 1535. Exactly 400 years later he was canonized (for a saintly life and as a Catholic martyr).

While Henry's powers were not as absolute as those of an Italian despot, it was still dangerous to cross him, and More's fate illustrates the perils of criticizing a prince. However, it does seem that, within the limits set by his conscience, More made every effort to save himself: his refusal to obey Henry VIII was couched in language as conciliatory and carefully judged as anything Castiglione's courtier might have devised. But, despite this, Greenblatt suggests that More may have colluded in creating the role of martyr which political circumstances offered him:

> More's writing and behaviour in his final months suggested that here too he is adapting himself to the play in hand, though the play is a more solemn and fearful one than any in which he had ever performed.

> (1980, p.71)

Utopia was written early in More's career, just before he joined the king's council. 'Utopia' now generally means an ideal state or society; but More's *Utopia*, though it describes an imaginary commonwealth, was not intended to depict an ideal one (the word is a coinage from Greek and literally means 'nowhere'). It was first published in Louvain, under the supervision of Erasmus, in December 1516, and More had probably started writing it about a year earlier. More also wrote a history of Richard III, a pamphlet against Luther, poems and devotional works, and published various translations, but of his writings it is *Utopia* for which he is remembered.

In Utopia private property is unknown and it is a relatively egalitarian society (by the standards of sixteenth-century Europe). It is headed by a chief magistrate or prince chosen for life by magistrates from a panel elected by popular vote. Lower-level magistrates are also elected to represent various divisions of the people. The lives of citizens are strictly regulated for the common good. All learn a craft and agricultural skills and have to spend time working on collective farms. While they can choose their craft, the normal practice is to follow that of their father. Men marry at the age of 22, women at the age of 18, and prospective marriage partners have to be displayed to each other naked by sober elders before the marriage is finalized. Utopians live communally and have ample leisure for study and games because of the frugality of their needs, which can easily be met by moderate amounts of their own labour. Food is provided freely in generous quantities and people are encouraged to eat it at communal meals for which the women cook. Ostentation in dress and attachment to useless 'valuables' like gold and jewels are regarded contemptuously as foolishness. Since there is no property, there are few laws, but social infringements are punished with reduction to slavery. Utopians make war against other communities if necessary, in self-defence or to plant colonies to support their surplus population, but are skilled at minimizing bloodshed which they always try to do.

Figure 5.9 *Utopia*, 1516, engraving, frontispiece of Thomas More, *Libellus ... Insula Utopia (Book on the Island of Utopia)*. Mary Evans Picture Library

The extract from More that you will read in the next exercise contains the heart of More's conception: the account of Utopian religion and moral philosophy, that is, the principles underlying the organization of Utopian society. The description of Utopia has the essential features of the theoretical construction of a 'best commonwealth' as described by Aristotle. The best commonwealth contains only those things necessary for the happiness of its citizens, so human happiness must first be defined (the job of moral philosophy), which in turn defines the commonwealth's goals. These in turn determine necessary material conditions for the achievement of those goals. The best means to achieve them, given those material conditions, can then be devised and built in to the structure of the ideal society. Thus the character of the society ultimately depends on the foundational moral philosophy.

Exercise

Read the first four paragraphs of the extract from More's *Utopia* (Anthology, no. 18). How would you describe the arguments used by the Utopians about what is good?

Discussion

More rather gives himself away in the first sentence when he writes that the Utopians 'carry on the same arguments as we do'. For most of this passage he seems more concerned to rehearse the unsatisfactory nature of both the classical and scholastic solutions to the question of what is good than to add to his picture of Utopia. The first paragraph with its praise of pleasure has an Epicurean tone, the second sounds more like Christian, scholastic reasoning and the third and fourth bring in Stoic doctrine, the 'school which declares that virtue is itself happiness'. Yet this last view, taken to extremes, encourages people to cultivate misery for its own sake and to harm themselves while they help others. The conclusion of paragraph four leads back to one of the defining characteristics of the good as it is practised in Utopia: nature warns 'not to seek your own advantage in ways that cause misfortune to others'. None of the philosophies he has considered have presented More with the solution to the problem. He thus comes up with a radical series of measures which owe something to Platonism, Epicureanism, Stoicism, but most of all to Christianity. ❖

The big puzzle about Utopia is how far we are meant to admire it – even though it is the result of a 'best commonwealth' exercise. More, as his life makes clear, was a devout Christian, but the religion and moral philosophy of Utopia are distinctly unchristian. The description of the commonwealth is introduced by a lengthy dialogue between More, his friend Peter Giles (*c*.1486–1533) and an imaginary character called Raphael Hythloday who has visited Utopia. The dialogue concludes with More doubting the viability of an egalitarian society in which property is held in common. Hythloday retorts by citing the example of Utopia:

> I lived there more than five years, and would never have left, if it had not been to make that new world known to others. If you had seen

> them, you would frankly confess that you had never seen a well-governed people anywhere but there.
>
> (Logan, 1995, p.105)

But we should not necessarily take his introductory words at face value. Humanists enjoyed using the rhetorical play of irony – a favourite device of Socrates in Plato's dialogues – to tease their readers and conceal their own position. The name Hythloday is another coinage from the Greek meaning something like 'peddler of nonsense' or 'fool'. Not that we are necessarily meant to take this at face value either: 'Raphael' is, after all, the name of an archangel. This invented name is itself a learned tease and the character More disagrees with him at every turn! It has been suggested that it belongs to the tradition of ancient rhetoric, which was well known to humanists. Book 1 of *Utopia* is an example of deliberative oratory: should Hythloday join a royal council, and how persuasive are his reasons for deciding not to do so? This form, intended to influence the hearer to favour a particular policy, was especially important in political life. Book 2, which contains the description of *Utopia*, is an example of display or epideictic oratory which enabled the speaker to show off his skill and even to attract patrons. In this case, the subject chosen would not necessarily be a serious one.

There may be a clue to More's intentions in the introductory dialogue. It opens with a discussion of whether or not someone as widely travelled and as knowledgeable as Hythloday should join a royal council, so that his experience may benefit as many others as possible. (At the time of writing More may already have received an invitation to join Henry VIII's council and it may have reflected his own deliberations on whether or not to accept a position that would enable him to give moral advice to a prince.) Hythloday disclaims having any real wisdom to offer, and doubts that real wisdom would make any headway in royal councils in any case, since courtiers are typically motivated by self-interest rather than concern for the good of the commonwealth or the virtue of the prince. Good advice will always be drowned out by bad. To illustrate the effects of bad advice, Hythloday cites the failure of the rigorous punishment of thieves by hanging in England. This is bad policy, because hanging is unjust as a punishment for theft, and, in any case, 'no punishment however severe can restrain men from robbery when they have no other way to eat'. Theft is caused by social inequalities and the only way to eradicate theft is to eradicate the inequalities.

> [This may seem extreme, but] if we dismiss as outlandish and absurd everything that the perverse customs of men have made to seem

alien to us, we shall have to set aside, even in a community of Christians, most of the teachings of Christ ... [which] are far more alien from the common customs of mankind than my discourse was.

(Logan, 1995, p.99)

We then move to More's scepticism about the practical possibility of creating an egalitarian polity in Utopia.

What might we conclude from this? Is More teasing us again? Hythloday seems to be suggesting, paradoxically, that a non-Christian commonwealth can be more Christian than a Christian one and that good counsel is wasted on a Christian prince. Yet More went on to try and give that good counsel. Perhaps, after all, his ambivalence is not a mere tease but rather what it appears to be – ambivalence. He may have thought that the arguments for and against advising princes were pretty evenly balanced, that Utopia was both good and bad, and that its moral philosophy was partly right and partly wrong.

Perhaps some of the arguments about the nature of More's intentions in composing *Utopia* concentrate too exclusively on the nature of the polity in the mythical island rather than on the devastating condemnation of contemporary European society with which Book 2 ends:

the rich constantly try to grind out of the poor part of their daily wages, not only by private swindling but by public laws. Before, it appeared to be unjust that people who deserve most from the commonwealth should receive least. But now, by promulgating law, they have transmuted this perversion into justice.

(Logan, 1995, p.243)

Taken from this perspective, the description of Utopia may seem to be geared principally to pointing to the selfishness and corruption of contemporary sixteenth-century society, by contrasting it with the organization of an ideal state. As James Hankins asks:

What would it take for society to reward people according to their merit and their contribution to the common good, not according to their wealth and ancestry? Clearly, educating princes and oligarchs in the classics is not going to do the job. If we analyse the defects of human society, they can all be traced to money and pride. Through the mouth of Hythloday, More suggests that the only way to rid European society of these evils would be to effect a radical social revolution, abolishing social rank and private property. Only thus can Christendom achieve the *optimus status rei publicae*, the best constitution of the commonwealth.

(1996, pp.138–9)

A further problem encountered in *Utopia* is that of reconciling the well-known (although recently challenged by authors such as Greenblatt) *persona* of the author – More the devout Catholic statesman, who was prepared to sacrifice his life for a principle – with the ironic philosophical eclectic of 1516. Yet the circumstances of 1535, when More was executed for treason, were very different from those which prevailed 20 years earlier. More had experienced high office with all its temptations and pressures, the termination of communion with Rome and the destruction of his own career. He had intimated in 1516 that no ancient philosophy constituted a satisfactory guide to what was good, despite the fact that, as a humanist, he had an understanding of the whole range from Plato to Epicurus. It is hardly surprising that he eventually made his choice in favour of the certainties of the orthodox religion in which he had been raised.

Burckhardt and humanist philosophy

As well as providing examples of humanist moral philosophy, the above texts shed light on two aspects of the Renaissance that are specifically excluded from Burckhardt's study, namely, the Renaissance in northern Europe and philosophy. In *The Civilization of the Renaissance in Italy*, Burckhardt conceives the Renaissance to be a manifestation of the specifically *Italian* spirit (1990, pp.1–15). So the question arises as to whether and how his characterization of the Renaissance applies to the northern Renaissance. This question is not considered by Burckhardt because for him, given his view of history as the history of peoples, and his belief that the Italian and Germanic peoples were very different from each other, the northern Renaissance must have been a different phenomenon from its Italian counterpart. He seems to have seen it as the product of cultural diffusion from Italy, rather than as an indigenous manifestation of local genius.

Philosophy is omitted from consideration by Burckhardt for a different reason: no study, he says, can encompass everything. So although Burckhardt recognizes that the rise of humanism affected philosophy, he counts philosophy as one of the 'special sciences', excluding detailed consideration of it from his study and referring readers instead to specialist literature (1990, p.163). Perhaps another reason for its omission is Burckhardt's acknowledged lack of interest in philosophy. He reveals in an aside that he finds its main humanist vehicle, the treatise, 'a bore' (p.159).

However, Burckhardt does not exclude philosophy from the general remarks he makes about the relation between humanism and the Renaissance, although his view of that relation is noticeably different from modern accounts. The term 'Renaissance' is now often taken to refer to the rebirth of antiquity which is identified with humanism and humanism is seen as a major, perhaps *the* major, cultural influence. Burckhardt, in contrast, while recognizing the contribution that humanism made to the background culture, assigns it a relatively minor role in the Renaissance, and seems to give a rather low rating to the achievements of the humanists themselves.

The reason for this could be the centrality of the visual arts to his thesis. For Burckhardt the Renaissance was not primarily a historical but rather a spiritual and cultural phenomenon, a burgeoning of the spirit whose 'type', or most essential manifestation, was the personality and visual creative achievement of the great universal master artists of the period. Burckhardt's prime example is Leon Battista Alberti (1404–72) (pp.102–4). We can also find him excluding a particular work from 'the Renaissance' on the grounds of its literary character, despite the fact that it falls within the period from which he draws his examples. He comments with surprise that 'epochs far above our own in the sense of beauty – the Renaissance and the Greco-Roman world' could not dispense with didactic poetry, a humanist form which he clearly finds unappealing. He says of a didactic poem, *The Zodiac of Life,* written in 1528 by Marcello Palingenio Stellato:

> On the whole ... his work must be considered as lying outside the boundaries of the Renaissance, as is further indicated by the fact that, in harmony with the serious didactic purpose of the poem, allegory tends to supplant mythology.

(p.172)

So Burckhardt's account of humanism consists largely of an assessment of its creative achievements in the form of Latin literature. What he seems interested in assessing is how humanist productions rate as works of art, that is, in his terms, as high achievements of the human spirit. A cultural historian of the twenty-first century would be more likely to treat humanist works as sources of information about the mentality of the time. As a result of his approach, Burckhardt gives relatively little space to the impact of humanist scholarship on the many aspects of culture, including philosophy, which a modern study would feel obliged to treat. He is only interested in the background culture as the soil from which sprang *his* conception of the Renaissance: the burgeoning of the Italian spirit which produced great art.

Burckhardt's appeal to aesthetic judgement creates a further difficulty specific to philosophy, for it is not now regarded as central to the historical study of philosophical texts. This is not to suggest that aesthetic judgement is irrelevant to the study of either history or philosophy, but there is a danger in relying too much on such personal judgement when bringing art to the service of history – a danger from which Burckhardt does not always escape. These problems are also illustrated by Burckhardt's attitude to the philosophical treatise. Renaissance philosophy tends to divide into moral philosophy on the one hand, and metaphysics, natural philosophy and logic on the other. The latter were mainly the preserve of the scholastic philosophers of the universities, and it may be these that Burckhardt has in mind when he reserves philosophy for specialist treatment. The standard humanist vehicle of moral philosophy was the treatise, which he does consider, despite admitting to finding much of this material 'commonplace'. He acknowledges, however, that this is not how it would have seemed to contemporaries:

> much which appears to us as mere commonplace in their writings was for them and their contemporaries a new and hardly won view of things upon which mankind had been silent since the days of antiquity.

(p.159)

Nonetheless, Burckhardt is still not willing to grant humanist achievements in this sphere a very high place. This may seem an ill-advised judgement but there is a plausible explanation for it. Part of the programme of some humanists was to change the method of philosophical argument. The central place given to formal logical procedures by the scholastics was to be assigned instead to rhetoric, which persuades by literary as opposed to logical means. Judging the success of such a form of reasoning involves aesthetic as well as philosophical judgement, though some humanists would not have recognized this distinction. In the humanist treatise, literary form and philosophical argument were interrelated in ways that have since become unfamiliar: by Burckhardt's time, these rhetorical forms and conventions had fallen out of use, especially in philosophy. To understand what is going on in a humanist philosophical treatise, and exactly what the argument is, can require expert knowledge of rhetoric, and this makes it very difficult to judge the work's success, including its aesthetic impact. This demands that we treat the work on its own merits, for which detailed historical knowledge is required, and this was something Burckhardt regarded as unnecessary in making his judgement.

Burckhardt appears to believe that true artistic quality is timeless and can be recognized across centuries: the test of time, in other words, is a *reliable* test of artistic quality. So he is prepared to dismiss most Renaissance philosophical treatises simply because he finds them boring, outdated and uncongenial. But this assessment by the later judgement of one individual is a very feeble version of the test of time. Only if both style and content match Burckhardt's personal tastes does philosophical writing meet with his approval, as being truly of the Renaissance. Only one of our texts falls into this category: Castiglione's *The Courtier*, which earns Burckhardt's admiration at least as much because of its literary qualities as because of its philosophical content, and even that is probably gained mainly because he is sympathetic to its religious conclusion. He also saw it as contributing to the construction of the state a 'work of art'. If we read humanist philosophical treatises as philosophy rather than as literature, Burckhardt's judgements seem more questionable.

Conclusion

There is good reason to pay more attention than Burckhardt does to the content of humanist moral philosophy. His aesthetic focus has its drawbacks even when such considerations are relevant to the understanding of philosophical texts. Too much emphasis on stylistic criteria may lead to an underestimation of the relation between style and content. The inadequate attention he paid to philosophical content may be explained by his self-confessed distaste for it, but this distaste hardly seems a sufficient reason for ignoring humanist philosophy. This is particularly so given the importance Burckhardt attached to the role played by the philosophical treatise in the crisis of values which he saw as the result both of the moral bankruptcy of the Catholic church, and of the political and social instability of the time:

> The century which escaped from the influence of the Middle Ages felt the need of something to mediate between itself and antiquity in many questions of morals and philosophy; and this need was met by the writer of treatises and dialogues.

(p.159)

This transformation of morality is an important part of Burckhardt's account of the Renaissance, and one of the places where it emerges most clearly is in humanist moral philosophy, which actively set out to effect this transformation. By paying only cursory attention to humanist philosophy, then, Burckhardt seems to deprive himself of an important source of evidence, which is highly relevant to his own conception of the Renaissance. You will probably have realized by now that we think Burckhardt is almost completely wrong about humanist philosophy. So which of the four humanist texts considered above do you think make the most successful contribution to solving the moral difficulties, or crisis of values, that Burckhardt saw as intrinsic to Renaissance culture?

The author admired by Burckhardt, Castiglione, may be an enchanting writer and a popularizer of genius, but he contributed little to the philosophical treatment of the moral difficulties of his time. His version of the relation between theory and practice in moral education – which seems eminently sensible and realistic – actually makes the project of ethical re-education of an adult and immoral prince a hopeless endeavour. Contemporaries would have admired the Platonic ideal of spiritual love as an eloquent exercise rather than a serious moral programme.

The other three texts, by Valla, Erasmus and More, are related, and all in their different ways try to wrest and reshape something new and usable out of Epicureanism and Platonism. It is interesting to compare and contrast their versions of these schools of ancient philosophy. Valla and Erasmus were professed humanists who lived by their writings. Neither found a satisfactory formula among the ancient philosophers with which to resolve the moral dilemmas of their time. Both took seriously the challenge of reconciling the desire to achieve goodness with the pressures of expediency. Valla does not emerge as the immoral sensualist he can easily be mistaken for; his Christianity seems to have been genuine. Erasmus may have claimed to be praising folly but his satirical wit repeatedly damaged its target, such as the scholastics and the corrupt clergy of his day. More published his *Utopia* long before his rapid rise to high office and subsequent disgrace. If Henry VIII took his castigation of contemporary society and proposals for a totally different social order seriously, they did him no harm, nor ultimately did they achieve any tangible results.

So Valla and Erasmus seem to have been the humanists who made the strongest contribution to solving the moral difficulties that Burckhardt thought were intrinsic to Renaissance culture. Both took what was usable from ancient ethics but grounded it firmly in Christian morality: the only solution which was acceptable to contemporary opinion.

Bibliography

ACKRILL, J.L. (1981) *Aristotle the Philosopher*, Oxford, Oxford University Press.

BAINTON, R.H. (1969) *Erasmus of Christendom*, Fontana Library, London, Collins.

BULL, G. (trans.) (1976) *Castiglione: The Courtier*, London, Penguin Classics.

BURCHARDT, J. (1990) *The Civilization of the Renaissance in Italy*, trans. S.G.C. Middlemore, Harmondsworth, Penguin; first published 1858.

COLISH, M. (1985) *The Stoic Tradition from Antiquity to the Early Middle Ages*, Leiden, Brill.

GREENBLATT, S. (1980) *Renaissance Self-fashioning: From More to Shakespeare*, Chicago, University of Chicago Press.

HANKINS, J. (1990) *Plato in the Italian Renaissance*, vol. 1, Leiden and New York, Brill.

HANKINS, J. (1996) 'Humanism and the origins of modern political thought' in J. Kraye (ed.) *The Cambridge Companion to Renaissance Humanism*, Cambridge, Cambridge University Press.

HOBY, T. (trans.) (1975) *Castiglione: The Book of the Courtier*, introduction by J.H. Whitfield, London, J.M. Dent; this translation first published 1561.

JARDINE, L. (1988) 'Humanistic logic' in C.B. Schmitt, Q. Skinner, E. Kessler, J. Kraye (eds) *The Cambridge History of Renaissance Philosophy*, Cambridge, Cambridge University Press.

JONES, H., (1992) *The Epicurean Tradition*, London, New York, Routledge.

KNOX, D. (1989) *Ironia: Medieval and Renaissance Ideas on Irony*, Leiden, Brill.

KRAYE, J. (1988) 'Moral philosophy' in C.B. Schmitt, Q. Skinner, E. Kessler, J. Kraye (eds) *The Cambridge History of Renaissance Philosophy*, Cambridge, Cambridge University Press.

KRAYE, J. (1994) 'The transformation of Platonic love in the Renaissance' in A. Baldwin and S. Hutton (eds) *Platonism and the English Imagination*, Cambridge, Cambridge University Press.

KRAYE, J. (1996) 'Philologists and philosophers' in J. Kraye (ed.) *The Cambridge Companion to Renaissance Humanism*, Cambridge, Cambridge University Press.

KRISTELLER, P.O. (1991) 'Humanism and moral philosophy' in A. Rabil (ed.) *Renaissance Humanism: Foundations, Forms and Legacy*, vol. 3, Philadelphia, University of Pennsylvania.

LEVI, A.H.T. (ed.) (1971) *Erasmus: Praise of Folly*, trans. B. Radice, Harmondsworth, Penguin.

LOGAN, G.M. et al. (eds) (1995) *More: Utopia*, Cambridge, Cambridge University Press.

MILLER, C.H. (ed./trans.) (1979) *Erasmus: The Praise of Folly*, New Haven and London, Yale University Press.

WOODHOUSE, J.R. (1979) 'Book four of Castiglione's *Cortegiano* – a pragmatic approach', *Modern Language Review*, vol. 74, pp.62–8.

Anthology and Reader sources

Plato, Socrates Second Speech from *Phaedrus*: *Phaedrus; and the seventh and eighth letters*, trans. and intro. W. Hamilton, Penguin Classics, Harmondsworth, 1977, pp.46–58, 61–3, 65. (Anthology, no. 13)

Marsilio Ficino, Commentary on Plato's *Phaedrus*: *Marsilio Ficino and the Phaedran Charioteer*, ed. and trans. M.J.B. Allen, Center for Medieval and Renaissance Studies, University of California, Los Angeles, 1981, pp.82–6 (English text only). (Anthology, no. 14)

Lorenzo Valla, *Of the True and False Good*: (i), (ii) and (iii) *On Pleasure: De Voluptate [Of the True and the False Good]*, ed. M. Lorch, trans. A. Kent Hiett, M. Lorch, Albaris Books Inc., New York, 1977, pp.49–65, 73–7, 91, 121–3, 133–37, 167, 235–7, 259–65, 269–79, 299–301 (English text only). (Anthology, no. 15)

Jill Kraye, The transformation of Platonic Love in the Italian Renaissance: Jill Kraye, 'The transformation of Platonic Love in the Italian Renaissance' in *Platonism and the English Imagination*, ed. Anna Baldwin and Sarah Hutton, Cambridge University Press, Cambridge, 1994, Chapter 8, pp. 76–85. (Reader, no. 6)

Baldassare Castiglione, from *The Courtier*: *The Courtier*, trans. and intro. G. Bull, Penguin Classics, London, 1976, pp.288–9, 291–5, 301–2, 324–8, 333–40. (Anthology, no. 16)

Desiderus Erasmus, *The Praise of Folly*: (i) Desiderius Erasmus, *The Praise of Folie*, trans. Sir Thomas Chaloner (1520–65), ed. C.H. Miller, EETS, OUP, 1965, pp.3–6. (ii) Desiderius Erasmus, *The Praise of Folly*, ed. and trans. C.H. Miller, Yale University Press, New Haven and London, 1979, pp.17–23, 87–93, 136–8. (Anthology, no. 17)

Letizia Panizza, Valla's *De voluptate ac de vero bono* [Of the True and False Good] and Erasmus' *Stultitiae Laus* [Praise of Folly]: Reviewing Christian Ethics: Letizia Panizza, 'Valla's *De Voluptate ac vero bono* and Erasmus' *Stultitiae Laus*: Reviewing Christian Ethics, Erasmus of Rotterdam Society Yearbook 15, 1995, pp.1–25. (Reader, no. 7)

Thomas More, from *Utopia*, Book II: (i) and (ii) *Utopia*, Latin text and English translation, eds G.M. Logan, R.M. Adams, C.H. Miller, Cambridge University Press, Cambridge, 1995, pp.159–69, 185–97 (English text only). (Anthology, no. 18)

CHAPTER SIX

Machiavelli's *Prince*: the dilemma of Italian politics

BY LUCILLE KEKEWICH

Objectives

The objectives of this chapter are that you should:

- further develop your skills in reading and analysing historical texts;
- be able to describe the political situation in Italy and its interaction with the rest of Europe from the late Middle Ages to the early sixteenth century;
- understand how ideas about good government, inherited from ancient and medieval thinkers, developed during the Renaissance;
- read *The Prince* and be able to explain how it relates to other contemporary works concerned with good government;
- be able to describe the impact of the political ideas generated in Italy on the rest of Europe;
- engage with the various historical interpretations of the significance of Machiavelli's works.

Introduction

> One ... should admire those who know how to govern a kingdom, not those who, without knowing how, actually govern one.

> (Machiavelli, 1970, p.94)

The career and writings of Niccolò Machiavelli (1469–1527) coincide exactly with a particularly volatile period in the history of Europe. In this chapter we will discuss his interaction with that period, both as a politician and a writer, principally through a close reading of *The Prince*. In doing this we will also address the great dilemma of Italian politics at that time, that is, how strong, stable government could be achieved without sacrificing the republican inheritance. So far much of this book has been concerned with interpretation: what Burckhardt and his successors thought about the Renaissance and how humanists and philosophers interpreted the past, defined the present and anticipated the future. Here we will look first at the political situation in Italy which, it is suggested, gave rise to a new way of looking at how good government could be achieved. Next, the traditional Christian moral code of political conduct will be contrasted with the ideas which culminated in the writings of Machiavelli and his contemporaries in the early sixteenth century. Finally, the impact of Machiavelli's ideas on later generations will be assessed.

From the early nineteenth century, when political thought became a subsidiary discipline for historians and political scientists, there has been a tendency to assume that it was fairly autonomous. After a brief look at the life and times of the 'great thinker' under consideration, the scholar set about describing and analysing his ideas. The treatment of Machiavelli by Burckhardt is an example of this approach (1990, pp.19–97). Although most writers did cover the influence of scholarly tradition, they were disinclined to dwell on the effects of government structures, propaganda and political tensions. Historians writing during the Renaissance, such as Leonardo Bruni, were probably largely to blame for this: they tended to shun anything that seemed trivial or squalid in their narratives and emphasized the importance of noble deeds and lofty sentiments (see Chapter 3). As the study of political ideas in their own right emerged in the nineteenth century, this attitude was perpetuated in the cult of the 'great thinker' and its rejection of the possibility that innovative thought could be the product of political circumstances. The continued importance of the art of rhetoric meant that it was a conscious aim of historians to write elegant, persuasive prose and this was much easier to achieve with elevated subject-matter.

In Chapter 3 you encountered the work of Hans Baron, who in the 1940s adopted a different approach. He still presented men like Bruni and Coluccio Salutati as great writers, but insisted that the times in which they lived and the impact of political events on the development of their ideas were of crucial importance. For instance, he saw the threat to Florence from the autocratic Milanese regime as instrumental in producing Bruni's praise of republican liberty. Although Baron's interpretation has been much questioned in recent decades, it remains a useful way of approaching the dilemma of Italian politics (see the article by A. Rabil in the Reader, no. 3, discussed in Chapter 3). The work of John Pocock (1975) in the decades after the Second World War extended the possibilities for studying Renaissance political ideas by concentrating on the interaction between the use of political terms and contemporary circumstances. Quentin Skinner has used and extended that methodology for studying the thought of the early modern period (from the late fifteenth to the eighteenth

Figure 6.1 Santo di Tito, *Niccolò Machiavelli*, Palazzo Vecchio, Florence. Photo: Alinari

centuries) and has also stressed the importance of looking for continuities between the legal and scholastic writers of the late Middle Ages and Machiavelli and his circle. The concerns of these historians will set our agenda for the study of Machiavelli's *Prince* in its material and ideological context. But first the political background will be established along with the ideas it generated.

City-states, princes and the papacy

During the late Middle Ages the Italian peninsula was a microcosm of western Europe. It contained infertile areas, especially in the kingdom of Naples where most inhabitants lived by subsistence farming; rich, expansionist states like Milan; the papal territories in and around Rome; and prosperous, commercially oriented republics such as Venice and Florence. 'Italy' was simply a geographical expression, the states existing either as independent entities or ruled by foreign powers such as the Spanish state of Aragon. The possibility that the whole area might have one national identity giving it a common culture and political interest was only just beginning to emerge.

The dominant idea throughout Europe during the previous millennium was that it had been chosen by God to bear witness to the truth and supremacy of the Christian faith. Indeed Europe was often referred to as 'Christendom'. Italy enjoyed a special status because, as the seat of the Roman empire, it had been the first part of Europe to be converted, with Rome becoming the headquarters of the church hierarchy, surmounted by the pope. While this inheritance may have enhanced the status of Italy it also involved the peninsula in a series of bitter struggles which lasted for several centuries.

When the ancient Roman empire finally succumbed to the barbarian invasions of Italy in the fifth century CE, there were three claimants to its defunct powers (*imperium*). For some time the eastern part of the empire had been ruled separately by a succession of imperial families from Constantinople (Byzantium) and they regarded themselves as the heirs to the Roman empire. The same claim was made by successive northern monarchs who ruled the western part of the

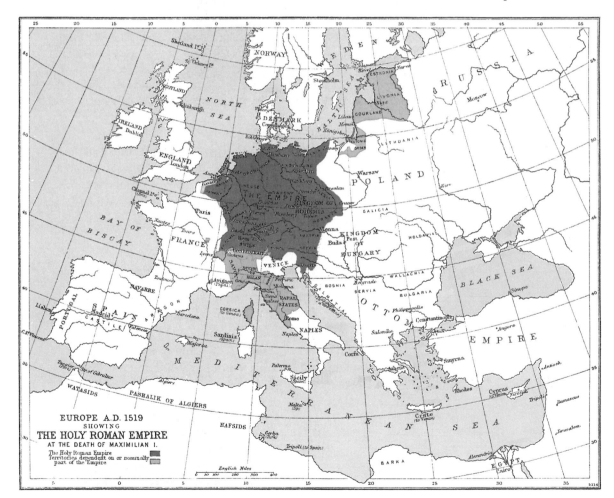

Figure 6.2 Map of the Holy Roman Empire in 1519. Reproduced and adapted from James Bryce (1968) *The Holy Roman Empire*, London, Macmillan; first published 1864

empire. The papacy also laid claim to the *imperium* through such myths as the *Donation of Constantine* (see above, pp.76–8).

Exercise Now turn to the Anthology and reread the text of the *Donation of Constantine* (no. 4).

1 What powers and privileges were claimed for the papacy?

2 Why do you think that such claims were made?

Discussion 1 The Emperor Constantine was said to have conceded to the pope 'the power of a supremacy greater than the clemency of our earthly imperial ... power'. This massive concession was then translated into a number of practical gifts: supreme rule over all Christian churches; lands and other possessions to maintain them; the Lateran palace in Rome; and all the trappings of imperial rule including the purple mantle and the diadem. The pope could admit anyone he pleased to the priesthood without interference. Constantine had apparently decided to retreat to his new city of Constantinople so that the pope could rule Rome and the western provinces of the empire directly 'under the law of the holy Roman Church'.

2 It was unlikely that even the most ambitious and worldly pope would really want or expect to exercise all the powers so optimistically listed in the *Donation*. Its main use during the Middle Ages was as a piece of case law when jurisdictional disputes arose between the empire and the papacy. These usually centred on two areas covered in the document: lordship of territory and the ordination of priests. The first carried the right to levy taxation, which was essential for the church if it was to fulfil its many functions; the second bestowed not only powers of patronage but also the chance to wield enormous influence as the clergy were the most educated element in a mainly illiterate society. ❖

The emperors in Constantinople controlled the eastern branch of the Christian church but could not assert credible claims to supremacy in the west during the Middle Ages. They were too busy fighting off the encroachments of the Saracens and, later, the Turks. The threat to the *imperium*, which the papacy aspired to exercise in western Europe, came from the northern monarchs who claimed the title 'Emperor of the Romans'. The position was elective and as the princes or electors who had the vote came from Germany and Bohemia, most of the emperors came from that area too. This presented both an opportunity and a danger to the Italians. They could petition the emperor as their overlord to come south to settle their internal disputes, but when he did so they could become embroiled in further conflicts as his allies. Involvement in war was notoriously dangerous to the preservation of citizens' liberties. During the thirteenth and fourteenth centuries many of the Italian states took sides, more or less willingly. Those who supported the papacy were called **guelfs** and imperial partisans were known as **ghibellines** (both names were Italian versions of the names of German dynasties who had been involved in the conflict). The main interest in these matters from our point of view lies not in the complexities of the long struggle but in the political ideas that they generated.

The situation in the Italian peninsula (see map, p.xii) during most of the fifteenth century was as follows: the islands of Sicily and Sardinia were ruled from Spain by the kings of Aragon, while Naples was an independent kingdom which, after a tumultuous period, fell in the middle of the century to a junior branch of the house of Aragon. Rome and much of central Italy belonged to the church, although a number of cities were virtually self-governing. Adjacent to these were small city-states, some of which were ruled by princes like those of the family of Este of Ferrara, while others were republics such as Genoa. The two largest and most important of the republics were Florence and Venice. Both were uncomfortably near the militaristic duchy of Milan, which was ruled first by the Visconti dukes and later by the Sforza. At this time the Roman imperial title almost invariably went to a member of the house of Hapsburg, a German dynasty which ruled Austria and possessed tenuous claims to other parts of northern Europe and Italy. Fortunately for the Italians the Hapsburgs had the financial resources of a duchy rather than an empire and were not readily able to engage in transalpine adventures.

The Florentine historian Francesco Guicciardini (1483–1540) was a contemporary of Machiavelli, who spent much of his career in the service of the Medici family. When they dispensed with his services he used his leisure to write *The History of Italy*, a pessimistic work in which, unlike Machiavelli, he saw the prudent rule of aristocracies as offering the best chance of stability for the Italian states.

Exercise

Read the extract from Guicciardini's *History of Italy* (Anthology, no. 19).

1 How does Guicciardini account for the peaceful condition of the Italian peninsula during most of the second half of the fifteenth century?

2 Would you describe the passage as objective?

Discussion

1 Fear seems to have been an important factor in keeping the peace. Florence recognized its limited capacities to use force and the king of Naples feared his own subjects who might support the French if they asserted their claim to the throne. Lodovico Sforza ruled Milan on behalf of his nephew who was 'of very limited intellectual capacity'

Figure 6.3 Giuliano Bugiardini, *Francesco Guicciardini*, 1531–4, oil on wood, 114.9 x 84.8 cm, Yale University Art Gallery. The Rabinowitz Collection, gift of Hannah D. and Louis M. Rabinowitz

and feared that the youth's father-in-law, the king of Naples, might intervene on his behalf. All three states were apprehensive about the intentions of the Venetians, who were known to have expansionist ambitions. The other reason given for the accord was the unique position and abilities of Lorenzo de' Medici (the Magnificent), who was related to the pope by marriage, and who was sufficiently respected by the rulers of Naples and Milan to forge a long-term alliance, which it was in all their interests to maintain.

2   Guicciardini's interpretation of the motives of the powers seems to ring true but, as a Florentine aristocrat who had served the Medici for many years, he is likely to have exaggerated the importance of the role played by Lorenzo the Magnificent. He also betrayed animosity towards Venice, a state which would have good reason to feel vulnerable to attack, especially from its neighbour Milan. ❖

Florence often occupies a privileged position in studies of the Renaissance on account of the scholars and writers, including Machiavelli, that lived and worked there. Therefore an understanding of the way in which the Florentine government functioned is essential background to a study of the ideas of Machiavelli and other contemporary thinkers. Florence had a republican form of government which was conducted by a number of elected assemblies and groups of magistrates. You should bear in mind that the word 'republic' carries a particular anti-monarchical connotation today that dates only from the late eighteenth century when first the Americans and then the French rejected their monarchs in favour of forms of government which they described as 'republics'. However, the word 'republic' is taken from the Latin *res publica*, and simply means 'public interest'. In medieval and early modern times it was used to describe princely regimes as well as non-monarchical forms of government. A further important difference in the understanding of the use of the term 'republic' now and during the Renaissance is that we usually take it as a radical kind of regime, excluding nobles and other privileged groups (an exception to this generalization is in the United States of America, where the Republican party is perceived as being more attached to the *status quo* than the Democrats). During the Renaissance, however, the idea of republican government included the participation of nobles and other elites, although debates were held about the extent of the influence they should be allowed to enjoy.

In Part 1 of *The Civilization of the Renaissance in Italy,* 'The state as a work of art', Burckhardt describes the rule of the Italian princes or 'despots' as he calls them and then goes on to describe the republics of Florence and Venice.

Exercise

Read Burckhardt's description of the Florentine republic (1990, from the final paragraph on page 65 to page 73). What were the features that he believes made it so admirable?

Discussion

'That wondrous Florentine spirit, at once keenly critical and artistically creative, was incessantly transforming the social and political condition of the state, and as incessantly describing and judging the change. Florence thus became the home of political doctrines and theories, of experiments and sudden changes, but also, like Venice, the home of statistical science, and ... the home of historical representation in the modern sense of the phrase' (pp.65–6). Burckhardt spends the rest of the section devoted to Florence exemplifying the claims made in this opening eulogy by citing the work of writers like Dante, the Villani and, at the greatest length, Machiavelli. ❖

Rather than following Burckhardt's example and looking at contemporary literature, we will take a less inspirational but, by modern standards, more historically correct approach. We will examine the political institutions of the Florentine republic and their relationship to the strength or weakness of the state.

In common with other north Italian city-states, the class structure in Florence reflected the importance of commerce to its well-being and status. Outside the boundaries of the city itself, landowners, some of them nobles, and peasants maintained feudal relationships similar to those in other parts of western Europe. Within the city, wealth and political power were distributed according to the economically determined structure of society. The most influential men, such as the Medici (see Figure 6.4), belonged to the great guilds, although members of the smaller guilds were also citizens. Citizenship gave many the right to hold office and regular office-holders formed the inner circle which ruled Florence. Power was mostly wielded by those who belonged to wealthy **patrician** families, which enjoyed longstanding rights to hold office. Members of the priesthood, whether or not they belonged to prominent citizen families could also be influential, as could well-educated men who were not native Florentines: Leonardo Bruni, for example, originally came from Arezzo. The poor, who were not members of guilds, were excluded from political power, except in times of disorder when their cries and

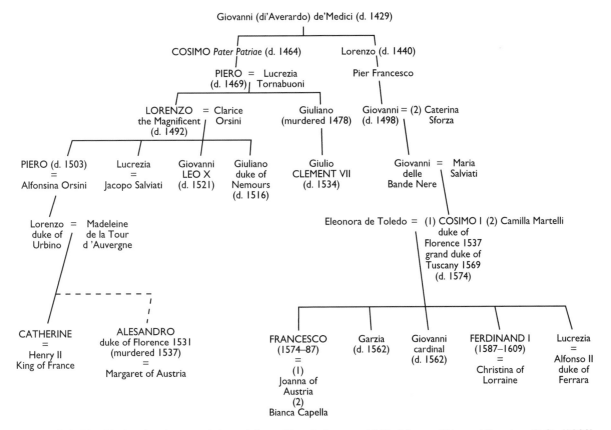

Figure 6.4 The Medici family tree. Adapted from Koenigsberger, H.G., Mosse, G.L. and Bowler, G.Q. (1989) *Europe in the Sixteenth Century*, London, Longman. Reprinted by permission of Pearson Education Ltd

blows could have the same impact as those of their masters. Women were not expected to take any part in public affairs. In fact the possibility of female political activity was never considered by Machiavelli and his contemporaries, although sometimes writers quoted past examples of the evil consequences of rule by women.

The way in which Florence was governed under the Medici was the subject of a considerable body of research undertaken by Nicolai Rubinstein (1997). Rubinstein used his extensive knowledge of the city archives to answer some of the important questions about that period. One of these questions focused on the role of the Medici in Florentine politics. From your reading of the extract from *The History of Italy* (Anthology, no. 19) you will have gathered that Guicciardini tended to attribute the course taken by political events to the intervention of the Medici. And, like him, most twentieth-century writers saw the mid and late fifteenth-century history of Florence in terms of the able manipulation of republican institutions by the Medici. This made them in practice, though not in name, the rulers of the city-state. Rubinstein realized that only a close study of those institutions and, in particular, of those who held office, would enable him to test the validity of the traditional interpretation. This study brought forth solutions to other questions about the political abilities of various members of the Medici dynasty and the extent to which their policies proved to be beneficial both to Florence and to the whole Italian peninsula. We need to have a view on these matters as they may throw light on how Machiavelli's ideas can be explained and interpreted. However, for an understanding of the Renaissance, or indeed of Machiavelli's political theories, it is not necessary to acquire a detailed knowledge of the workings of the Florentine government. This is fortunate because the workings were extremely complex and were constantly adjusted throughout the century in response to changing pressures. Indeed their very complexity was probably one of the safeguards for civil liberties: any attempt to make radical changes could be negated by the great array of assemblies, committees, restrictive procedures and regulations which were intended to achieve exactly that result. Only after the Medici regained power by force in 1530 was the whole system disbanded and citizens' liberties finally destroyed.

In 1434, when Cosimo de' Medici was recalled from a period of exile to play a major part in governing the state, there were two well-established assemblies which had to ratify new laws and taxes: the councils of the People and of the Commune. The chief magistrates responsible for policy and the regular business of government were known as the *Signoria*. The personnel of the assemblies and of the *Signoria* were changed regularly, in some cases as frequently as every two months. The

Figure 6.5 Giorgio Vasari, *The Signoria deliberate on the war against Pisa*, Salone dei Cinquecento, Palazzo Vecchio, Florence. Photo: Alinari

choice of new members was usually made by drawing lots: bags for each office were filled with the names of all those eligible and names were extracted under strict supervision. From time to time the lists of the names that went into the bags would be reviewed by formal scrutinies and some would be added and some withdrawn in accordance with the regulations. To qualify for inclusion, men had to be taxpayers and of a certain age (which varied according to the office). The age qualification was linked to the idea that it was important to take mature and measured decisions after due reflection and consultation. This also accounts for the existence of the ***pratiche*** (advisory commissions), which gave their views on any major policy developments. The records of these views are one of the most useful sources of evidence for the workings of the government and the ideas behind it. For example, in 1499 the *condottierre* Paolo Vitelli was suspected of disloyalty to Florence, but this could not be proved. To continue to employ him could lead to disaster, to ask him to defend himself would make him an enemy, so he was summarily executed. This is how the action was justified by one speaker in the ***pratica***:

> I feel one should not proceed in this case according to the usual standards of fairness, as one does not usually proceed in such a way in affairs of state.

(Gilbert, 1973, p.43)

The intricate system, which is only described here in outline, could be by-passed in times of emergency, such as enemy attack or civil unrest, by the *balia*, a special council with extensive powers. In the name of the safety of the state, it could set aside the usual provisions and create new bodies and offices which were calculated to serve factional interests. Once such interventions had been made and officials put in place who were favourable to the predominating faction, power could be prolonged indefinitely. Rubinstein's research shows that the Medici and their followers did this from time to time: consolidating their position after Cosimo's return in 1434, strengthening it again in 1458 and 1466 when internal and external pressures threatened it, and in 1478 when their rivals the Pazzi family nearly succeeded in destroying them. Only in 1494 did a combination of the inexperience of the new young Medici leader Piero (son of Lorenzo the Magnificent), and the military intervention of the French in Italy, make the usual constitutional adjustments inadequate for dealing with the crisis.

So was Guicciardini correct in assigning such a central position in the government to the Medici? Now that more is known about the workings of the Florentine government and the identity of its personnel, it is clear that the Medici did indeed dominate Florentine affairs for many decades, and there is evidence available as to how this happened. In discussing the way in which the lists of potential candidates for office were scrutinized Rubinstein writes:

> While single families or individuals are subjected to discrimination on political grounds, and while new men and families are admitted, the scrutinies [of who was eligible for office] remain firmly rooted in the oligarchical foundations of Florentine government.

(1997, p.67)

His findings in this respect were replicated by investigations of other aspects of the system and have led to the conclusion that the Medici ruled as the leading members of an oligarchy of great Florentine families. They had their enemies within this elite but its predominant desire was for self-preservation from external threat, both from the less-important citizens and the poor as well as from hostile powers which menaced the state. Provided that they were prepared to work within the traditional forms of government, the best interests of the elite were served by supporting the Medici. It was only in 1494, when Piero de' Medici showed himself incapable of protecting those interests, that he was allowed to fall from power. Despite the institutional changes which accompanied his fall and the disgrace of some of his followers, the same inner group retained its control of power. They did so because republican government had a long and respectable pedigree and had traditionally been praised as the best means of achieving virtue and justice for all its citizens.

Making sense of politics: the writers

Machiavelli's *Prince*, though original in its extreme realism and exclusive stress on expediency, is linked in its themes and problems with the late medieval and early humanist literature on the best prince.

(Kristeller, 1997, p.135)

Like his contemporaries who concerned themselves with theories of how good government could be achieved, Machiavelli was influenced by the two great political thinkers of classical antiquity, Plato and Aristotle. Their prestige as philosophers had continued to be high throughout the Middle Ages but Aristotle's works were only fully known by the end of the thirteenth century, and, in some cases, they were only available in overly literal versions. By the end of our period, however, humanists like Bruni had translated a number of works such as Plato's *Phaedo* and Aristotle's *Ethics*, Ficino had translated all Plato's dialogues, and the writings of Cicero, especially *On Duties* (*De Officiis*), were also influential and enjoyed wide currency. These works counteracted the prevailing tendency, for which the writings of St Paul and St Augustine were largely responsible, to see life in this world as an unpleasant but unavoidable prelude to the life to come. The attitude of these fathers of the church to the organization of political life was that it was a necessity which must be structured in such a way as to discourage sinful behaviour. Most churchmen believed that a hierarchical form of government, such as princely rule, was likely to be the best since it mirrored the arrangements described in the books of the Bible and in Christian tradition, that is, the Holy Trinity presiding over all the orders of angels, prophets, saints, martyrs and confessors. Only in Italy, once the seat of the Roman republic, did an alternative to princely rule survive into the Middle Ages in the shape of the city-states (or communes). While some did, from time to time, fall under the control of a prince, there was never a time when the possibility of self-government by citizen republics was completely destroyed.

By the mid thirteenth century the assumptions that princely rule was the best form of government and that it should be exercised without the constraint of legal limitations were being challenged and debated throughout western Europe. Scholastics such as Thomas Aquinas absorbed these ideas from the newly available texts of classical philosophers and developed theories which attempted to reconcile them with Christian theology. Despite this, Aquinas remained a traditional thinker in that he maintained that of Aristotle's three categories of government – monarchy, oligarchy and democracy – monarchy was the best.

Exercise

Read the extract from Aquinas's 'Commentary on the *Sentences* of Peter Lombard' (Anthology, no. 20). On what grounds did he claim that tyrannicide could be justified?

Discussion

Although Aquinas stressed the Christian's obligation to obey political authority – which derived from God – there were two cases when it could be defied. These were when political authority had been wrongfully obtained and when it was put to evil use. He said those who obtained power by violence were not true rulers. When they obtained power against the will of their subjects and when there was no possibility of making an appeal against their action to a higher power, it was lawful for tyrants to be killed. ❖

Not all thinkers went as far as Aquinas in questioning the right of rulers to impose their will, but even the most traditionally minded used treatises such as Aristotle's *Ethics* and *Politics* to prescribe the moral characteristics which would make a good ruler. This genre of literature was known as '**mirrors for princes**'. In addition, in Italy, with its small self-governing city-states, a particular kind of handbook, the *ars dictaminis*, (the art of letter writing) was produced which catered for civic needs such as the writing of official letters, propaganda and speech making, and guides were also produced for the conduct of the *podestà* (chief magistrate). The art of eloquence or rhetoric was an important element in these books and classical models were widely used to provide historical parallels and examples of wise and foolish policies. This technique was one of the precursors to that used by Renaissance humanists including Machiavelli.

The political situation in the Italian peninsula determined that writers should have another motive for questioning the traditional support given to the idea of unlimited princely power. One of its strongest sources of authority was the civil code of law which dated from the time of Emperor Justinian (527–65). It was also reflected in the provisions of the canon or church law, which owed its origins to the period when Christianity had become the official religion of the empire: its authoritarian nature suited the papacy very well. The basis of the civil code was the precept: 'what pleases the prince has the force of law'. This gave very little room for manoeuvre to Italian jurists who wished to question the rights of emperors or local princes to ignore the traditional liberties of their states. The best-known and most often cited justification for the assertion of civic liberties was produced by the jurist Bartolus of Sassoferrato (*c*.1314–57). He claimed that although the emperors were *de iure* (by right) sovereigns in northern Italy, many cities had for a long period *de facto* (in fact) ruled themselves. Prescription, or the validation of a practice by long usage, is a common argument in law. Bartolus encapsulated his new account of how authority could be exercised in the city-states in the principle: 'the people themselves constitute *sibi princeps*, an Emperor unto themselves' (Skinner, 1978, p.12).

The papacy, which was so often in conflict with the emperors over jurisdiction, was usually quick to lend its support to the city-states. Yet such support was not given freely, and, by the end of the thirteenth century, it seemed to contemporaries that much of central and northern Italy was falling under papal domination. When the Italian poet Dante Alighieri (1265–1321) was exiled from Florence by the *guelf* faction, his response was to write the *Monarchy* in support of the emperor's right to sovereignty, even though this would simply replace one great power with another. The formula offered by the *ghibelline* Marsiglio of Padua (*c*.1275– *c*.1342) was more profitable for republicans: in his *Defender of Peace* he suggested the transfer of the prerogatives for exercising the functions of a lay government, claimed by the papacy, to the highest civil authority. This could benefit the emperor where he enjoyed supreme power, but in practice such a system would usually serve the interests of self-governing city-states.

The work of early writers such as Bartolus and Marsiglio is seen by Skinner (1978) as an example of the 'civic consciousness' which Baron (1966) claimed as a characteristic of early Italian humanism. These writers thought that civil discord was the main threat to the liberty of the city republics and to avert such disasters the people themselves, through their magistrates, should be responsible for defending the peace. This was precisely how Florentine citizens, in the fifteenth century, thought their government should function. This statement begs an important question about political ideas and the influence they exercise over people's values and actions. Just because some late medieval writers questioned the extent of the sovereignty claimed by the empire, papacy and other princes, does this account for the popular tumults, diplomatic exchanges and wars which related to these issues during the Renaissance? Conversely, did theorists feel the need to account for these cataclysmic events and justify or condemn them by designing appropriate political systems? These are questions to keep in mind as you read the rest of this section and the one that follows, at the end of which some tentative suggestions will be offered. They have to be tentative as there is no prospect of achieving a definitive solution to the problem. In the meantime some evidence will be discussed, most of it drawn from the writings of Machiavelli. We also need to consider the circumstances of the political writers: whether they spent their lives remote from practical government or were directly involved in it may have some bearing on the issue.

Otium (leisure) and *negotium* (business) have been contrasting ways of life since people with the means and education to choose between them have existed: the dilemma of this choice already preoccupied writers in the ancient world. Today we take certain images and situations as emblematic of escape from pressing affairs and crowded cities, perhaps studies furnished with antiques, wide empty landscapes or secluded gardens. For many people these do not simply represent holidays and leisure pursuits but the opportunity to reflect upon personal preoccupations, to study, to

Figure 6.6 Anon., *Scholar at his lectern in a library*. Mary Evans Picture Library

extend experience and to re-evaluate attitudes. Men of the Renaissance had similar feelings about the merits of a calm and remote situation, divorced from worldly cares. Women had a rather different problem since few had the opportunity to play a part in public life: for them the best escape from domestic cares was offered by the conventual life. In both cases personal preoccupations would usually be expressed in terms of a quest for a better spiritual life. In the prevailing Christian ethos anything else would have seemed unacceptably self-indulgent. The search for knowledge, however, could and did serve secular as well as religious purposes. By the time of Petrarch classical writers were invoked to praise and justify the *otium* enjoyed by scholars. And in the late sixteenth century, Michel de Montaigne was to show in his *Essays* what an individual could achieve by solitary study (see Book 3 in this series, Chapter 8).

While the values accepted in the Middle Ages, still dominated by those of St Augustine and St Paul with their dislike of the material world, accorded well with the notion of *otium*, it was an inappropriate goal for humanists. Salutati, Poggio and Bruni were deeply involved in *negotium*, the affairs of state. During the violent upheavals of the fifteenth century the worst thing that could happen to a disgraced citizen, who was not actually killed, was to be sent into exile, away from the civic spaces, the churches, town halls and piazzas where political life was lived and individuals could achieve power, wealth, and fame.

Humanists constantly made comparisons between the high standards of civic behaviour and the greatness enjoyed by ancient Rome and dwelt on the possibilities presented for similar achievements in contemporary republics. The virtuous citizen should not hold himself aloof from affairs but should seek office or military service in order to do his duty to his state. Included in this definition of good citizenship was the need to subdue smaller cities to which the state held a claim and, if possible, to expand at the expense of neighbouring states. This aspect of an ideology which favoured the values of the ancient Roman empire, was, however, directly opposed to the need for internal stability, which Guicciardini had identified as the key to the peaceful condition of Italy in the second part of the fifteenth century.

Exercise

Writers on good government in fifteenth-century Italy combined several traditions in their work. Based on what you have read so far in this chapter, suggest what they might be.

Discussion

They combined their knowledge of classical authorities such as Plato, Aristotle and Cicero with the Christian scholastic tradition, which saw government as hierarchical and monarchical. Since the thirteenth century, however, some thinkers, while adhering to those two sources of authority, had suggested that there should be limitations to the exercise of power. Thomas Aquinas thought tyrants should not necessarily be obeyed if they violated the Christian moral code and legists like Bartolus of Sassoferrato and Marsiglio of Padua vindicated the rights of the citizens of Italian states on the grounds of prescription. By the early fifteenth century a heightened awareness of Italy's cultural and moral heritage from the ancient Roman republic led humanist writers like Bruni to link political regeneration with the emulation of its customs and achievements. ❖

The distinctive nature of Italian political thought, at least in the early Renaissance, can best be demonstrated if it is contrasted with the kind of treatises that were being written in other parts of western Europe at the same time. Although many of these recognized that a ruler was limited by the demands of the Christian moral code and by the laws and customs of his subjects, the conclusion that was drawn from this situation in most of the 'mirrors for princes' literature was that the ruler must seek to acquire the virtues that would enable him to govern well. Most highly valued of these were the cardinal virtues: justice, prudence, temperance and fortitude. Other virtues were also recommended but these four were thought to be particularly princely and many works were structured around them. Clerics were still active in producing such treatises, Nicolas de Clamanges in France and the poet John Lydgate in England, for example. The fallacy inherent in their approach was readily apparent since both the recipients of their good advice, Charles VI in France and Henry VI in England, turned out to be insane.

An alternative available to Italian humanist writers, many of whom lived in republics rather than kingdoms, was to advocate the pursuit of a different kind of virtue for secular rather than religious purposes. This quality, which was greatly valued by Machiavelli, has a different meaning from the traditional Christian 'virtue'. To distinguish it we will use the Italian term *virtù* which was derived from the Latin word *virtus* which means 'strength'. While Burckhardt was not much concerned with the term itself, he recognized its manifestations and believed that it was an essential component in the success of the Renaissance. Of Leon Battista Alberti he wrote: 'an iron will pervaded and sustained his whole personality; like all the great men of the Renaissance', adding, 'men can do all things if they will' (1990, p.103).

So *virtù* signified the effective exercise of the will, but this should not be done for evil or selfish purposes, unless a public good arose out of such actions. The goal should typically be the pursuit of civic benefits, including creative enterprises (which often involved court patronage), good government and military triumphs over the enemies of the state. Although most writers assumed that they were working within a Christian context, and even paid lip service to the needs of the church, the ethos was essentially secular, grounded on the pagan values of ancient Rome. In his 'Oration at the funeral of Nanni Strozzi', Bruni declared:

> our commonwealth requires *virtù* and *probitas* [honesty] in its citizens. Whoever has these qualifications is thought to be of sufficiently noble birth to participate in the government of the republic ... This, then, is true liberty ... to enjoy equality among citizens before the law and in the participation in public office.

> (Baron, 1966, p.419)

The word 'Fortune', like 'virtue', was another pagan concept which survived from classical times but in this case its meaning did not change. What did change was the attitude people adopted towards the disasters or benefits which it could bring them. Stoic philosophers like Seneca believed that they should be regarded with indifference as trivial matters in comparison to humanity's quest for equanimity through the achievement of wisdom. For Christians in the Middle Ages, by contrast, happiness was a gift from God and misfortune a sign of his displeasure; but old habits died hard and many authors

Figure 6.7 Marcantonio Raimondi, *Herculean virtue destroying vicious Fortune*, engraving. *Journal of the Warburg Institute*, vol. 1, 1937–8, plate 52A. Reproduced by permission of the Warburg Institute, University of London

still wrote in terms of the favours or displeasure of Fortune: '*O Fortuna, velut Luna, statu variabilis*' (O Fortune, changeable like the Moon) (from *Carmina Burana*, anon., twelfth century).

A popular illustration in European books, often those with a moral purpose, was the goddess Fortune turning her wheel so that her favourites rose to the top and those she rejected fell to the bottom. Humanist writers on government questioned the use of behaving with *virtù* if the operation of Fortune or chance could ruin the most public spirited exercises of the will. The rational response was to invoke the cardinal virtue personified as Prudence: with her help it should be possible to anticipate and even overcome the vagaries of Fortune. This was how the Neapolitan Giovanni Pontano responded to Charles VIII's invasion of 1494. In his treatises on *Fortune* and *Prudence* he suggested that the latter could conquer the former by daring or ingenious courses of action. This was later to be a line of action favoured by Machiavelli when he faced the potentially disastrous interventions of Fortune. Some political writers hoped knowledge of astrology (the influence of the planets on human conduct), might help to control Fortune, although Machiavelli had little time for such superstition (De Grazia, 1989, p.65).

By the mid fifteenth century clerics no longer monopolized literary debates about good government. Even in northern Europe nobles like Hughes de Lannoy could write political treatises for the dukes of Burgundy, and a lawyer, Sir John Fortescue, did the same for the English kings. They had no difficulty in detaching Christian ethics from the consideration of the best policies for their states, yet, until recently, the contents of their works and those of their southern equivalents such as Bruni and Pontano were not well known. This may account for the great impact that the writings of Machiavelli had upon Burckhardt and his preoccupation with the 'state as a work of art'.

Violent changes and deep thought, 1494–1530

Fortune has determined that since I don't know how to talk about the silk business or the wool business or about profits and losses, I must talk about the government; I must either make a vow of silence or discuss that.[1]

(Gilbert, 1989, pp.900–1)

[1] From Machiavelli's letter to Francesco Vettori, 9 April 1513.

The political background

The years 1494 to 1530 were a dangerous and volatile period in the history of the Italian peninsula. The first of the French invasions was followed by other major interventions by the German emperor and the kings of Spain and France. The Medici and the Sforza dynasties fell from power, although both were restored with external support. By 1530 only Venice and Genoa remained as independent republics and they survived by placating the great foreign powers that controlled most of Italy. Florence, which had possessed such intellectual and artistic prestige during the previous century and whose diplomacy was perceived to have promoted peace and stability during its final decades, proved an impotent commentator on the processes which were taking place. The city's main spokesman for posterity was Machiavelli, yet, because of one little treatise that he produced among a mass of worthy reports, histories and writings on military affairs, his testimony was suspect for subsequent generations. 'Machiavellian' is still a term of abuse applied to duplicitous politicians and others who achieve their goals by cunning. By the end of this chapter you should understand why Machiavelli gained this reputation and will be able to decide if such notoriety is justified.

Exercise

Read Anthony Grafton's introduction to *The Prince* (Bull, 1999, pp.xiii–xvii), which gives an outline of Machiavelli's career. Then, concentrating on pages xx (final paragraph) to xvii, explain why the work and its author have been so harshly criticized since it was written.

Discussion

Machiavelli had served the Florentine republic and yet *The Prince* explained how an absolute ruler could take over such a state. He expressed admiration for the brutal tactics which were required to establish and safeguard the authority of a prince and many have seen this as deliberately advocating a policy of immorality. In this regard *The Prince* presented a sharp contrast to previous books of advice which had recommended that successful rulers should practice the Christian virtues. Instead Machiavelli advised that rulers must adapt their conduct to different circumstances rather than following the guidance of set moral criteria: 'reasons of state' must be their supreme justification. ❖

A number of questions are being raised in this chapter and evidence can be found in *The Prince* to answer them. You may find it useful to note down the questions as headings and keep them in sight as we continue with this study of Machiavelli. Then as evidence pertinent to a particular question is considered you can make a note under the relevant heading. The questions are:

1   Is Machiavelli genuinely advocating autocratic government, or is *The Prince* a satire on princes behaving badly and a ploy to discredit that form of government?

2   To what extent was *The Prince* innovative – did it really represent a departure from traditional thought about politics?

3   What is the relationship between Machiavelli's *Prince* and his works, such as the *Discourses,* that are republican in tone?

4   Was Machiavelli trying to create a new system of government or was he reacting to existing circumstances by suggesting a rationale for current political realities?

5   To what extent were Machiavelli's ideas indebted to humanism?

In 1494, after the flight of Piero de' Medici from Florence, several of the councils and committees which had assisted in his exercise of power were abolished and a Great Council was established. This was composed of about 3,500 citizens whose families had the right to hold office, dating back to the time of their great-grandfathers. The Council's main functions were to vote on taxation (without discussion, it merely rubber-stamped decisions), and to choose the members of a series of executive committees. In a study of the constitutional significance of this period, R. Pesman Cooper (1981) echoes the conclusions drawn by Rubinstein about the hegemony of the Medici. He found that much of the real power continued to be exercised by a small group of wealthy guild members. Only about 1,000 members of the Great Council were habitual office holders and they formed an inner circle which conducted the government and employed civil servants to assist it. Apart from men who had been prominent Medici supporters, very few of the 'top' families lost their influence under the new regime. A new 'Hall of the Great Council' was built in the Palazzo Vecchio (Old Palace), the city hall, to accommodate up to 1,000 members of the council at one time. Frescoes by Leonardo de Vinci and Michelangelo, commemorating the victories of the Florentine republic, were designed to decorate the walls.

During the first three years of government without the Medici the degree of continuity with the past was masked by the phenomenon of Girolamo Savonarola (1452–98), a charismatic Dominican friar whose prophecies of divine retribution against the rulers of the Italian peninsula seemed to be fulfilled with the French invasion. He enjoyed a large following among all orders of society and presented a threat to the inner circle of government. He castigated the papacy for its worldliness, at a time when the Florentines were trying to preserve peaceful relations with it. He also preached to the common people as if they, as well as their betters, were capable of hearing the voice of God and interpreting it through political action:

> this government of the people is more natural and proper to you than all the others. So I want to tell you that although the government of the Hebrews was popular because the people ruled and the judge didn't command but advised, yet it could be called royal because it depended on the mouth of one person, that is God's.[2]

> (Brown, 1988, pp.61–2)

This may seem pretty tame stuff at the beginning of the twenty-first century, but five hundred years ago it would have sounded like subversive rabble-rousing. Anxieties were not allayed by Savonarola's fanatical followers who prowled round the city as self-appointed guardians of morality, castigating anyone who infringed their strict moral code. Machiavelli, whose attitude to Savonarola was ambiguous, gave an account of two of the friar's sermons. Although he respected Savonarola as a good man who was closely identified with republican liberty, his writings recommended amoral behaviour which negated the friar's ethical system. By 1498 Savonarola had made one criticism of the papacy too many and his followers were unable to save him from arrest, condemnation and execution (Plate 11). This served to demonstrate the limits that were set on the republic's precious liberty and the danger presented by Rome, where Giovanni, the brother of Piero de' Medici, was an influential cardinal. This situation had enabled the friar's enemies among the ruling elite to use a papal decree of excommunication to bring about his downfall.

Three weeks after the death of Savonarola, on 19 June 1498, Machiavelli was appointed second chancellor (secretary) to the Florentine republic. It is clear from his father's account book and the early official reports which survive that he had received a good education, an advantage for entering a service where humanists were valued (both Poggio and Bruni had been first chancellors). Bartolomeo Scala, who held that post for many years and had recently died, had been an associate of Machiavelli's father (Scala had cast him as an interlocutor in a dialogue on law which he had written), and the young man's preferment could have been due to his patronage. As Robert Black has observed:

> In his education, in his literary interests, in his technical command of language and style, Machiavelli was a fully-fledged humanist when he entered the chancery.

> (1990, p.75)

---

[2] From Savonarola's sermon on Ruth 1.1.

Figure 6.8 Pinturicchio and followers, *Pope Alexander VI kneeling*, detail from the *Resurrection of Christ*, Sale Borgia, Palazzo Vaticano, Rome. Photo: Alinari

Machiavelli's family had been active citizens for several generations but they were not rich or particularly influential, so the appointment would have been welcome. He serviced various committees, especially the **Ten of War** whose main function was to avoid expensive and dangerous military entanglements. He was also sent on numerous diplomatic missions and compiled detailed reports, not only on what took place but also on the social, political and economic conditions in some of the states he visited. These provide excellent evidence of some of the influences which must have contributed to the formation of Machiavelli's political ideas, ideas that he was unable to set down systematically at that time because he was far too involved in public affairs (*negotium*). His other preoccupation grew in importance as the external and internal threats to the stability of the republic increased. He believed that a citizen *militia* (armed force mustered for the defence of their own country) would provide much better protection than a mercenary army led by unscrupulous *condottieri*.

Even if he had not attained such notoriety through his political writings, Machiavelli's prolific output of reports and letters would have been an important source for historians of this period. His abilities constantly put him at the centre of Florentine affairs and were fully recognized by the Chief Magistrate Piero Soderini (1452–1522), whose title was *Gonfaloniere di Iustitia,* literally 'standard bearer

Figure 6.9 Raphael, *Cesare Borgia*, Galleria Borghese, Rome. Photo: Alinari-Anderson

of Justice', and who held office from 1502 until the return of the Medici in 1512. Throughout this period the Florentine government was trying to avoid irrevocable commitment to any of the changing alignments of Italian and foreign powers. The French had traditionally been their friends and were credited by many with the removal of the Medici. However, they were not proving helpful in the campaigns to recover Pisa, which had managed to regain its independence from Florence during the last days of Piero de' Medici's regime (the republic's ideals of liberty did not extend to such subject territories). To complicate affairs further, Cesare Borgia (1476–1507, duke of Valentino from 1498), the son of Pope Alexander VI (1492–1503), was waging a belligerent and effective series of minor wars to subdue all the papal states to obedience.

Technically much of central Italy, including the prosperous Romagna, should have been ruled directly by the pope, but over time many city-states had become either self-governing or controlled by despots. Florence was terrified of Borgia's ambition, backed as he was by the strength of the papacy, and wished to divert him from its borders. Even if Borgia did not aspire to conquer the state, the wealth of Florence made it a potential victim of blackmail. Despite all this you will see Borgia quoted as a role model several times in *The Prince*, so what was the extent of Machiavelli's practical knowledge of his capabilities?

Exercise

Read Burckhardt's account of Borgia (1990, pp.86–90) and an extract from Machiavelli's 'Reports on a mission to Cesare Borgia' (Anthology, no. 21). What is your view of the conclusions that Burckhardt and Machiavelli drew about Borgia?

Discussion

Burckhardt painted a very grim picture of the duke indeed, but on what grounds? While most of the evidence does seem to have been based on contemporary records we could question whether or not Burckhardt's sources were reliable (for example, the Venetian ambassador, p.88 and Corio and Malpiro, notes 27 and 28, p.358). But a further aspect of the narrative undermines Burckhardt's credentials as a historian: his value judgements. Phrases such as 'devilish wickedness', 'the great criminal' and 'insane thirst for blood' are disturbing to modern scholars. Not only do they seem misplaced in a serious study but they call in to question the judgement of the person who wrote them.

Modern readers may find Machiavelli's account of Borgia chilling, especially as we know that Machiavelli was quite favourable to his subject. The way in which the blame for difficulties in relations with Florence was thrown on Borgia's Roman enemies (some of whom Borgia later murdered), the half-placatory, half-threatening tone Borgia adopted and the boasting about his powerful friends were menacing diplomatic ploys. At the end of the letter of 9 October 1502, Machiavelli approvingly remarked that Borgia reviewed 'six thousand infantry selected from his cities'. The success of Borgia's military strategy was one of the reasons why Machiavelli so persistently advocated the use of *militia* rather than mercenaries. A positive evaluation of Borgia is also given at the beginning of the letter of 27 October 1502. At this time Borgia was at the height of his power and no one could have predicted how quickly he would fall after his father's death the following year. Throughout the report Borgia's enemies were blamed for his hostility and his purposes were interpreted in a positive light, although the potential danger he posed to Florence was not ignored. Some writers have charged Machiavelli with gullibility in his diplomacy but it must be recognized that he was a relatively minor official from an unimportant family and was often given assignments where he lacked the authority to conclude business. Machiavelli's appreciation of the limitations of his position was clearly expressed at several points including in the last letter of 3 November 1502. ❖

The death of Alexander VI in 1503, and the succession to the papal throne of an enemy of Borgia, Julius II (1503–13), solved one problem for Florence, yet posed another. Julius was as expansionist as Borgia in his ambitions and possessed formidable diplomatic

Figure 6.10 Raphael, *Pope Julius II*, detail from Raphael room, Vatican. Photo: Alinari

capacities. These he displayed by forging the so-called Holy League, professedly to protect the church but actually to promote his domination of the Italian peninsula. Florence was uncomfortably near to some of the territories he ruled directly, thanks to the successful papal campaigns of the previous decade, and Machiavelli was again dispatched, with others, to do his best to maintain a friendly neutrality. He succeeded for a time and the French, desperate to keep their allies in Italy, finally supported the reconquest of Pisa, which was effected by *militia* from Florentine territories. This was to be the last success of Machiavelli's patron, Piero Soderini, for they both put excessive faith in the effectiveness of the *militia*. The king of Spain needed the support of Julius II for his designs on Italian territories and could easily please him by reinstating the family of the two influential Medici clerics in Florence, Giovanni and Giulio. Now read Guicciardini's account of the sack of Prato in August 1512 (Anthology, no. 22), which was the occasion of the flight of Soderini and the return of the Medici to power. This demonstrates both how unrealistic it had been to expect a citizen *militia* to stand up to seasoned professional troops and how much control the papacy could exercise in Italy as a result of its expansionist policies in the previous decade.

The most famous, although not the most important, casualty of 1512 was Machiavelli himself, who was dismissed from his post as second chancellor. Soon afterwards he was wrongly accused of involvement in an inept plot against the Medici and was imprisoned and tortured. He was soon released, but remained unemployed for nearly a decade and was forced to support himself and his large family on the meagre income from his small estate just outside Florence.

Exercise

In the Anthology (no. 23) read Machiavelli's letter to Francesco Vettori (see Figures 11–13 for photographs of Machiavelli's house and the inn he frequented). How does this description of Machiavelli's life in disgrace relate to the concepts of *otium* and *negotium*?

Discussion

The first part of the letter to Vettori could be taken as a kind of satire on the life of a man of affairs, of *negotium*; instead of writing reports and carrying out the policies of the republic, Machiavelli now caught thrushes and haggled over loads of wood. He used to visit princes, generals and popes; now he played games with artisans in the local tavern. Vettori had offered him the chance to return to Florence and seek restoration to favour, but, perhaps wisely, Machiavelli saw the dangers of making a move which could be misinterpreted. His preferred approach was to use his leisure, or *otium*, to compose *The Prince* which drew on his communion with the great minds of the past and also on his long experience as a public servant. He proposed to present it to Giuliano de' Medici in the hope it would gain him some employment, no matter how humble. Machiavelli, despite his eulogy on the pleasures of study, did not see *otium* as an ultimately satisfactory way of life but rather as a means of thwarting the vagaries of Fortune and re-engaging him in *negotium*. ❖

Figure 6.11 General view of Machiavelli's house, S. Andrea in Percussina. Photo: Index/Cantarelli

Figure 6.12 Machiavelli's study, S. Andrea in Percussina. Photo Index/Cantarelli

Figure 6.13 The inn frequented by Machiavelli, S. Andrea in Percussina. Photo: Index/Cantarelli

After the return of the Medici, government was a compromise between the republican liberties that had been enjoyed, at least by full citizens, during the past eighteen years and despotism. A pro-Medici *balia* was convened and the Great Council was abolished, but the traditional assemblies of the Commune and the People were retained along with the *Signoria*, various ruling committees and the complicated method of choosing new office holders. Cardinal Giovanni de' Medici visited Florence to oversee the reinstallation of his family and the return of their property, but he soon returned to

Rome. In 1513, on the death of Julius II, he became Pope Leo X and he lost no time in making his cousin Giulio a cardinal. Giuliano, duke of Nemours, younger brother of Leo X, had some voice in the government, but he too preferred to spend most of his time in Rome. Perversely this proved annoying to the Florentines as it showed how second class their state had become. Lorenzo, duke of Urbino (son of Piero, who had been expelled in 1494), an arrogant young man, also tended to leave the city too often for his family's good. Although his mother, Alfonsina, did as effective a job as her sex permitted in looking after their interests, republican forms could still flourish while this complex arrangement continued and no real attempt was made to suppress political discussion, provided criticism was not translated into plots to oust the Medici. Votes in the councils and committees were by no means unanimous in their support of the policies proposed by the Medici, although if their interests looked like being seriously threatened, Leo X, Giuliano or Lorenzo intervened.

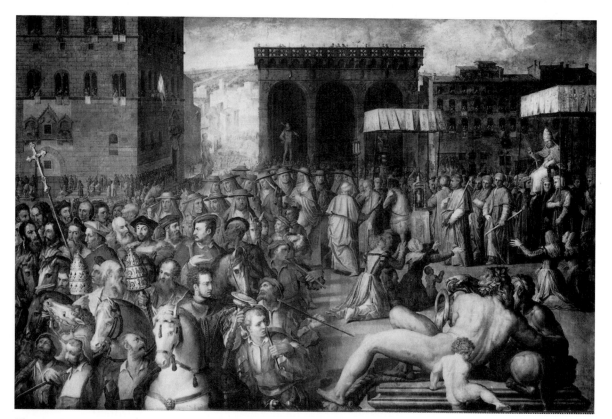

Figure 6.14 Giorgio Vasari, *Triumphal entry into Florence of Pope Leo X*, Sala di Leone X, Palazzo Vecchio, Florence. Photo: Alinari

The Prince

Machiavelli's letter to Vettori (Anthology, no. 23) indicates that he composed *The Prince* in 1513, soon after the return of the Medici to power. He states that he intends to dedicate it to Giuliano de' Medici, but he died in 1516 and the surviving version of the treatise is dedicated to his nephew Lorenzo, duke of Urbino. *The Prince* remained in manuscript form during Machiavelli's lifetime and was first published, with some other minor works, in Rome in 1532. It was composed in the Italian vernacular, a departure from tradition as most books of advice to princes were still written in Latin. Now turn to *The Prince* (Bull, 1999). The exercises that follow will guide you through a close reading of the text.

Exercise

Read the dedicatory letter to Lorenzo (pp.1–2). What strikes you about its tone and contents?

Discussion

You probably felt that the tone was sycophantic. Machiavelli grovels to Lorenzo, giving him his grandfather's title, 'Your Magnificence', and implying that he was a prince, when in fact he only became duke of Urbino a few years later. This was the usual way in which subordinates addressed their superiors, the normal language of courtiers seeking patronage. The meaning behind the conventional terms, however, was less flattering, as Machiavelli contrasted his own 'long acquaintance with contemporary affairs and a continuous study of the ancient world' with Lorenzo's inexperience. He had yet to prove himself an effective ruler and it was Machiavelli's 'urgent wish that you reach the eminence that fortune and your own accomplishments promise you'. ❖

Machiavelli carried out his promise to write his treatise in plain language and began in a manner which would have been reassuringly familiar to those who had read 'mirrors for princes'. In Chapter 1, following a model which derived from Aristotle's *Politics* and had been emulated by authoritative scholastics, he distinguished the principal types of dominion as either republics or principalities, the latter being either hereditary or new. In the first sentence of Chapter 2, Machiavelli stated that he would not be discussing republics since he had 'discussed them at length on another occasion' (p.5). This statement is of great importance to our understanding of the development of Machiavelli's political ideas. 'On another occasion' is almost certainly a reference to his much longer work, *Discourses on the First Ten Books of Titus Livy* (the *Discourses*), which was completed in about 1519. That the *Discourses* should have been written, even in part, by the end of 1513 is surprising for many reasons, and we will consider this later in the chapter when we look at Machiavelli's other writings. At the end of Chapter 2 Machiavelli gave an optimistic forecast for the survival of hereditary princes, saying that as long as they avoided 'extraordinary vices' they should be able to hold on to their territories (p.6).

Chapter 3 goes straight to the main topic of the treatise, namely, how princes could hold on to newly conquered lands (the title, 'Composite principalities', refers to new appendages to old states). According to Machiavelli, it was easier to hold lands which shared a common language and had the same customs and institutions than it was to hold those which differed in these respects. One solution to the problem of holding lands was for the prince to live in his new domains or, if that was impossible, to make settlements there. The latter expedient would avoid the need to keep expensive and unpopular garrisons, but would alienate those whose lands and houses were taken by the new inhabitants. The dispossessed, however, would be poor and scattered and would not be in a position to harm the new prince. The prince should befriend small neighbouring states and try to weaken those that were strong. The Romans observed these rules in their successful domination of Greece, but Louis XII of France did not. He allowed Spain and the papacy to profit by his activities and, as a consequence, twice lost the duchy of Milan.

In Chapter 4 Machiavelli drew a distinction between states in which the prince ruled alone, supported by servants whom he had appointed and who could easily be dismissed, and states where the prince ruled with nobles who did not depend on him for their rank, wealth or prestige. The Turkish empire was an example of the first kind of regime and the kingdom of France an example of the second. He felt that it was difficult for princes to conquer the former kind of state as they would receive no encouragement from its subjects, but, once conquered, such states would be easy to hold. In the second case, disaffected nobles might readily invite a prince to invade, but, if he did so, he would encounter endless difficulties in subduing that same nobility. Machiavelli suggested in Chapter 5 that once a principality had been conquered there were three possible ways of holding it: by devastating it, by living there in person or by allowing it to keep its own laws. The most effective method was devastation and several classical examples were cited to support this. States which had already been ruled by a prince would be more amenable to the new regime but, Machiavelli concluded:

> in republics there is more life, more hatred, a greater desire for revenge; the memory of their ancient liberty does not and cannot let them rest; in their case the surest way is to wipe them out or to live there in person.
>
> (p.17)

This sounds very much like a warning to the absentee Medici family who aroused much resentment, even among their supporters, by their preference for Rome.

Up to this point in the treatise contemporary readers would not have found any radical departure from the traditional description of different forms of government developed in classical times and revived by scholastic writers. Some of the sentiments were brutal, but they were no worse than the discussions in the *pratiche*, discussions which, as in the case of the unfortunate Vitelli, would relate to real rather than hypothetical situations. The rest of *The Prince* was more innovative and covered the following subjects: the different means of acquiring principalities (Chapters 6–8); the nature of certain kinds of principalities (Chapters 9–11); military organization (Chapters 12–14); and the qualities princes should possess and devices to help them govern (Chapters 15–23). Concluding the treatise, Chapters 24 to 26 introduced a wider view of contemporary political affairs culminating in a rhetorical, visionary appeal for a prince to liberate Italy from the barbarians.

Exercise

Read Chapters 6 to 9 (pp.17–34) and answer the questions that follow.

1 What did Machiavelli believe were the best ways of securing new principalities?

2 Comment on the role of Fortune and *virtù* (usually translated by Bull as 'prowess').

Discussion

1 The most successful new princes were invariably those who had considerable personal ability, men like Moses and Theseus. Many were assisted by favourable circumstances, or Fortune, but they also needed force to ensure that their regimes would last. In recent times, Savonarola had lacked the sanctions which might have ensured his survival. Able princes who relied both on Fortune and the arms of others might easily acquire a new territory but would find it hard to keep, since those who had helped them would not be reliable. Francesco Sforza of Milan was successful and Cesare Borgia was a model for a new prince: he did all the right things to build up a

principality in the Romagna but the double ill-fortune of the death of his father, Alexander VI, and his own serious illness deprived him of everything. It was also possible to win principalities by criminal means. For example, Agathocles, king of Syracuse, rose to power by the use of violence 'inflicted once for all' and Oliverotto held Fermo for a year by nefarious actions. Once in power, a prince should distribute his favours gradually so that they were fully appreciated. Finally Machiavelli addresses the case of constitutional principalities where a private citizen was elevated by the favour of the people or the nobles. The latter constituted an unreliable and self-seeking basis for authority but 'a prince who builds his power on the people ... will be found to have established his power securely' (pp.33–4). Their faithfulness could best be insured by keeping them dependent on his authority: magistrates who were allowed too much licence could turn against him in a crisis.

2   Fortune often formed a necessary component of a prince's success but he also had to have the ability to take advantage of its benefits. This ability or prowess was the same as *virtù*, but even a combination of fortune and ability could not ensure a prince's survival, as in the case of Borgia. Machiavelli had more to say on these matters later in the treatise, but he clearly felt that Borgia lacked *virtù* when he foolishly made the decision to allow Julius II to become pope. ❖

The advice given by Machiavelli in Chapter 9 must surely have been intended specifically for the attention of the Medici. As a public servant under a republican government that was dominated by an inner clique of rich citizens Machiavelli had flourished, but the flaw in the situation for Florence was its weakness in international power politics. Now both a brother and a nephew of Pope Leo X were available to achieve in northern and central Italy what Borgia had so narrowly missed: the creation of a strong, united state which could assume the leadership in the Italian peninsula. However, Machiavelli's view of how this could be achieved – a citizen prince ruling with the support of his people – is somewhat simplistic. In his account of government in early sixteenth-century Florence, H.C. Butters (1985) describes the difficulties the Medici experienced in getting their way even in minor matters. For example, Antonio Gualterotti was a rich citizen who was opposed to the Medici. Lorenzo wished to humble him by ensuring that he lost a suit which was being pressed against him by some other citizens, who claimed that he owed them a large sum of money. It took requests to three successive *Gonfaloniers* over a six month period, 1514/15, before Lorenzo's wish was granted and those who had failed to co-operate with him were not punished.

Machiavelli was not the first to pride himself on his practical approach to political reality. About 20 years earlier in his *On Rulers and on the Duties of a Good Prince* Diomede Carafa had written:

> you should take thought of those who, you hope, would aid you in need, as much as of those whose disposition toward you is in doubt, and certainly about those who are neither friends nor enemies ... those are to be thought of more value to you whose fortunes are joined with yours than those who are bound to you by kindred or any other necessary link, especially if from your calamities some advantage can come to them.

> (Gilbert, 1968, p.57)

In Chapter 10 Machiavelli went over some of the details that princes should consider when assuming power, such as the need to build adequate fortifications to resist attack. He was at his most cold-hearted in this respect: the countryside should be sacrificed to an adversary and all resources put into making the city strong. The consequent devastation would soon be over and would bind his subjects more securely to the prince. Chapter 11 continued with the line of argument that he had started in his analysis of constitutional principalities, and again was aimed specifically at the Medici. The subject was ecclesiastical principalities and after a pious first paragraph, 'they are sustained by higher powers which the human mind cannot comprehend' (p.37), he got down to business. He reverted to one of his favourite subjects, the *virtù* of Alexander VI and his son, and showed how they had turned the papacy from impotency to become a major power. This good work had been continued and improved upon by Julius II. Leo X had then found the papacy in a strong position and it was to be hoped that he would 'make it very great and revered' (p.37).

In Chapters 12 to 14 of *The Prince*, Machiavelli deals with military organization. This is another subject close to his heart and it occurs not just in this treatise but in his other major works, including *The Art of War*, as well as in his reports and letters. He first launches into a condemnation of the contemporary practice in Italy of employing mercenaries (troops usually led by *condottieri*). He describes mercenaries as 'disunited, thirsty for power, undisciplined, and disloyal' (p.39) and uses extended anecdotal evidence to illustrate the evils which arose from using them. According to Machiavelli, mercenaries so ordered affairs that: 'they might escape both exertion and danger: and as a result they have captained Italy into slavery and ignominy' (p.43). Auxiliaries (foreign troops called in to assist a prince) were almost as bad. 'You are left in the lurch if they are defeated, and in their power if they are victorious' (p.44). The conclusion is drawn that it is much the best thing for a prince to employ his own forces, which Machiavelli defines as the prince's own subjects or an army of citizens (*militia*) or dependants. Borgia had graduated from auxiliaries via mercenaries to using only his own soldiers with spectacular results. In Chapter 14 the prince is advised to practise the art of war assiduously, as nothing is more important for the extension and defence of his state. Francesco Sforza's conquest of Milan and its subsequent loss by his son were a recent illustration of this maxim. The prince should keep in good physical shape and constantly think about the practicalities of waging war. For intellectual exercise he should study history, seeking examples of great leaders who were either successful or suffered defeat in war.

Early modern readers of this section of *The Prince* would not have found its contents particularly startling, apart perhaps from the strong emphasis put on the danger of employing mercenaries. The art of war had always been considered an important area of expertise for a prince to master and it was frequently included in 'mirrors for princes'. It was usually founded on a collection which originated from Flavius Vegetius, a late classical writer. Versions of his work had been produced throughout the later Middle Ages (one of the most popular was by Christine de Pisan). And as recently as the end of the fifteenth century Bartolomeo Sacchi (known as il Platina), in his *Principis Diatuposis*, had anticipated Machiavelli's advice:

> [A prince] should be skilful in guarding beforehand against all contingencies. He may do this easily if he has become acquainted with districts, roads, mountains, valleys and rivers.

(Gilbert, 1968, p.71)

The most controversial material in *The Prince* is in Chapters 15 to 19. It is often thought to surpass anything else suggested by Machiavelli or any other contemporary writer in cynicism and amorality. Yet the content of previous chapters has shown that many of Machiavelli's ideas were to be found in the work of earlier theorists and in the words of practical politicians. There was nothing particularly new in the idea that *virtù* could combat the evil effects of Fortune or that reasons of state could override conventional standards of morality.

Exercise

Read Chapters 15 to 19 (pp.49–67). Why do you think that the ideas in these chapters have often been viewed as particularly objectionable?

Discussion

You will recall that princes were traditionally believed to rule well if they possessed the four cardinal virtues, justice, prudence, temperance and fortitude, and their associated qualities. Machiavelli warned his readers that this system was about to be stood on its head:

> the gulf between how one should live and how one does live is so
> wide that a man who neglects what is actually done for what should
> be done moves towards self-destruction rather than self-preservation
> ... if a prince wants to maintain his rule he must be prepared not to
> be virtuous ...

(pp.49–50)

Machiavelli was using the term 'virtuous' here in its conventional
Christian sense and in the following chapters he demonstrated that
the practice of the cardinal virtues and their associated qualities,
while desirable, could be harmful to the prince and his subjects.
Princely generosity was traditionally valued as an attribute of the
virtues of prudence and justice but Machiavelli warned of its
dangers, especially if goods belonging to subjects were taken to
enable the ruler to give freely. It was only wise to be generous when
using the possessions of conquered foreigners, otherwise it was
better to risk the shame of being called a miser than the hatred
incurred by the appropriation of other citizens' goods.
Compassionate behaviour was an aspect of the virtue of justice, but a
new prince could not afford to practise it. It was often necessary to
gain a reputation for cruelty and to be feared as long as this did not
cause the prince to be hated:

> [for he] can always avoid hatred if he abstains from the property of
> his subjects and citizens and from their women ... men sooner forget
> the death of their father than the loss of their patrimony.

(p.54)

Although it was praiseworthy for princes to honour their word and
to be straightforward in their dealings, it was sometimes prudent to
combine the cunning of a fox with the might of a lion. They should
appear to be compassionate, faithful, honest and pious, but if the
need arose they should know how to abandon these virtues and
practise their opposing vices instead. They should shun undignified
vices such as fickleness, frivolity, effeminacy and cowardice and could
afford to cultivate the virtues of justice and fortitude: provided they
possessed the good will of their people they had no reason to fear
conspiracies. To illustrate these arguments Machiavelli uses the lives
of some of the later Roman emperors to show that scorn and hatred
could be equally fatal to rulers who did not possess sufficient *virtù* to
be effective. ❖

Even in this section of the treatise, however, Allan Gilbert has shown
that Machiavelli was not the first to expose these brutal political
realities. Rather, he was restating the ideas of previous writers in a less

circuitous fashion. His advice that princes should not alienate their subjects by the consequences of prodigality was close to that to be found in one of the best-known scholastic 'mirrors', Egidio Colonna's *The Rule of Princes*. Even the much condemned sentiments in Chapter 18 of *The Prince*, about the circumstances in which a prince was justified in not keeping his word, had been anticipated by Giovanni Pontano in 1490:

> It is the act of a wise man when two ills are put before him, always to choose the smaller one. Hence it is permissible for the sake of the state and of a king who is father of his people sometimes to tell falsehoods; though when time and circumstances require silence about the truth especially when the safety of the king, the kingdom and the fatherland is in question he who prudently keeps still certainly does not seem to be a liar ... since he acts like a prudent man who balances utility and necessity with the true and the false.
>
> (Gilbert, 1968, p.127)

Chapters 20 to 23 may broadly be described as offering devices to help new princes govern effectively. Machiavelli starts with an analysis of the best methods of defence for princes. Mercenaries had already been shown to be useless, so the princes' own subjects should be their most reliable protection. Undue trust should not be given to those who had assisted in the overthrow of the previous government, for they could easily turn against the new one. The best supporters were likely to be adherents of the old regime as they would be temperamentally disposed towards stability and would be anxious to ingratiate themselves with the new prince. Sometimes it could be useful to build fortresses but: 'I censure anyone who, putting his trust in fortresses, does not mind if he is hated by the people' (p.71). Machiavelli, a citizen of Florence, was familiar with the walls and fortified gates which surrounded the city: they had been built with the purpose of providing protection against external enemies not to subjugate the native population.

In Chapter 21 Machiavelli deals with how a prince should win honour, and the career of Ferdinand of Aragon is taken as an exemplar. His calculated cruelty and hypocrisy gave him a reputation for conducting pious and victorious campaigns and strengthened his position at home. This demonstrated that it was always better to take sides firmly in conflicts: indecision would gain the enmity of both parties. A prince should not make alliances with those more powerful than himself, but if it could not be avoided (a recent predicament for Florence) then he should accept it as the lesser evil. In a break from this consistently gloomy account of power politics, Machiavelli concludes the chapter by encouraging the prince to patronize talent, stimulate commerce and agriculture and entertain his people with shows and festivities. He should 'give an example of courtesy and munificence, while all the time, none the less, fully maintaining the dignity of his position' (p.74). This echoes sentiments voiced by many political commentators in the late Middle Ages.

The quality of a prince's ministers and his capacity to follow their advice reflected his own judgement. It was wise to reward a good minister generously so that he would have no incentive to desert his master. It was a cliché of the traditional 'mirrors for princes' that flatterers were to be shunned as they presented a moral threat to the prince. Machiavelli takes the matter further by pointing out that the reverse of flattery was plain speaking, and that if this was indulged in too freely by ministers the prince could lose respect. The solution to this dilemma was to employ wise ministers and to take advice only from them and permit them to offer it only when asked. An example of a contemporary prince who failed to ask for advice, kept his purposes secret and constantly changed his mind was the emperor Maximilian. Some historians have taken Maximilian's behaviour for cunning, but Sydney Anglo describes it as 'the impenetrable secrecy of those who haven't the faintest idea of what they are doing' (1969, p.23). Machiavelli was not optimistic about the chances for an unwise prince, however good the advice he received: 'good advice, whomever it comes from depends on the shrewdness of the prince who seeks it' (p.77).

The final three chapters of *The Prince* change in subject and in tone so radically that it is tempting to suggest that Machiavelli's heart rather than his head set the agenda. Whereas the previous chapters were balanced and neutral in tone, the style here has rhetorical flourishes which were clearly intended to persuade the Medici to adopt a particular policy. Machiavelli's harping throughout the treatise on the unedifying career of Cesare Borgia would have given some intimation that *The Prince* was not exclusively about endearing the author to the restored Medici. He believed that if bad Fortune had not intervened and had Borgia displayed more *virtù* when the crisis of his father's death occurred, he might have succeeded in setting up a powerful state in central and northern Italy which could have resisted incursions by foreign powers.

Exercise

Read Chapters 24 to 26 of *The Prince*, and answer the following questions:

1 How realistic a solution do you believe Machiavelli offered for contemporary problems in the Italian peninsula?

2 What light do the final three chapters throw on Machiavelli's political values at the time he was writing?

Discussion

1 It is always tempting for historians to speculate on alternative outcomes to the events of the past and this can seem to be a great waste of time. However, attempting to test the validity of political theories of the kind offered by Machiavelli is legitimate. No Italian saviour emerged to chase the foreigner from the peninsula until the time of the *Risorgimento* (uprising for liberty) in the nineteenth century, but this does not mean that it was an impossible aspiration. The flaw in Machiavelli's plan was rather one of motivation: Alexander VI, Cesare Borgia and Julius II all fought and intrigued for their own ends, not with an altruistic concern for national solidarity and salvation. We should also be aware of the dangers of hindsight. Nationalism was a rudimentary concept in the sixteenth century; the great series of wars between authoritarian, expansionist monarchies which saw its development over the next few centuries were only just beginning. What Machiavelli had in mind was more likely to have been a return to something like the *status quo* of two decades earlier, when a few influential states such as Florence and Naples maintained a diplomatic balance in the peninsula and avoided major wars and the large-scale involvement of foreign powers.

2 This is part of the larger problem, which relates to all Machiavelli's political writings, of reconciling Machiavelli's advice to new, despotic princes with his long allegiance to the Florentine republic and its values. He makes no judgement in *The Prince* about which form of government is preferable, simply saying that he has written about republics elsewhere. He suggests a whole range of the most arbitrary measures that a prince could adopt but warns against assaults on property or the virtue of women and long drawn out acts of cruelty. The Florentines had just experienced a traumatic period when it had become clear that they were no longer truly independent: any major foreign power which bothered to make the effort could subjugate them. Under such circumstances, and with the experience of Piero Soderini's dismal failure to protect them from foreign coercion, the creation of a powerful native dynasty must have seemed the most realistic option. And Machiavelli prided himself on being a realist. ❖

Exercise

You should now be in a position to answer the first of the five questions posed earlier: Is Machiavelli genuinely advocating autocratic government, or is *The Prince* a satire on princes behaving badly and a ploy to discredit that form of government?

Discussion

Machiavelli certainly had a sense of humour, as you will have gathered from his letter to Vettori (Anthology, no. 23), but a treatise addressed to a ruler from whom he was desperate to gain employment was scarcely the place to display it. When you read extracts from his other works you will see that the anecdotal approach to making his points employed in *The Prince* is entirely typical of his style (indeed many of his anecdotes were recycled). The evidence of his embassy to Borgia shows his admiration for a ruthless man of action who could adapt to circumstances and achieve his goals by the use of force. As for seeking to discredit princely government, the nature of the new regime had scarcely been established when he wrote in 1513. Florence remained a republic in theory until the 1530s and it has been remarked above that much continuity existed with the period before the fall of Soderini. The sack of Prato must have led to great disillusionment on Machiavelli's part, since a popular government using a native *militia* proved incapable of standing up to foreign professional soldiers. His goals when he wrote *The Prince* were two-fold: first to get employment, and that entailed placating the Medici; and second, to find a means of returning the Italian peninsula to the equilibrium that it had, in retrospect, enjoyed in the days of Lorenzo the Magnificent. He was not to know when he wrote *The Prince* that, with the exception of Leo X, the Medici would prove themselves to be incompetent or tyrannical rulers. ❖

Exercise

Scholars such as Allan Gilbert and Quentin Skinner have traced many continuities between *The Prince* and earlier writing in the genre. In the light of this you should be able to answer the second of the questions posed earlier: To what extent was *The Prince* innovative – did it really represent a departure from traditional thought about politics?

Discussion

There was a long tradition of such writing going back to classical Greek writers like Plato and Aristotle and their Roman followers. The work of scholastic translators and commentators revived this type of literature and it was still flourishing in Renaissance Europe. A new spirit of realism and scepticism about formerly authoritative precepts already informed such thinking and writing by the end of the fifteenth century. This can be seen in the work of Diomede Carafa and Giovanni Pontano and in the debates about policy that are recorded in meetings such as the Florentine *pratiche*. The writers were careful, however, to couch their ideas in circumspect language, while Machiavelli firmly stated that he was going to deal with forms of government as they really existed, not as they should be in an ideal world. His treatise was first published in 1532. It was short and written in the vernacular so it could be easily read, and thus was perceived as being more unique than it really was. Despite all this, however, there remain features of *The Prince* which were truly innovatory and they hinge, as Skinner recognized (1988, p.434), on

Machiavelli's analysis of *virtù*. For him it consisted in putting the good of the state above all preconceived systems of morality and thus, by implication, above Christian doctrine as well. The best strategy for a new prince was to be free of any such preconceptions: ideally he would act in accordance with conventional virtue; but, should necessity dictate it, he should be prepared to be ruthless and amoral. ❖

Machiavelli's later works

It is not known whether Giuliano or Lorenzo de' Medici ever read *The Prince*, but if they did it failed to impress them sufficiently for Machiavelli to be rescued from his enforced *otium*. Instead he continued the life he had described so graphically, although he did attempt to improve his finances by writing. Apart from various short studies and satires he composed a poem, *The Ass*, which he never completed. It was based on a lascivious prose satire by the Roman author Apuleius, but it was also intended as a parody of Dante. After a mildly erotic beginning it turned into a gloomy tirade on contemporary politics. A more successful literary venture was a play, *La Mandragola* (*The Mandrake Root*), which was performed in front of Leo X in 1520, a sign that the author's standing was improving. Anglo quotes a typically negative Victorian response to the indecency of the plot and then goes on to reprove equally unreasonable and excessive praise:

> Symonds[3] was badly hemmed in by the moral preoccupations of his time, and by a rigid preconception of what constituted the Italian Renaissance and Machiavelli's place therein. But this mode of self-indulgent literary response, which can discern hidden meaning in a laundry list – provided only that it emanate from the household of a great man – is, unfortunately, still with us. As far as the *Mandragola* is concerned things have scarcely improved since Symonds's day. Ridolfi [writing in the 1950s] is almost equally fanciful, and a good deal more hyperbolic. He assures us that, if there were a purpose behind the play, it could hardly be merely to make people laugh, 'when the comedy has far more the effect of making people think' ... Machiavelli is, of course, the greatest Italian everything ever.

(1969, p.120)

All this debate hinges on a tale of an old man with a virtuous young wife who is seduced by an attractive young man with the help of a mandrake. Such stories were common in the Middle Ages and the

---

[3] John Addington Symonds, an English scholar, who published a series of books on the Italian Renaissance during the mid 1870s (see Chapter 3).

Renaissance, and most were drawn from classical sources. We are not obliged to decide on Machiavelli's motives in this case, and he stated his attitude to the project pretty clearly in the prologue:

> And if this seems too light and frivolous
> For one who likes to be thought serious,
> Forgive him: for he tries with idle dreams
> To make the hour less bitter than it seems.
> – Bitter, for he can turn no other way
> To show a higher worth, do what he may;
> For graver themes
> He sees no chance of patronage or pay ...
>
> But he who thinks this author can be wrung
> By malice, or be made to hold his tongue,
> I warn him: this man is malicious too;
> Malice, indeed, his earliest art, and through
> The length and limits of all Italy
> He owes respect to none; though I agree
> He'll fawn and do
> Service to richer, smarter folk than he.
>
> (Hale, 1966, p.187)[4]

Anglo discerns a number of sentiments in the play which echoed points that Machiavelli had made either in *The Prince* or in the *Discourses*. He never seemed able to desert his overwhelming preoccupation with politics for long.

Soon after his loss of office, Machiavelli found a congenial outlet for continued discussion and speculation at the *Orti Oricellari* (Gardens of the Rucellai). The patrician Bernardo Rucellai had been a Medici supporter up to 1494. He had not resisted their overthrow, although he later went into exile for differing with Soderini. He was to die soon after the Medicean restoration but his garden remained a gathering place for writers, philosophers and politicians, including his invalid grandson Cosimo:

> It was between the inner and outer circuits of the walls, looking up to Fiesole. There was a summer-house, and beside the paths were marble benches and busts of great figures from the Roman past, statesmen and men of letters. The beds were full of rare flowers, for it had been Rucellai's fancy to collect as many as he could of the flowers mentioned in classical literature.
>
> (Hale, 1966, p.171)

---

[4] The entire play has been translated into English: D. Sices and J.B. Atkinson (1985) *The Comedies of Machiavelli*, Hanover, NH, University Press of New England.

The inception of both Machiavelli's *Discourses on the First Ten Books of Titus Livy* and *The Art of War* is attributed to the cultivated and relatively free environment of the *Orti Oricellari* (for an example of a Renaissance garden, see Plate 12). He never finished the *Discourses* – hardly surprising when we reflect on the scale of the work which does survive. It was dedicated to Cosimo Rucellai and Zanobi Buondelmonti, another member of the humanist circle, (the death of the former in 1519 provides the latest date for its completion). It was noted above (p.223) that in Chapter 2 of *The Prince*, Machiavelli states that he had already discussed republics and that this was almost certainly a reference to the *Discourses*. It is just possible that Machiavelli could have written another piece which has not survived, but, given his notoriety and the care with which even his trivia were preserved, this is not likely. If he bothered to mention the *Discourses* at all in 1513 they must have been in an advanced state of preparation; but how did he have time to achieve that during the busy public life he had lived, and why write a potentially subversive book when he was trying to ingratiate himself with the Medici? A solution to these problems was offered by Baron in an article entitled 'Machiavelli: the republican citizen and the author of *The Prince*' (1961). Previously, a notable Machiavelli scholar, Federico Chabod, had suggested that the *Discourses* might have been started in 1513, left unfinished while Machiavelli took up the more urgent task of writing *The Prince*, and resumed a year or so later. Chabod saw these works as a kind of biography of Florentine politics, charting a hopeful approach towards the possibilities of a classically based republic, disillusion and a final return to the republican ideal. But Baron would have none of this:

> instead of so many efforts to harmonize Machiavelli's thought, we ought to face the obvious differences and explore whether their secret may, after all, yield to a generic approach.
>
> (1961, p.228)

Baron's solution to the conundrum was to study the text closely and to postulate that the sentence at the beginning of Chapter 2 of *The Prince* was a later insertion. Machiavelli had mentioned *The Prince* in his letter to Vettori at the end of 1513 (Anthology, no. 23). If he had also been in the process of composing the *Discourses* why did he not also refer to it? It is only from the letter to Vettori that we know of Machiavelli's original intention to dedicate *The Prince* to Giuliano de' Medici. The dedication in the earliest-known version of the treatise is to Lorenzo and would have been substituted after Giuliano's death in 1516. The first draft of *The Prince* from around 1513 may have differed from the version of 1516. Between these times Machiavelli had failed to get a new post and the Medici had disappointed him, showing themselves to be self-seeking rather than dedicated to the interests of Florence. Following his own precepts he maintained a show of loyalty to their house but aired his true views about the superiority of republican government in the *Discourses*, which he composed during the next few years. Part of this change of direction Baron attributed to the influence of the traditions of civic humanism which Machiavelli absorbed from the circle of humanists in the *Orti Oricellari*.

Before formulating a response to the possibilities outlined above, it will be helpful to look at some of the key ideas in the *Discourses*. Livy wrote his *History of Rome* under the patronage of the Emperor Augustus although much of the work was devoted to the origins of Rome's greatness in the time when it was a republic. Machiavelli probably only ever intended to deal with the first ten books of Livy, as they covered the republican phase of Rome's development. Producing a commentary on a traditional authority was a well-established medieval and humanist genre and most writers who did so kept closely to their original text. Machiavelli, however, diverged from that practice and used Livy merely as a departure point for developing his own views about how contemporary government should be conducted. As in *The Prince* he started with a conventional description of the principal forms of government, based on Aristotle's *Politics*, and the perversions into which they could decline. You can read Book 1, Chapter 2 of the *Discourses*, 'How many kinds of state there are', in the Anthology (no. 24i). Machiavelli described the different forms of government as characteristically following each other in a cycle (an idea which had been developed by the ancient Greek historian Polybius). He proposed that the best way to avoid this unsatisfactory situation was to design a form of government which combined the best elements of the princely, aristocratic and democratic regimes.

In the chapters that follow Machiavelli formulated one of his most innovative ideas. To the objection that the coexistence of aristocratic and democratic forms in one regime could lead to civil conflict he responds with the assertion that this was a positive good for 'they led to laws and institutions whereby the liberties of the public benefited' (Gilbert, 1989, p.114). A few chapters later he offers advice to princes who might rule over a combination of the best forms of government (which could also be a solution to the question of reconciling the contents of the *Discourses* with the ideas found in *The Prince*).

Exercise

Read Book 1, Chapters 9 and 10 of the *Discourses* (Anthology, no. 24ii). How do they relate to Machiavelli's advice in *The Prince*?

Discussion

In Chapter 9 Machiavelli states that if a republic was to be founded or radically reformed it was often necessary for one man to take on the job. In Chapter 10 he concedes that there is always a danger that the rule of such princes could degenerate into tyranny, but they would be well-advised to resist such temptation for then 'in life they rest secure and in death become renowned'. Machiavelli drew his illustrations of these precepts from classical times, but there can be little doubt that this advice was intended for Florentine citizens living under the Medici just as surely as were the contents of *The Prince* aimed directly at the dynasty. In other words, whatever the chronology of his composition of the two works may have been, there was no essential contradiction in the advice they offered. Machiavelli tacitly recognized this in the famous reference in Chapter 2 of *The Prince*: if he had thought that the work negated his views on the excellence of government by the people, why mention it at all? The situation of Florence and other parts of Italy in 1513 fitted exactly the kind of emergency he envisaged and illustrated at length in the *Discourses*, using both ancient and modern examples. A man of *virtù* was required to establish stability and security so that the institutions of government could function properly. Ideally such a man would be a reasonably selfless republican like Soderini, but if the citizens had to put up with autocrats like the restored Medici for a while it was a price worth paying. According to the cyclic theory of political change, it would only be a matter of time before a truly republican government was restored. ❖

It is just possible that Machiavelli did produce an early draft of the *Discourses* before he was sacked by the Medici in 1512, but Baron's suggestion that the reference to it in *The Prince* was a later insertion seems much more likely. We do not, however, have to accept the other part of his hypothesis, that Machiavelli changed from being a pragmatic supporter of the hegemony of the Medici to an idealistic republican in the space of the next few years. This becomes even less likely if other continuities of thought between the two works are identified. The methodology is the same: Machiavelli illustrated his ideas about government from ancient examples, he used material drawn from all parts of the classical period, not confining himself to Livy's narrative and included, as appropriate, contemporary material as well. His use of the concepts of Fortune and *virtù* is the same as in *The Prince* and he gives similar, arresting examples of its manifestations. The story of Romulus in Book 1, Chapter 9 of the *Discourses* concludes with the maxim that: 'reprehensible actions may be justified by their effects, and that when the effect was good, as it was in the case of Romulus, it always justifies the action'. This sentiment closely corresponds to much of the reasoning in *The Prince* and there are many more examples of similarity of thought to be found in the works. The scholar Pasquale Villari even went as far as to suggest that if *The Prince* was lost it could be reconstructed from the *Discourses* (Chabod, 1965, p.40, n.2). The *Discourses* may be seen as extending many of the ideas that appear in *The Prince* and also as adding to the advice it contains (see the *Discourses*, Book 1, Chapter 55 in the Anthology, no. 24iii).

The *Discourses* can be presented as a reaction to the kind of thinking which was characteristic of the patrician sentiments to be found among some members of the circle in the *Orti Oricellari*, including Francesco Guicciardini. Guicciardini and his fellow patricians believed that Venice, the only republic which retained a semblance of independence, exemplified in its constitution the mixture which so many theorists proclaimed was ideal: the doge (chief magistrate) exercised the function of the prince, the Senate represented the aristocracy and all Venetian citizens made up the people. While Machiavelli rejected this analysis on the grounds that ordinary citizens were excluded from office and thus not truly free. Pocock suggests that the *Discourses* 'are best interpreted as a systematic dissent from the Venetian paradigm and a diffuse pursuit of the consequences of that dissent' (1975, p.186).

Another big idea found in the *Discourses* which represented further continuity of thought with *The Prince* was the great importance that Machiavelli attached to the need to organize and maintain an effective *militia* to defend the chosen form of government. Many of the points made are similar, although in the *Discourses* they are illustrated with more extensive examples; a large part of Book 2 is devoted to these and Machiavelli reverted again to the subject for part of Book 3. References to a particular sequence in the *Discourses* can, however, be misleading: early printed and manuscript versions differ from each other and it is not always clear how far they had been revised by the author or edited by others. Pocock complains about their diffuseness and modern scholars have presented their various editions with the commendable intention of making them as coherent as possible. However, we must still consider the possibility that we are not now studying the *Discourses* in the order intended by Machiavelli, who may not have had a master plan in his head as he wrote them. The writers of the early modern period did not always give priority to symmetry or consistency in their arguments, as some of the jottings and epigrams of Machiavelli and his contemporaries testify.

Machiavelli's *The Art of War* was dedicated to Lorenzo di Filippo Strozzi, a Florentine patrician from a family which played a prominent part in the city's affairs and had recently supported the Medici. It was the most successful of Machiavelli's treatises in the sense that it was finished in 1520, published a year later and soon came to be regarded as one of the principal authorities on the subject. This was perhaps, as Anglo suggests, because his contemporaries had not come to terms with the realities of the technological changes in warfare which were rapidly taking place, and remained psychologically rooted in a chivalric mode of thinking which Machiavelli's book reinforced (1969, p.157). Chabod was of the same opinion:

> he who was in political thought a man of the Renaissance, became a man of the thirteenth century when he turned to military matters.
>
> (quoted in Mallett, 1990, p.173)

Michael Mallett (1990) takes a rather different view, emphasizing the importance of his conceptual grasp of the art of war he refers back to Chapter 12 of *The Prince*:

> The main foundations of every state, new states as well as ancient or composite ones, are good laws and good arms; and because you cannot have good laws without good arms, and where there are good arms, good laws inevitably follow, I shall not discuss laws but give my attention to arms.
>
> (Bull, 1999, p.39)

Here Machiavelli, obsessed by military prowess, gleefully puts the practice of arms at the very heart of his advice about state-building. He adopted the same attitude throughout the *Discourses* (indeed they are principally an illustration of how Roman republican prowess or *virtù* led to the establishment of a mighty empire through the victorious use of arms). You will find an illustration of this approach in an extract from *The Art of War* (Anthology, no. 25). The fact that Machiavelli draws most of his examples from types of warfare that were outdated by the early sixteenth century does not undermine the importance of this aspect of his thought. The power wielded by ambitious princes, however morally reprehensible, was a fact of political life: good citizens should recognize this and use it to establish strong states. Despite the disaster of Prato in 1512 Machiavelli persisted in urging that the most practical way in which citizens could do this was by the organization of a *militia*. The esteem in which the book was held by his contemporaries since its inception in the *Orti Oricellari* implies that they were no more prepared than the author to counterbalance theory with pragmatic experience.

The political situation in Florence changed in 1519 with the death of Lorenzo, duke of Urbino, the unappreciative recipient of the second dedication of Machiavelli's *Prince*. Cardinal Giulio de' Medici proved a more accessible ruler, who valued the lustre that men of letters could give to the regime. Machiavelli was presented to him in the *Orti Oricellari* in March 1520 and at about the same time Machiavelli submitted to Cardinal Giulio and to his cousin Leo X a *Discourse on Florentine Affairs after the Death of Lorenzo*. This was extraordinarily optimistic in its assumption that, on the death of the two prelates, Florence could revert to the republican institutions that had flourished after 1494. As with the case of the *militia*, it was another example of how extreme cynicism and sophistication could coexist in Machiavelli's writings with an almost unworldly idealism. The Medici must have drawn the same conclusion, for instead of being punished for anticipating the demise of their house, he was commissioned to write *The Florentine History*, receiving an annual fee equivalent to half the salary he had lost in 1512. By the time he started work on it, he was also resuming the life of *negotium* which had eluded him since the fall of Soderini. He was first sent on private missions concerned with commerce rather than politics, but these led to official employment by the Medicean government, first on fairly trivial matters but eventually involving more important commissions.

Figure 6.15 Bronzino, *Giulio de' Medici, later Pope Clement VII*, Palazzo Medici-Riccardi, Florence. Photo: Alinari

Machiavelli's rehabilitation could have been threatened by a plot to assassinate Cardinal Giulio in 1522 involving the exiled Soderini and members of the *Oricellari* circle including Zanobi Buondelmonti. He managed to distance himself from the conspiracy but it brought the gathering, from which he had drawn so much intellectual sustenance, to an end. Was his survival through prudent disengagement reflected in a new circumspection in his writings? Certainly the dedication to Giulio de' Medici, who had become Pope Clement VII by the time *The Florentine History* was completed in 1525, had a conventionally sycophantic tone:

> I was particularly charged and commanded by your Holiness to write in such a manner of your ancestors that I could in no way be accused of flattery ... [I] greatly fear, however, that in describing the goodness of Giovanni, the wisdom of Cosimo, the affability of Piero, and the magnificence of Lorenzo, I may appear to your Holiness to have transgressed your commands ... If under their noble deeds there lay concealed an ambition contrary to the welfare of the commonwealth, as some have said, I have not found it.

> (Machiavelli, 1912, pp.xv–xvi)

Machiavelli was writing within a well-established historiographical tradition (see Chapter 3), and there would have been some expectation that he would provide a comprehensive account of the city's origins, set in a wider political context.

Exercise

Read the introduction to *The Florentine History* (Anthology, no. 26i).

1 What were Machiavelli's motives for structuring *The History* as he did?

2 Do these motives throw any light on his approach to the exercise of political authority in the 1520s?

Discussion

1 Machiavelli had originally intended to start *The History* in 1434, when the Medici emerged as the most powerful family, thinking that earlier times had been fully covered by his predecessors, such as Bruni and Poggio. But on reading their histories he discovered that they had neglected to cover the internal dissensions which had been a longstanding characteristic of the state and which, he believed, had exercised such an important influence on the formation of the capacities and valour of the citizens of Florence. Studying these processes would be most 'profitable to citizens who may be called upon to govern republics'. The earlier historians may have avoided these topics either because they thought them unworthy of consideration or because they feared to offend the descendants of certain families involved in the conflicts.

2   The tone of the introduction is considerably more objective than the dedication to the pope. Machiavelli recognized the fact that he would have to record matters which would be unpalatable to the Medici and their supporters. In identifying civil strife as the most interesting and, perversely, fruitful aspect of his city's recent history he was harking back to the argument of the *Discourses*, a work which had not been intended to please the Medici. Once he became engaged in the past affairs of Florence he seemed incapable of putting his own interests above an objective analysis, and he presumably still believed in the future that he had mapped out in the *Discourses on Florentine Affairs*: that Medici power would eventually fade away and be replaced by a wholly republican constitution. ❖

About half of *The History* is devoted to the period up to 1434 and the rest deals with the affairs of Florence in a wider European context, from then until the death of Lorenzo the Magnificent in 1492. The major preoccupation of the second part is, as Anglo suggests, to complement the thesis he had developed in *The Art of War* with more historical evidence. Anglo gives instances of shocking economies with the truth made with the intention of proving Machiavelli's obsessive thesis about the uselessness of employing mercenaries:

> the battle of Anghiari in 1440, as described by Machiavelli, is worthy of the Keystone Cops ... after four hours' stiff combat and a great victory, 'not more than one man died: who expired, not from a wound or any honourable blow, but through falling off his horse and being trampled on'. This is a good story; but it is disturbing when one notes that Machiavelli's sources clearly state that as many as seventy men were killed and six hundred wounded, together with some six hundred horses shot down by the artillery. Similarly, the battle of Molinella in 1467 is described by Machiavelli as an encounter in which no one was killed, and only a few horses wounded – despite the fact that contemporary sources suggest that several hundred troops were slain. Scipione Ammirato, writing later in the sixteenth century, was highly irritated by the constant errors in the *Florentine History* and when dealing with the various casualties at Molinella, as listed in the original sources, he especially notes Machiavelli's falsification and 'customary sneers at the expense of hired troops'.

(1969, p.185)

All this sits uneasily with the claims made about the enlightening powers of history in the introduction. Similarly, Gisela Bock (1990) has perceived a disparity between the positive claims made there for civil strife and its actual treatment in the body of the work where it was invariably contrasted unfavourably with a stable, well-ordered city.

Exercise

Read Machiavelli's description of the Pazzi conspiracy of 1478 and its failure (Anthology, no. 26ii). Does this example support Bock's suggestion that civil discord was presented in an unfavourable light?

Discussion

The first point to note must be that Machiavelli is describing the process which led to the death of the pope's father Giuliano de' Medici. This in itself made it more likely that the Pazzi and their followers would be portrayed as troublemakers. It is surprising, therefore, that quite a neutral tone is employed in describing the events and their causes: some pity is even expressed for particular conspirators. Lorenzo's speech to the *Signoria* and leading citizens was evidently an opportunity to justify and reinforce the Medicean hegemony: he represented a return to order and stability after a dangerous interlude. Yet there is some ambiguity even in the attitude towards civil strife which Machiavelli attributes to Lorenzo, 'when I remember with what readiness and earnestness, and with what sympathy and unity, the whole city has risen to avenge my brother and defend me, I am disposed not only to rejoice but to feel honoured and exalted'. So a response to the question will be that while the terrible events of the conspiracy and the ensuing war with the pope were deplored, it also served as an opportunity for the Medici and their supporters to demonstrate *virtù*, and the incident ultimately confirmed the strength and solidarity of the state and its leaders. ❖

These kinds of contradictions are recognized by Bock at the end of her article. What she says also harks back to a point made earlier about it being unrealistic to expect total consistency from early modern writers, especially from Machiavelli, who had abandoned the certainties of Christianity as the criteria for acceptable political action:

> Precisely because he was a convinced republican – in respect to the city state – he perceived and analysed the fact that in republics there are contrasting interests, harsh conflicts, power relations, tyranny and amorality. But it is only in the republican order that the discords among the various human *umori* [humours] can and must be expressed; on the other hand, it is these very discords that continually threaten it. They are both the life and the death of the republic.

(1990, p.201)

Despite the ambiguities in the treatment of his family's history, Clement VII seems to have been well pleased with *The History* when Machiavelli presented it to him in Rome in 1525. Perhaps he had really meant what he had said about flattery in his dedication (see above, p.242). The impact of Clement's papacy on Florence was not good for republicans, however, as he designated the governing role to the two young illegitimate sons of Giuliano, duke of Nemours, and Lorenzo, duke of Urbino. Neither of them showed any aptitude for the task and the state of Florence looked progressively more like a satellite of the papacy. It was a further sign of papal approval that Machiavelli was sent to Faenza to organize a mercenary force to defend the Romagna. Nothing came of this opportunity, but another chance arose in 1526 for Machiavelli to indulge his love of military affairs. Knowing that further conflict was imminent between the Emperor Charles V (1519–56) and the Medici's French ally, Francis I, the pope considered strengthening the defences of Florence, especially the great fortified wall which surrounded it (see Figure 6.16). Machiavelli inspected the wall in April in the company of a well-known military engineer, Pietro Navarra, and sent a report to Clement VII which made a number of recommendations: shortly afterwards he was made chancellor to the five Procurators of the Walls.

Machiavelli was asked by the *Signoria* on two occasions to go to the army of the French king and his allies to consult with Guicciardini, who was representing Clement VII, about how Florentine security could best be preserved. John Hale comments on the difficulty of a situation, 'where the city's interests had to be pressed half-surreptitiously past the wider interests of the Medici family' (1966, p.227). The weakness of his state meant that Machiavelli achieved nothing practical; but the fact that he was entrusted with such an important mission showed how he had returned to the centre of Florentine politics. The immediate danger of an imperial invasion of

Figure 6.16 Lucantonio degli Uberti, *Chain plan of Florence*, 1482, wood engraving from eight blocks. Kupferstichkabinett. Staatliche Museen zu Berlin – Preussischer Kulturbesitz. Photo: Jorg P. Anders

Florence passed as the ill-disciplined army swept on to Rome. However, the sack of Rome, while Clement cowered in the Castel Sant' Angelo and the Spanish troops and Protestant mercenaries indulged their 'nun-raping, priest-bating, church-stripping fervour', weakened the Medici and led to the fall of their regime in Florence in May 1527 (Hale, 1966, p.232).

After this, a republican constitution was restored with the kind of attributes that Machiavelli had always wanted: a Great Council and a commission, the Ten of War. Ironically, once again, his lack of wealth or lineage left him without a post, although others who had collaborated with the Medici, like Vettori and the Strozzi, joined the inner circle. Machiavelli had been suffering from stomach trouble for some time, possibly an ulcer, so it would perhaps be over sentimental to suggest that disappointment contributed to his death on 21 June 1527. He was buried in Santa Croce, Florence.

Figure 6.17 Ignatio Spinazzi, *Monument to Niccolò Machiavelli*, Santa Croce, Florence. Photo: Alinari

Exercise

To put this study of *The Prince* into a wider context I would like you to reread the last section of the Rabil article (Reader, no.3). Then answer the third of the questions posed earlier: What is the relationship between Machiavelli's *Prince* and his works, such as the *Discourses,* that are republican in tone?

Discussion

You have probably already gathered that historians will go on arguing about this issue until Hell freezes over. Much hangs on chronology: if the reference in Chapter 2 of *The Prince* was inserted after 1513 a case could be made that he completed this work before he wrote the *Discourses.* We could then demonstrate that he had become so disillusioned with the prospect that the Medici would lead the states of Italy in a crusade to expel the foreigners (barbarians) that he reverted to the more popularly based republicanism under which his career had flourished. This approach discounts the many continuities to be found in the thought of the two treatises and the fact that many of the same ideas recur in the works specifically intended for the Medici in the 1520s: *The Discourse on Florentine Affairs* and *The History of Florence.* Machiavelli was in a strange position throughout his adult life. His powerful intellect and strong ambition distanced him from the minor citizenry from which his family came, yet his lack of wealth and family position meant that he could never fully belong to the inner circle of the governors of Florence. This may sometimes have given his writings the freedom and inconsistency which have caused debates as to their meaning. ❖

The impact of Machiavelli's ideas

'A scurvie schollar of Machiavellus lair'[5] (Raab, 1964, p.58)

During his lifetime Machiavelli's works were not greeted with unanimous approval. His circle in the *Oricellari* certainly encouraged him, *The Art of War* was immediately regarded as authoritative and Clement VII seems to have welcomed *The History of Florence.* The thinking in *The Prince* and the *Discourses,* however, was too much at variance with the norms of Christian morality, the traditional virtues to be found in 'mirrors for princes' and the interests of the inner circle of government to be generally acceptable. The best-known of a number of contemporary and near contemporary Italian commentators on his work was the Florentine patrician and writer, Francesco Guicciardini.

---

[5] The Scottish statesman William Maitland of Lethington (*c.*1528–73) was called this as early as 1570 for his part in negotiations between Elizabeth and Mary, Queen of Scots.

Guicciardini was by no means hostile to republican institutions: as a young man he had lived well under the rule of Soderini. However, he soon entered the service of the restored Medici and served for many years as a go-between for them with the *Signoria*, in their absence from Florence. Consequently he suffered exile when they were expelled in 1527 and his later works date from that period. His admiration for the patrician nature of the Venetian constitution has already been mentioned, and another characteristic which divorced him from Machiavelli's statecraft was the value he set on prudence. While the former wished to create citizen *militias* strong enough to repel invaders from Italy, seeing this as the greatest possible manifestation of *virtù*, Guicciardini believed *virtù* to be much closer to prudence than to prowess. The prudent governor would adapt himself to circumstances and concentrate on developing a political system which delivered a strong and stable state. Arming the poorer citizens, exactly those who had often caused civil strife in the past, was hardly likely to produce that result. He also criticized Machiavelli for using Roman incidents as models through which to address current problems:

> Before he wrote the *Ricordi* [Maxims and Reflections] Guicciardini had completed the *Dialogo* [Dialogue] in which he considered and rejected the Roman paradigm and settled for the *Città disarmata*, [unarmed state] where the essential skill was that of adaptation to the environment through prudence. Consequently *virtù* had no meaning for him outside the civic setting, where it was identical with prudence; and when the republic and its *virtù* had vanished together, prudence remained the instrument of the post-civic individual.
>
> (Pocock, 1975, p.270)

Further examples of Guicciardini's thought can be found in the extract from his *Maxims and Reflections* (Anthology, no. 27). Other contemporaries were more positive about Machiavelli's contribution. Antonio Brucioli, an *Oricellari* regular who was exiled after the anti-Medici plot of 1522, produced *The Dialogues on Moral Philosophy* just after Machiavelli's death. As Delio Cantimori has shown Brucioli deplored the demise of the robust and independent republic defended by a *militia* and made an explicit 'connection between political consciousness as personified in Machiavelli, and the literary and rhetorical tradition of the humanists' (1937–8, p.86). This civic humanism directly linked Machiavelli to the rhetorical tradition of political writing whose introduction Baron attributed to Bruni (see Chapter 3).

Yet the eventual fall of the Florentine republic in 1530 and the second restoration of the Medici, who soon turned the state into a duchy, gave rise to a darker development in political thought. In 'The end of republican liberty', Skinner suggests Guicciardini wrote his *History of Italy* in a mood of despair at the helplessness of humanity in its subjection to the vagaries of Fortune. Far from adopting the humanist method of using history to provide a model for conduct, his narrative recounted 'the tragedy of Italy's progressive exploitation and collapse' (1978, p.188). Trajano Boccalini, writing at the end of the sixteenth century in his *Advertisements from Parnassus*, lined up the rulers of Europe, including Italian princes and the Ottoman Turks, and arraigned them for the corruption and follies of their rule. Some admitted their faults but those (including the Turks) who put up a defence did so using the kind of arguments Machiavelli had employed: nothing could better illustrate how discredited his ideas had become even among his own countrymen.

During the reigns of Henry VIII and his children in England, Renaissance humanism and all things Italian were very much in vogue. Machiavelli's writings at first enjoyed a positive reception, although Reginald Pole's *Apology* (*De Concilio*) (1562) was an exception since he roundly condemned them (Kraye, 1997, pp.274–84). The Protestant Reformation gradually caused a general change of attitude, and after the massacre of Protestants on St Bartholomew's day in Paris, for which the French dowager queen, Catherine de' Medici, was blamed, Machiavelli became the epitome of evil for many writers. French writers like François Hotman and Innocent Gentillet (1535–88) were particularly vociferous in their condemnations.

Exercise

In the Anthology (no. 28), read the extract from Gentillet's *Against Nicholas Machiavell* (1576), a commentary on Machiavelli's *Discourses*, Book 2, Chapter 2 and Book 3, Chapter 3.

1 On what grounds did Gentillet condemn these chapters of the *Discourses*?

2 Is the condemnation justified by what Machiavelli wrote?

Discussion

1 Gentillet charged Machiavelli with setting out a programme which would enable a prince to rule tyrannically. He goes on to suggest that, even if princes did become powerful tyrants, the fear of destruction would never give them any contentment. He ends with a condemnation that 'this wicked man' should, 'pluck out from the hearts of men, all hatred, horror and indignation, which they might have against tyranny, and to cause princes to esteem tyranny, good, honourable and desirable'.

2 Gentillet's tone is extremely vituperative and that in itself might cause unease in his readers. He assumes that Machiavelli was writing

advice for tyrants, while the principal theme of the *Discourses* was the desirability of republics: the rule of one man might have to be a transitional stage but it should certainly not be tyrannical even if it had to be ruthless. Machiavelli had specifically condemned acts of needless cruelty in *The Prince*, while recognizing that an omelette could not be made without breaking eggs! ❖

With the onset of a more secular age in the seventeenth and eighteenth centuries, Machiavelli's writings once more came back into favour. His formulae for strong, effective rule were emulated, although most writers would not acknowledge him as a source except to condemn him. While his work could be used to support absolute monarchies, it could also offer wisdom to republics. Pocock has traced its progress in England from the speeches of anti-royalists like John Pym (1584–1643) before the Civil Wars to the republican theories of Algernon Sidney (?1622–83) and the first Earl of Shaftesbury (1621–83) after the Restoration. The *Leviathan* of Thomas Hobbes (1588–1679) with its rationale for strong, authoritarian rule, has not been identified as containing either a specifically monarchical or a republican ideology, but its assumption of the autonomy of politics, divorced from any particular system of morality or belief, was Machiavellian. This possibility was also welcomed by the thinkers of the Enlightenment. Another facet of Machiavelli's thought, the collective *virtù* required of good republicans, was influential with the founders of the American Constitution after they had broken with British rule and with the leaders of the French Revolution.

By the nineteenth century very different reactions to the ideas of Machiavelli were possible. Those who held strong views about religion and morality were likely to condemn them, while those for whom the Italian Renaissance represented the peak of human achievement could tolerate or even applaud them. Burckhardt, as we have seen, was never backward in handing out praise or blame and, on the whole, Machiavelli was a recipient of the former. Several reasons for this can be suggested: he was writing at a time when nationalism was a great force in Europe, and the last chapters of *The Prince*, along with other of Machiavelli's writings, could be interpreted in that light. As a citizen of the Swiss republic, Burckhardt could be expected to warm to the kind of republicanism most of Machiavelli's works promoted and, finally, there was his great love for all aspects of the Italian Renaissance.

Exercise

Reread *The Civilization of the Renaissance in Italy* (1990) from page 69 (final paragraph) to page 73.

1   What aspects of Machiavelli's work did Burckhardt praise?

2   Did Burckhardt criticize any of Machiavelli's advice?

Discussion

1   Burckhardt praises Machiavelli as the first modern historian to describe the development of his city as if it were a living organism. His statecraft is also admired: he takes 'a large and an accurate view of alternative possibilities, and seeks to mislead neither himself nor others'. Despite his laxity in morals and speech (and this was characteristic of his time), he was an objective and patriotic writer who always put the welfare of his state first.

2   Machiavelli is obliquely accused of naivety in a blanket criticism of those who thought that they could manufacture constitutions from 'existing forces and tendencies'. Burckhardt is also affronted by Machiavelli's populism, but suggests he might have been misled 'by his imagination and the pressure of events' into thinking that the people could be trusted with choosing its own officials. ❖

The twentieth century witnessed a move away from a judgemental approach to the works of Machiavelli, although Herbert Butterfield, a Christian writing under the shadow of Nazi and Communist totalitarianism, was a notable exception. The great extension of Renaissance scholarship which took place in the decades after the Second World War, much of it connected with the Warburg Institute in London, encompassed the life and works of Machiavelli. The publication of the account book of his father, Bernardo, increased knowledge of Machiavelli's early life and confirmed his humanist education. New and fuller editions of his works were produced and more extensive research was carried out into the ideas of his antecedents and contemporaries. Some of the particular issues of interpretation which have preoccupied scholars such as Baron, Pocock and Skinner have been discussed in this chapter. At the time of writing it is not easy to discern what turn Machiavelli studies will take next. Sebastian de Grazia (1989), in *Machiavelli in Hell,* stresses the importance of Machiavelli's literary and festive works, and claims him as Italy's greatest prose writer. He also lays more emphasis than has been customary on the role of religion in his work. In *From Poliziano to Machiavelli,* Peter Godman (1998) stresses the impact of the Florentine Chancery on Machiavelli's career and writings and, later, the duplicity with which Cardinal Giulio de' Medici manipulated him. Nigel Warburton observes in his *Reading Political Philosophy: Machiavelli to Mill* (forthcoming) that: 'although he was not a philosopher, Machiavelli's ideas have deep philosophical implications'.

Machiavelli's ideas had an impact on his circle of influential friends during and soon after his lifetime and knowledge of them soon extended to a wider European audience. Even those who vociferously condemned Machiavelli's ideas often showed in their writings that they were subject to their influence. Both as handbooks for absolute princes and prescriptions for republican ideology, Machiavelli's major works remained of great importance. With the severance of the link between church and state in most modern democracies, he retains the capacity to clarify thinking about the great issues of the day. Indeed, a lecturer in strategic management at a conference in 1998 feared that writers on management were quoting aphorisms from *The Prince* too frequently (*The Times*, 22 May 1998).

Exercise

Now read Maureen Ramsay's essay 'Machiavelli's political philosophy in *The Prince*' (Reader, no. 8), which shows how Machiavelli's ideas can fit into both the modern tradition of liberal thought and a utilitarian consequentialist ethical system (i.e., one based on the belief that even inherently bad actions are justified if their result adds to the total of human happiness). The first part of the essay summarizes what was new about the thinking in *The Prince* and the second part explores its philosophical implications. When you have read the essay, answer the final two questions posed earlier:

1 Was Machiavelli trying to create a new system of government or was he reacting to existing circumstances by suggesting a rationale for current political realities?

2 To what extent were Machiavelli's ideas indebted to humanism?

Discussion

1 Baron, on the evidence of Machiavelli's writings, claims his work as the culmination of an ideology based on civic humanism. This leads to the conclusion that rather than seeking to create a new system of government, Machiavelli wished to restore one, that is, the republic, which he believed had been eroded by the patricians, especially the Medici. However, since he was living under the Medici regime and hoped to get employment from them, he also had to take on board existing circumstances. *The Prince* and *The Discourse on Florentine Affairs* both accepted Medici rule but, taken in the context of his other writings, his ultimate hope was that it would be replaced by a popular republic of the kind that he believed had flourished intermittently in the later Middle Ages. This question raises again the issue that has lain under much of this study: do writers on politics try to make sense of the system as it operates in their time or do they seek to design a new one? There will never be a definitive answer to this question but perhaps it has always been possible for visionaries like Savonarola to ignore the harsh realities of life and strive for ideal constitutions. Pragmatists such as Machiavelli could hope, at best, to introduce better standards of citizenship and to reform existing structures. Only in his belief that a saviour might be found to free Italy from foreign

incursions did Machiavelli seem to transcend or, perhaps, to ignore reality.

2   Put more plainly, 'was Machiavelli a man of the Renaissance?' The answer must surely be that in literary matters he was one of the first to use Italian rather than Latin for his major works (a notable precursor in this respect was Leon Battista Alberti). He also made liberal use of classical examples, to such an extent that his friend Guicciardini criticized him for it. He was a typical humanist in the way in which he discussed the relative importance of Fortune and *virtù* and in his conclusion that sufficient exercise of the latter could invariably conquer the former. Many of his contemporaries would not have followed him in the most daring and plainly stated of his conclusions: that religious codes were irrelevant to the practice of politics, where the statesman's first duty was to preserve his country and its institutions, regardless of the means which he was obliged to use. Ironically, whatever they may have claimed in public, the rulers of the great nation states which were emerging in the sixteenth century, France, Spain and England, frequently achieved success by the means advocated by Machiavelli. ❖

Along with Shakespeare and Leonardo da Vinci, Machiavelli is one of the best-known figures of the Renaissance, one who can still arouse strong emotions. Why do his ideas remain so controversial long after the political conditions in which they were produced have ceased to exist? Ramsay (Reader, no. 8) suggests that they have been adapted by liberal thinkers for their promotion of a broad-based republicanism, as well as appealing to those who subscribe to a consequentialist ethic. We all face dilemmas where there is an opportunity to achieve a good end by doing something which is contrary to our moral convictions: much of government policy is based on this principle. Belonging to one of the earliest state bureaucracies, Machiavelli was in a good position to predict the necessary criteria for future action by the state as it extended ever further into the lives of citizens.

Bibliography

ANGLO, S. (1969) *Machiavelli : A Dissection*, London, Victor Gollancz.

BARON, H. (1961) 'Machiavelli: the republican citizen and the author of *The Prince*', *English Historical Review*, vol. 76, pp.217–53.

BARON, H. (1966) *The Crisis of the Early Italian Renaissance*, Princeton, NJ, Princeton University Press.

BLACK, R. (1990) 'Machiavelli, servant of the Florentine republic' in G. Bock, Q. Skinner and M. Viroli (eds) *Machiavelli and Republicanism*, Cambridge, Cambridge University Press.

BOCK, G. (1990) 'Civil discord in Machiavelli's *Istorie Fiorentine*' in G. Bock, Q. Skinner and M. Viroli (eds) *Machiavelli and Republicanism*, Cambridge, Cambridge University Press.

BROWN, A. (1988) 'Savonarola, Machiavelli and Moses: a changing model' in P. Denley and C. Elam (eds) *Florence and Italy: Renaissance Studies in Honour of Nicolai Rubinstein*, Westfield Publications in Medieval Studies, London, Committee for Medieval Studies, Westfield College.

BULL, G. (1999) (ed./trans.) *Niccolò Machiavelli: The Prince*, introduction by A. Grafton, Harmondsworth, Penguin.

BURCKHARDT, J. (1990) *The Civilization of the Renaissance in Italy*, trans. S.G.C. Middlemore, Harmondsworth, Penguin; first published 1858.

BUTTERS, H.C. (1985) *Governors and Government in Early Sixteenth-Century Florence, 1502–1519*, Oxford, Clarendon Press/Oxford University Press.

CANTIMORI, D. (1937–8) 'Rhetoric and politics in Italian humanism', *Journal of the Warburg Institute*, vol. 1, pp.83–102.

CHABOD, F. (1965) *Machiavelli and the Renaissance*, New York, Harper Torchbooks.

DE GRAZIA, S. (1989) *Machiavelli in Hell*, Hemel Hempstead, Harvester Wheatsheaf.

GILBERT, A.H. (1968) *Machiavelli's Prince and its Forerunners*, New York, Barnes & Noble.

GILBERT, A. H. (1989) *Machiavelli: The Chief Works and Others*, vol. 2, Durham, NC and London, Duke University Press.

GILBERT, F. (1973) *Machiavelli and Guicciardini: Politics and History in Sixteenth-Century Florence*, Princeton, NJ, Princeton University Press.

GODMAN, P. (1998), *From Poliziano to Machiavelli: Florentine Humanism in the High Renaissance*, Princeton, NJ, Princeton University Press.

HALE, J. (1966) *Machiavelli and Renaissance Italy*, London, The English Universities Press.

KRAYE, J. (ed.) (1997) *Cambridge Translations of Renaissance Historical Texts*, vol. 2, Cambridge, Cambridge University Press.

KRISTELLER, P.O. (1997), 'The moral thought of Renaissance humanism' in J. Dunn and I. Harris (eds) *Machiavelli*, vol. 2, Great Political Thinkers Series, Cheltenham, Edward Elgar.

MACHIAVELLI, N. (1912) *The Florentine History*, trans. W.K. Marriott, London, J.M. Dent.

MACHIAVELLI, N. (1970), *The Discourses*, ed. B. Crick, trans. L.J. Walker, London, Penguin.

MALLETT, M. (1990) 'The theory and practice of warfare in Machiavelli's republic', in G. Bock, Q. Skinner and M. Viroli (eds) *Machiavelli and Republicanism*, Cambridge, Cambridge University Press.

PESMAN COOPER, R. (1981) 'The Florentine ruling group under the *governo popolare* 1494-1512', *Studies in Renaissance History*, vol. 7, New York, pp.69–181.

POCOCK, J.G.A. (1975) *The Machiavellian Moment: Florentine Political Thought and the Atlantic Republican Tradition*, Princeton, NJ, Princeton University Press.

RAAB, F. (1964) *The English Face of Machiavelli: A Changing Interpretation, 1500–1700*, London, Routledge & Kegan Paul.

RUBINSTEIN, N. (1997) *The Government of Florence under the Medici (1434–1494)*, Oxford–Warburg Studies, Oxford, Clarendon Press.

SKINNER, Q. (1978) *The Foundations of Modern Political Thought*, vol. 1, Cambridge, Cambridge University Press.

SKINNER, Q. (1988) 'Political philosophy' in C.B. Schmitt, Q. Skinner, E. Kessler and J. Kraye (eds) *The Cambridge History of Renaissance Philosophy*, Cambridge, Cambridge University Press.

N. WARBURTON, AA311, *Reading Political Philosophy: Machiavelli to Mill*, Chapter 1, 'Machiavelli', London and Milton Keynes, Routledge/The Open University, forthcoming.

Anthology and Reader sources

Lorenzo Valla, from *The Treatise of Lorenzo Valla on the Donation of Constantine*: *The Treatise of Lorenzo Valla on the Donation of Constantine*, ed. and trans. C.B. Coleman, Yale University Press, New Haven, 1922, pp.11–19, 24–9, 63–7, 115–17, 177–83. (Anthology, no. 4)

Francesco Guicciardini, from *The History of Italy*: *The History of Italy*, ed. and trans. S. Alexander, Macmillan Co., New York and London, 1969, pp.4–8. (Anthology, no. 19)

Thomas Aquinas, Commentary on the *Sentences* of Peter Lombard: *Aquinas: Selected Political Writings*, ed. A.P. D'Entreves, trans. J.G. Dawson, Blackwell, Oxford, 1954, pp.181, 183, 185 (English text only). (Anthology, no. 20)

Niccolò Machiavelli, Reports on a mission to Cesare Borgia: *Machiavelli: The Chief Works and Others*, trans. A.H. Gilbert, Duke University Press, North Carolina, 1965, vol. 1 (3 vols) pp.121–4, 128–9. (Anthology, no. 21)

Francesco Guicciardini, The Sack of Prato and the return of the Medici to Florence, from *The History of Italy*: *The History of Italy*, ed. and trans. S. Alexander, Macmillan Co., New York and London, 1969, pp.261–7. (Anthology, no. 22)

Niccolò Machiavelli, Letter to Francesco Vettori: *The Prince*, ed. M.L. Kekewich, Wordsworth Classics of World Literature, Ware, Hertfordshire, 1997, Appendix C, pp.126–9. Reprinted from *The Letters of Machiavelli: A selection*, ed. and trans. by A. Gilbert, Capricorn Books, New York, 1961, Letter 137. (Anthology, no. 23)

Niccolò Machiavelli, from the *Discourses*: (i) Book 1, Chapter 2, (ii) Book 1, Chapters 9 and 10 and (iii) Book 1, Chapter 55, Niccolò Machiavelli, *The Discourses*, ed. B. Crick, trans. L.J. Walker, Penguin Classics, London, 1970, pp.104–9, 111, 131–8, 243–8. (Anthology no. 24)

Niccolò Machiavelli, from *The Art of War*. *Machiavelli: The Chief Works and Others*, trans. A.H. Gilbert, Duke University Press, North Carolina, 1965, vol. 2 (3 vols), pp.568–70, 636–9. (Anthology, no. 25)

Niccolò Machiavelli, from *The Florentine History*: (i) Machiavelli's Introduction and (ii) The Pazzi conspiracy, *Florentine History*, trans. W.K. Marriott, J.M. Dent, London, 1912, pp.1–3, 317–18, 321–9. (Anthology, no. 26.)

Francesco Guicciardini, from *Maxims and Reflections*: *Maxims and Reflections of a Renaissance Statesman (Ricordi)*, trans. M. Domadi, intro. N. Rubinstein, Harper Torchbooks, New York, 1965, pp.45–7, 49. (Anthology, no. 27)

Innocent Gentillet, from *Against Nicholas Machiavell: A Discourse upon the Means of Well Governing. Against Nicholas Machiavell the Florentine*, in *Culture and Belief in Europe*, 1450–1600, ed. D. Englander, D. Norman, R. O'Day, W.R. Owens, Basil Blackwell, Oxford, 1990, pp.416–18, spelling modernized by David Englander. (Anthology, no. 28)

Maureen Ramsay, Machiavelli's political philosophy in *The Prince*: *New interdisciplinary essays*, ed. Martin Coyle, Manchester University Press, Manchester, 1995, Chapter 8, pp.174–93. (Reader, no. 8)

Glossary

academy associations, first made in France, for learned or cultural purposes.

all' antica art in the style of ancient Greece and Rome.

ars dictaminis handbook on the art of letter writing.

balìa council with extensive powers convened in emergencies under the republican government of Florence.

ballade type of medieval French song with the usual structure aab.

Baroque in western music the 'Baroque' period begins early in the seventeenth century, and lasts until roughly the middle of the eighteenth century.

cadence end of a **phrase**.

Calvinists followers of the sixteenth-century French Protestant reformer, John Calvin.

canti carnascialeschi carnival songs.

cardinal virtues derived from Aristotle, justice, prudence, temperance and fortitude (courage), characteristic of good governors.

Carolingian period, eighth to ninth centuries, when France and part of Germany were ruled by the dynasty of Charlemagne (Charles the Great).

chanson French song.

chord sound created by the simultaneous combination of notes.

city-state dominant political unit of northern Italy during the Middle Ages. Unlike the rule of monarchs and princes which characterized much of the rest of Europe and central and southern Italy at this time, the city-state was a semi-independent political entity in which authority was devolved on elected magistrates drawn from the ranks of the citizens. By the fifteenth century, such systems of communal government were increasingly falling under the control of powerful despots.

classical pertaining to the era of the ancient Greeks and Romans.

condottiere (plural *condottieri*) in Italy, mercenary captains or leaders who made a living by selling their military skills and armies to the highest bidder. Most were minor Italian noblemen who combined a military career with the concerns of governing their seigneurial estates and principalities.

contrapuntal see **counterpoint**.

counterpoint weaving together of independent melodic lines; related adjective is 'contrapuntal'.

cultural history general term used to describe an approach to the past which includes reference to the wider system of beliefs and values which characterize a society or period. For most historians, this includes not simply reference to 'culture' in the narrow sense of the word (i.e. elite concepts of the arts, learning and literature), but also to the manifestation and expression of popular as well as elite values in a wide variety of forms (e.g. religious devotion, popular pastimes and leisure, etc.).

dissonance jarring sound, as opposed to 'consonant' (pleasant, relaxed). Definitions of what constitutes a consonance or a dissonance have varied historically.

duple metre two or four beats in a bar of music, see **metre**.

duration note length.

encomium literary form of praise, the paradoxical encomium was made in jest.

epigraphy study of inscriptions.

Estates General assembly of representatives of the French clergy, nobles and commoners called periodically by the king.

feudalism social system of the medieval world. Its most fundamental feature was the ownership of land based on a contract between a lord and a vassal. Originally, the obligation of the vassal to a lord was performed through military service. During the course of the **Middle Ages**, however, this was frequently commuted to a money payment, or rent.

formes fixes fixed forms.

frottola Italian song, usually in several voices with a distinct tune and accompaniment.

Gallican relating to the belief that the church in France should be largely free from papal control.

German Romanticism cultural movement of the early nineteenth century rooted in the European-wide rejection of the values of the Enlightenment, which celebrated reason, scientific advancement and man's control over nature. Romanticism, in contrast, stressed the virtues of intuition and emotion. German Romanticism embraced similar themes and celebrated the spiritual and even mystical character of humankind. Typically, such phenomena as industrialism and liberalism were seen as potentially violating and undermining the cyclical patterns which German Romantics identified as the prime force in history.

ghibellines political supporters of the emperor in Italy.

Gothic style characteristic art-form of the **Middle Ages** characterized by an absence of **classical** features. Examples include: in architecture the use of the pointed arch, and in writing the use of Germanic as opposed to Roman or italic script.

guelfs political supporters of the papacy in Italy.

historiographical relating to the study of the way in which historians write history, and the dominant influences which help to shape their approach to the subject.

homophony parts moving together in **chords**.

humanism not coined until the late eighteenth or early nineteenth century, the phrase 'humanism' is loosely employed by historians to denote the revival of interest in the Renaissance in the values of a liberal arts education which stressed human as opposed to transcendental values.

imperium right to exercise imperial power.

Inquisition body set up by the Catholic church in the late **Middle Ages** to suppress heresy.

invective eloquent condemnation of a person or practice.

irony figure of speech in which the intended meaning is the opposite of that expressed by the words used; for example, condemnation disguised as praise.

Jesuits religious order founded in the sixteenth century by Ignatius Loyola mainly concerned to combat Protestantism.

lettera antica script in the style of **classical** antiquity.

l'uomo universale Italian for 'universal' or 'Renaissance' man; the idea, originating with Burckhardt and other nineteenth-century scholars, that man in the Renaissance was capable of achieving knowledge and accomplishment in a broad range of human activities, both social and cultural.

lute fretted, plucked string instrument.

madrigal setting of a short poem for voices of equal importance.

maestro di cappella musical director of the chapel.

Mass musical setting of the 'Ordinary' service of the Roman Catholic church, comprising the Kyrie, Gloria, Credo, Sanctus, Benedictus and Agnus Dei.

melismatic adjective derived from 'melisma', a term used of passages in which one syllable is sung over more than one note.

melody succession of notes having a recognizable musical shape.

mentalité assumptions and values common to a given period or place. Historiographically, the term is most often associated with the twentieth-century French school of history known as the *Annales* and is best represented in the work of such scholars as Marc Bloch, Lucien Febvre and Fernand Braudel.

metaphysics branch of philosophy which deals with first principles, including concepts such as being, substance, time, space and cause.

metre division of time into regular patterns – for example, four beats in a bar of music.

Middle Ages conventionally, the period in western Europe between the collapse of the Roman Empire (mid fifth century CE) and the onset of the Renaissance (fifteenth century). Like 'Renaissance', the usefulness of the term is much disputed, and the period itself is frequently divided and sub-divided into more manageable units (e.g. 'Dark Ages', 'low' and 'high' Middle Ages, etc.).

militia armed force of citizens mustered for the defence of their state.

mirrors for princes handbooks of advice for rulers.

moral philosophy concerned with how humanity can achieve a good life.

motet vocal setting of a Latin sacred text.

New Historicism movement of literary scholars designed to reassert the importance of history and historical awareness to the interpretation of Renaissance poetry, prose and drama.

papal nuncio papal ambassador to a foreign court or government.

patrician wealthy and influential Italian families.

philology critical analysis of texts both in respect of their content and the language in which they were expressed.

phrase short, distinct part of a **melody**.

Pléiade group of mid sixteenth-century French poets named after a constellation.

podestà chief magistrate in some Italian states (including Florence) in the **Middle Ages**.

polyphony many voices.

post-modern post-modernism is a reaction to modernism, which asserts confidence in human progress and the existence of objective knowledge of reality. Post-modernism questions the status of such knowledge stressing the transience of reality and the contingent nature of truth. Post-modernists routinely deny notions of fixed or permanent meaning or direct correspondence between language and the material world.

post-structuralist post-structuralism is a version of **post-modernism** which holds that we should understand the world through an exploration of the relationships between objects and concepts, rather than studying them in isolation. These relationships form a pattern or structure which are governed by laws. Such laws are seen as the constant in a world which is otherwise in a state of flux. Post-structuralists focus on, and celebrate, formlessness, subjectivity, transience and spontaneity making typically post-modernist claims such as the denial of objectivity, reality, or truth.

pratica (plural *pratiche*) advisory commission in the republican government of Florence.

Protestant Reformation religious movement, inspired by Martin Luther, which led to the rejection of Roman Catholicism and the dissolution of Christian unity in western Europe in the sixteenth century.

renovatio literally the Latin for 'renewal'; generally used by scholars as shorthand for the Renaissance rediscovery of the **classical** past.

rhetoric art of public speaking as it was developed in **classical** antiquity.

Risorgimento movement for the unification of Italy in the nineteenth century.

rondeau type of medieval French song with refrain.

Salic law French law which excluded women from succession to the throne.

salon meetings of cultured people, usually held in the homes of rich and witty women.

scherzo lively movement.

scholasticism system of enquiry emphasizing the study of dialectic and logic which dominated the medieval university curriculum.

sibyl prophetesses in ancient Greece.

signatures symbols indicating pitch and time.

Signoria chief magistrates making up the executive government of republican Florence.

sprezzatura studied negligence cultivated by courtiers.

staves lines and spaces onto which music is written.

strophic repeated verses.

tablature form of notation for lute and keyboard players whereby the pitches were intabulated, using either letters or numbers.

Ten of War committee of republican government of Florence concerned with war and peace.

texture ways in which voices and instruments can be combined; the word is derived from *texere*, 'to weave'. Composers may choose to weave melodies together in **counterpoint** or may combine notes simultaneously to form **chords**.

ultramontanism support for the interference of the papacy in the French church.

virelai type of medieval French song with the usual structure AbbaA.

virtù strength of will to serve the state loyally and selflessly.

Vulgate Latin version of the Bible attributed to St Jerome.

word-painting 'painting' of words with a suitable musical sound, such as a falling pattern for a sigh.

Index

Acknowledgements

Grateful acknowledgement is made to the following sources for permission to reproduce material in this book:

Gaudi, M.T. and Smith, C.S. (trans.) (1978) *Pirotechnia*, MIT Press; *Lancaster and Valois French and English Music, 1350–1420*, © Hyperion Records Ltd, London, translated by Dr Christopher Page; Sleeve notes for 'Gloria' from Ockeghem, *Requiem Missa Mi-mi*, © 1995 Virgin Classics Ltd; Claudio Monteverdi Canti Amorosi, 1975 Polydor International GmbH, Hamburg. English translation of the sung texts © 1972/1975 Lionel Salter © 1992 Dr Tim Carter, Verlag J.B. Metzler; *Appendix 1:* Turner, B. (ed) (1979) *Renaissance Performing Scores, Josquin Desprez: Absalon fili mi*, Series B: Franco–Flemish Church Music, no. 7, Vanderbeek and Imrie Ltd; *Appendix 2:* Josquin Desprez: Credo from *Missa 'Pange lingua'*, in Blume, F. (ed) (1929) *Josquin Desprez: Missa 'Pange lingua'*, Das Chorwerk, Wolfenbüttel, Karl Heinrich Möseler Verlag; *Appendix 3:* Josquin Desprez: 'Mille regrets', Dobbins, F. (ed) (1987) *The Oxford Book of French Chansons*, © Oxford University Press 1987. Reproduced by permission; *Appendix 4:* Josquin Desprez: 'Adieu mes amours', Lowinsky, E. (ed) (1976) *Josquin des Prez: Proceedings of the International Josquin Festival* – Conference held at The Juilliard School at Lincoln Centre in New York City, 21–25 June 1971. Reprinted by permission of Oxford University Press.